I'll Never See You Again

"There was a man – and behold, he is no longer there."
Chaim Nachman Bialik (1873-1934)

To my children

Originally published in German
by Bouvier Verlag, Bonn, 2008

English language version
published in 2012 by Pomegranate Books

Printed and bound in the UK

ISBN 978-1-84289-017-2

Pomegranate Books, Bristol
www.pomegranatebooks.co.uk

I'll Never See You Again
Memories for the future

by

Margot Barnard

Translated from the German
by Marion Koebner

Acknowledgements

I would like to thank Marion Koebner for her assistance with the editing of the English-language version of this book and to both Marion Koebner and Klaus Grosch for their support throughout.

Contents

1. Return to Bonn

It was a hot day in August 1955. I was on my way back to London from Bonn, via Ostend. The train had stopped at Cologne station for some time and I found myself dozing and mulling over the events of the previous two weeks. After my return to England from Nigeria, Uncle Simon – who had returned to Hamburg – wrote to me, saying Aunt Martha had survived the war and was still living in Oberdollendorf, a small village on the Rhine. There was also the matter of restitution and inheritance, which Dr. Meier, a solicitor and old friend of the family, had kindly offered to deal with for me. That was when I decided to go to Germany.

First, though, I headed for my old hometown of Bonn, or, rather, Beuel, which lies on the eastern (right-hand) bank of the Rhine, often referred to as 'the wrong side.' There I was, standing in front of our old cooperative shop in Wilhelmstrasse; as a child, I would be sent here almost daily on some errand or other and was always given a little toffee for my efforts. I entered the shop 'incognito' with the help of a pair of sunglasses. Nineteen years had passed since my departure, but there was no mistaking Frau Schuhmacher, the proprietor. She had hardly changed, except that her grey hair – which she still wore in a bun – had turned white. "What can I do for you?" I removed the sunglasses… A scream: "Kober's Marjötchen, Heinrich, Heinrich, come quick, Kober's Marjötchen!" In rushed Heinrich Schuhmacher and, 20 minutes later, the shop was crammed with old neighbours and people I had known as a child, and had always remembered with affection. And then it was down the Neustrasse, crocodile fashion, until we arrived at the house where I grew up. The Wandel family lived there now; their son, Paul, had been my childhood playmate. The door to number 6 opened – but it wasn't my 'Omama' or my mother or Gretchen standing there waiting to welcome me, it was Frau Wandel, who looked at me as if she had seen a ghost. Recalling that she had acquired the house under value when my parents had been forced to sell, I had to hide my inner turmoil as I greeted her warmly. I found myself being ushered into my childhood home by the Wandels, who proceeded to tell me how much they had suffered. Agreed – they had acquired the house cheaply, but their son Paul had been killed in Russia. A little later, their daughter, Adele, took me to one side and told me that the Hitler portraits had disappeared from the walls the moment news of Paul's death had reached her parents. At this point, I had to reassure the family that I had not come to dispossess them, but it took a telephone conversation with my lawyer, in their presence, instructing him that I intended to waive my claim for restitution of the house before they were persuaded.

I spent one night in the house, but I knew it would be the last: in that sense, there was no going back.

The compartment resounded with animated conversation, in Rhenish dialect. How I wanted to join in the conversation and repartee – it felt familiar, yet it awoke that fear of old. The compartment door opened and I heard someone asking whether the train was going to Ostend. "Yes," I replied, "I know it does because I'm going there myself." A woman wearing a little felt hat stood in the doorway. Her name was Grete Borgmann, and we were to become very good friends. "Please come in," I said. "There's still room here." Beaming, Grete pushed a massive, greenish-grey suitcase into the compartment. "Sorry, but could I ask you to help me manoeuvre my little case up there?" I responded: "Tell me, have you got a dead body in there?"... general laughter. Grete and I were soon sitting opposite each other and deep in conversation. I look back at the channel crossing from Ostend to Dover with pleasure. We fought hard for two sun loungers, lay in the sun, and exchanged life stories. Grete and her family were to help me rediscover the Germany I had lost, that I had had to give up.

2. Childhood

On 24 December 1919, as on every Saturday and before a Bank Holiday, my heavily pregnant mother went to help out in her older sister's butcher's shop in Bonn. She could not be dissuaded, even though the birth of her child was imminent. The shop was crowded with customers, all wanting to stock up for Christmas, when the labour pains set in. Mother had to be firmly persuaded to go home; otherwise she would have continued working, out of a sense of duty. Waiting at home were my grandparents, my father, my two and a half year old brother, Walter, our maid, Gretchen, and the midwife, who had been summoned at the last minute. It was probably around lunchtime – and, therefore, a few hours ahead of baby Jesus – surrounded by these people, that I came into the world.

In retrospect, my childhood was like a long summer's day. My earliest memory is sitting in my parents' bedroom playing with a basketful of money Mother had brought in. I was, of course, oblivious to inflation. Every Sunday morning, we were allowed to slip into bed with our parents and would listen, rapt, to Father's tales of the war, his escape from imprisonment in Russia, and his adventures with comrades. He was such a marvellous raconteur, his stories have remained with me to this day.

We lived immediately next door to the Protestant church, which had its own kindergarten run by Protestant nuns. I was three when I went there, by which time my brother Walter was already at primary school. The days followed the same pattern. After morning prayers came Froebel activities: dolls and some very simple wooden toys. The nuns were kind-hearted but strict and didn't differentiate in their treatment of Jews and Christians, rich or poor. I was happy there. Even when I was at senior school, I still visited the kindergarten from time to time.

Mother was friendly with the nuns. She played an active part in the annual ritual of giving Christmas presents to poor children, and always committed herself to crocheting dolls' clothes. Every year, I looked forward to the excitement of distributing the presents. We would assemble at the kindergarten in the morning, after which Sister Maria, wearing her dark blue Sunday robe, would escort the children to church. At a particular juncture, we had to sing "*Kling Glöckchen, klingeling…*" and when we got to the verse "open the doors for us", the doors to the church opened. The dolls and other gifts under the Christmas tree were distributed during the festivities.

At this point, I want to mention something about Mother I really admired but which, for her, was a matter of course. Every Wednesday, children from poor families, or who had been sent to us by Sister Maria, joined us for a meal. I also remember an ex-prisoner, a single man whom the Jewish community had decided to help, until he was capable of standing on his own two feet. Despite being rather eccentric, there was no question for Mother that he should be helped. As a child, I thought that all mothers acted in this way.

Mother had a cousin, Uncle Nathan, who lived in the United States with his American wife Rosalie. We were told, one day, that he and Rosalie would be coming to visit. They checked into the *Königshof*, Bonn's most expensive and luxurious hotel. Aunt Rosalie asked Mother if I could stay the night with her in the hotel, because Uncle Nathan had to go elsewhere on business. When I saw their suite of rooms, I could only imagine that a princess lived there. Going into the bathroom the next morning, I noticed that the light had been left on all night. "Aunt Rosalie," I said, "you forgot to turn the lights out." To my astonishment, she replied, "Not at all. I left them on deliberately, because the room is so expensive!"

My best friend was Agnes Lambertz – we were inseparable. She lived in a little house directly opposite us. Of her seventeen siblings, only five had survived tuberculosis. Agnes, the youngest, was a year older than me. She attended the Catholic elementary school and was very diligent. I would call for her after school using a special signal. Invariably, her mother would open the door and tell me that Agnes hadn't quite finished scrubbing and I would have to wait a little while. In those days, I had no idea just how poor her family was and thought nothing of it when Mother sent Gretchen over with food.

With the arrival of the long summer holidays, we children most looked forward to the hikes with Mother. Foreign holidays were very uncommon in those days. Frau Frank, mother's best friend, often joined us. We would don our walking boots, pack our rucksacks, and catch the train to Königswinter, from where we set off to a popular destination, such as the Drachenfels or the Petersberg. Even though the terrain was sometimes steep and the distances long, we didn't mind at all. The outings with Mother and Frau Frank were filled with laughter and song.

I shared my bedroom with my maternal grandmother. Grandfather had died some years earlier. My memories of 'Omama' have become intermingled with family anecdotes, but she also talked to me about her life herself. Every evening, as she stood in front of the washbowl, she would start with the same words: "Good night, my little lambkin." I would reply: "Good night, Omama" and then she would turn round and say: "Aren't you going to say 'good night' to me? I know... I won't be here much longer. I was the eldest of six and had to work hard in the vineyards back in Dettelbach." To me, she was old, grey-haired, wore long bloomers, a bodice and a blouse. To visualise her as the young, capable and good-looking girl who had left home to work as a maid in Bonn was beyond me. She married my grandfather, a cattle dealer, whose first wife had died in childbirth, leaving little Karl.

My grandparents, unassuming and hard-working people, had four children. Grandmother decided that there was no reason why they shouldn't slaughter their own cattle and sell the meat to the neighbours. And, like many other butchers, they also served lunch. So successful was the business, they could afford to send their eldest son, Simon, to university to study medicine. Nowadays that may seem unremarkable, but it should be remembered that Jews had been segregated and discriminated against for centuries. Depending on where they lived, they were restricted to certain occupations – trading or money-lending – and domicile. It was only with the unification of Germany in 1871 that they were granted full citizenship.

Omama gave her stepson Karl his own butcher's shop in Siegburgerstrasse. He was a cheerful soul. I often went to his shop, preferably on Tuesday afternoons when the butchering took place in the abattoir at the back. Of course, there was no 'kosher' slaughter where pigs were involved but, when it came to cattle, the *shochet* came to perform the ritual slaughter. The animal was laid on its side, a boy would hold its head steady and the *shochet* slit its throat with a knife. Blood spouted like a fountain and was caught in a bowl. After the animal was dead, the carcass would be hung up by its hind legs and split into two with an axe. After this spectacle, I would go into the shop and watch my uncle serve his customers with a joke and a smile. The children were given what he called a little "sausage sweet".

At the heart of our family life were the celebrations, particularly birthdays, which brought almost everyone together. My brother and I grew up with our cousins as if they were our siblings. We visited each other regularly and went on outings together. Most Saturdays were spent visiting our relatives in Bonn, Mother's sister, Aunt Jetta, and her husband, Leo, who had the butcher's shop. After the shop closed, we would sit together, eat and drink, play cards and laugh.

Uncle Simon, a doctor, lived in Hamburg with his family. Aunt Tilly, his wife, an emancipated woman for her time, was a paediatrician. All her emotional energy was channelled into Zionism. Mother and her brother, Simon, were very close, which is why the Hamburg relatives came to visit us so often. When they announced their visit, the cry would go up: "Hamburg is coming!" and the cooking, baking and general preparation began. Under normal circumstances, our house was filled from cellar to attic with provisions of all kinds, but the Hamburg visit resulted in the addition of their favourite foods.

Sundays followed a pattern. Lunch was frugal because we would go out later, but Mother always cooked something special. We took an afternoon nap until three and then usually drove to the Hotel Dreesen in Bad Godesberg. The Dreesen was the meeting place for the affluent Jewish middle class. Tea dances were laid on beneath chandeliers, and famous personalities frequented the hotel. It was there that I saw the film actor, Willy Fritsch, for the first time. The elegant ambience was still being carefully cultivated in the 1920s and early 1930s. The proprietors, Georg and Fritz Dreesen, invariably came to our table to greet us. We were good clients, and Father also had business dealings with them.

There was coffee and cake, and my parents danced and were in good spirits. We children were left to our own devices and went to play in the hotel garden. We usually left for home around seven but our parents sometimes treated us to dinner there – for us, there was nothing better than being allowed to order "Russian eggs."

Some of my childhood memories go back to the years after the First World War. I must have been six or seven when my brother and I went to 'the corner' to watch as the departure of French troops signalled the end of the occupation of the Rhineland. And there were always wreath-laying ceremonies for the fallen soldiers, at which, each year, the representatives of the three religious communities took it in turns to read the commemorative address. In 1931, it was the turn of our teacher, Herr Nussbaum. His speech was very emotional, patriotic, and full of words of gratitude for the soldiers who had fought on our behalf. It was around this time that Father and his comrades from the Reich Federation of Jewish War Veterans (RjF) decided to go to Verdun. This made a deep impression on my brother and me. What would they find there? We awaited Father's return, and his account, with bated breath. And, indeed, he told us that he had found his old dugout and also saw an old boot there that looked familiar.

Our Christmas always started with *Hanukkah*, the eight-day long Fes-

15

tival of Lights in remembrance of the dedication of the second temple after the Maccabean rebellion. At six o'clock in the evening, we were sent out for a walk with Gretchen. On our return, Mother, beaming, announced: "Just imagine, the little *Hanukkah* man was here!" There was a gift for each of us on the table. After dinner, the *menorah* was placed on the table and a candle was lit. Father took his fiddle out of its case and we sang the Maccabean victory song. On each of the next seven evenings, we lit an additional candle.

My birthday came immediately after *Hanukkah* and, to this day, I feel a sense of deprivation that there was no distinction between *Hanukkah* presents and birthday presents. We celebrated New Year and Carnival like everyone else. Occasionally, my parents went to a ball and they particularly enjoyed listening to carnival jesters' speeches on the wireless with friends. Sometimes we children were allowed to listen and get to know the latest hits. My grandmother was said to have gone out only once a year – on *Weiberfastnacht*, which falls on the Thursday before Shrove Tuesday.

Pesach, which commemorates the story of the Exodus and the liberation of the Israelites from slavery in Egypt, was the central festival of our year. The entire house was thoroughly cleaned for the occasion. Decisions had to be made about whom to invite, how many *matzos* – unleavened bread – should be ordered, and which of our relations would be coming. I would walk round the neighbourhood handing out *matzos*. At the *Seder*, Father related the history of the enslavement and suppression of the Jewish people and their ultimate liberation. Each of us had a book – the *Haggadah* – and read along. On the table was a platter with small dishes of food, each one symbolising an aspect of the misery the Jews in Egypt had been subjected to. A glass of wine was prepared for Elijah, should he arrive. As he never came to our house, the wine was mixed in with the food after *Pesach*. My role, as the youngest member of the family, was to pose the questions, in Hebrew: Why is this night different from all the other nights, why do we eat *matzos*, why do we eat bitter herbs? Everyone then rose and Father began the recitation: "We were slaves in Egypt..." a solemn monologue interrupted by short songs. We children found the whole ceremony very long. What kept us going was the prospect of the imminent feast. The big moment came when Mother stood up and instructed Gretchen to in bring the food. When I was older and ready to emigrate to Palestine, the passage "This year we are still slaves, next year we'll be in Jerusalem!" acquired a new and poignant significance. There is no doubt that the saying 'Celebrate festivals as they come' applied to assimilated Jewish families. Of course, Christian festivals, such as Easter and Pentecost, were official holidays for us, too, and we often went on outings.

One of the most important religious holidays for Jews is *Rosh Hashanah* – New Year – which ends with *Yom Kippur* ten days later – the Day of Atonement. In our home, too, the mood was festive and we dressed up. When the Kober family left the house to go to synagogue, the neighbours knew we were celebrating our most important festival. A few windows opened, Father doffed his hat, said a few words of greeting, and the neighbours nodded knowingly. We children walked ahead, our parents followed, and Father whispered "Walk tall". I maintained a solemn expression, as did everyone else that day, but couldn't help recalling a little nursery rhyme I had learnt at kindergarten: "First comes Daddy ladybird, then Mummy ladybird, and bringing up the rear, so sweet and dear, the little baby ladybirds…" We turned into Wilhelmstrasse and saw other members of the Jewish community heading for the synagogue in a similarly solemn manner. Men and women sat separately in synagogue, children in the front row; there was a smell of mothballs. It being autumn, the ladies had dusted down their fur coats and were eyeing each other. Around midday, Gretchen came to collect Omama and us children for lunch. We broke the fast traditionally, with pickled herrings and boiled potatoes in their skins. Children and old people excepted, almost every Jew, even the less observant, attended synagogue and fasted that day, which provoked such comments from people in the community as: "He wants to keep the door to the Jewish heaven open."

Even as a child, I was deeply moved by the solemnity of this high holiday, probably because it is a day of reflection and contemplation. The haunting sound of the *Shofar* – the ram's horn – at the end of *Yom Kippur* has remained with me to this day. Even our teacher, Herr Nussbaum, departing from his more familiar role, appearing more remote that day, as preacher and cantor. After the service, we all congregated outside and there was a sense of happy relief as we all engaged in lively conversation and wished each other *Shana tova* – Happy New Year. Of course, *Yom Kippur* also had a very real side. Every year, Mother insisted that I made up with any friend I had fallen out with. I thought it unfair that it was always me who had to initiate the process, but, looking back, I am grateful to her for the lesson it taught me.

The big events in those days were the family celebrations. My brother Walter's *Bar mitzvah* – the day a 13-year-old boy reaches religious maturity – was just such an event. Hosting a party for thirty or even forty people was not a problem for Mother, but preparations started almost two years earlier. The first sign was a Dresdner Bank silver savings tin, into which Father started to put money to finance the event. All the preparations for the big day were Mother's responsibility and she became completely absorbed. The closer the day drew, the more hectic things were at home. Conversations and telephone calls between Mother and Frau Frank became more frequent. She even employed a chef, who also served the food. Of course, Walter and I got new clothes, but it was Walter's day and I accepted it as such (*Bat mitzvah* – for girls – was unusual in those days). I remember how proud my parents were; Walter had sung well and read from the *Torah* during the ceremony, and many acquaintances who were members of the community came up to congratulate him.

3. School Days

The transition from kindergarten to primary school, which was only ten minutes from our house, presented no problems for me. On the contrary, I looked forward to learning to read at last. The surroundings were familiar, my parents knew the teachers, they met on the street and chatted, and my brother had already been at the school for two years. The students came from a variety of social backgrounds, well-to-do children mixing with children from Fabrikstrasse. My form teacher for the next four years was Fräulein Huber. The memory of her has been with me all my life. In retrospect, she was typical of German teachers then, who were expected to remain unmarried, asexual, and completely dedicated to their occupation. I can see her now, standing in front of the class, her hair tightly pulled back, wearing a white blouse, a long, black skirt and extraordinarily large lace-up shoes. She lived with Frau Stern, a distinguished Jewish lady. My parents knew the senior master, Herr Schneider, and they met frequently on the street. When I had written a good essay, Fräulein Huber would send me to the senior master, who was teaching the top class, where my essay was read out. I remember Herr Klein, one of the teachers I rather liked because he was good-looking, from the one and only time I had my ears boxed at school. I was skipping along the row of benches, giving each one I passed a high-spirited little tap, whereupon Herr Klein ordered me to the front of the class and boxed my ears in front of the whole class. Decades later, at the school's centenary celebrations, I was not surprised to hear he had joined the Nazi party.

Every year, at the school celebration of Christmas, to which all parents were invited, I had to recite the Christmas story. On one such occasion, I heard one mother ask: "Why does that Jewish kid always have to tell the story? One of ours could do it just as well!" To which the other mother replied: "Because that Jewish kid makes a pretty good job of it!" It was around this time I started thinking about religion. At school, we attended Christian scripture lessons and, once a week, the Jewish children had bible lessons from Herr Nussbaum in the synagogue.

Such was my insatiable appetite for reading that my parents simply couldn't provide me with enough books. Left undisturbed, I would happily enter the world of fairy tales, princesses and all kinds of heroes. Then came a series of books about girls at boarding school, *Der Kampf der Tertia* for example. One day, the mail coach brought a massive crate addressed to me. Mother commented how wonderful it was that Uncle Sim had sent me so many books. I was in paradise and, for the first time, became acquainted with Oscar Wilde and Charles Dickens. My nickname at the time was '*Chumash*' (the five books of Moses). Whenever I was sitting, walking or lying in the grass, engrossed in a book, people called out: "There she goes, '*chumashing*' again."

Until the age of nine, I regarded it as self-evident that I was German citizen of the Jewish faith, a state of mind I had adopted from my parents. Although not orthodox, the Beuel Jews observed the traditional Jewish festivals and attended synagogue. We were proud of our co-religionists who played a special role in public life. Father and his comrades from the RjF were proud to have fought for their fatherland and had been honoured for it: Father had been awarded the Iron Cross and Uncle Sim had even been awarded the Iron Cross 1st Class. He had been a doctor in the First World War and Father a paramedic.

On the whole, children from school and the neighbourhood were indifferent to the fact that I was Jewish, but I was aware that Jews in the Rhineland had a special word for anti-semites: 'Rischeskopp', and I knew there were people in Germany who didn't like Jews. I clearly remember the day my friend Luise announced that her parents had forbidden her to play with me because I was a Jew and that the Jews had crucified their Redeemer. Shocked, I told my parents who explained that this had happened two thousand years ago, that Jesus himself had been a Jew, that it was the Romans who had crucified him and that we had definitely not been there. I relayed this to Luise the next day. "Oh well" she replied, "if it was that long ago and you weren't there, we can play together again." As far as she was concerned, there was nothing more to be said, but I felt differently. From that moment, my life changed, eventually with catastrophic consequences.

One day, Father came home and told Mother that there was a new invention called 'the radio', which he had seen demonstrated in Cologne. He was so excited, he insisted on explaining it to her even before he had taken his coat off. "When someone speaks in America you can hear it here!" he said. "Oh, are you talking about the telephone?" asked Mother. Shortly after, Uncle Karl bought one and invited us over to marvel at the miracle. There stood a little box with strings hanging from it, at the end of which were headphones you pulled over your head. It was afternoon and we all sat round the radio listening to the story of Rumpelstiltskin during Children's Hour. Little did we realise we would soon be forced to listen to an entirely different kind of Rumpelstiltskin.

Friends of my parents discovered that I had a certain histrionic talent – I had performed a little piece for Grandmother's 80th birthday – and, as they had connections with the theatre, they promised to talk to a well-known director on my behalf. We had long forgotten about this when, one day, the telephone rang. It was Hans Dreier, inviting us to an audition. Immediately after the telephone conversation had ended, Mother was in a state of excitement, wondering what her talented 11-year-old should wear for the audition. She decided on a white pleated skirt, a lemon-coloured, crocheted pullover, black patent leather shoes and white socks. We met at the Metropole cinema, which had a cafe on the floor above. Hans Dreier was very kind and I was pleased when he offered me a part in the Christmas production, *The Adventures of Pulchinello*. In fact, I played two parts: a girl from the Black Forest and then a little angel. Selected school friends were given complimentary tickets, which considerably enhanced my reputation! There was no doubt in my mind that I was destined to become an actress. My parents, both amused and pleased at my little success, humoured me.

By now, I was struggling unsuccessfully with puberty, as was my brother. Our questions remained unanswered, and we were left to deal with our emotions with no help at all from our parents. The only enlightenment came from older playmates on the street. Gretchen also tried to induct me into the secrets of sexuality. She was engaged and told me a lot about her escapades with her fiancé. She also gave me some 'good tips', one of which I remember very clearly: an unwanted pregnancy could be avoided by simply not going to the toilet. The baby would then drown.

The attic, full of mysteries, played an important role at this time. It wasn't just full of all kinds of junk and homemade preserves; it was also where Walter – and our maid – had their rooms. A large box containing Uncle Simon's university medical reference books was also stored there. He had studied gynaecology so there were plenty of books to interest us. The illustrations taught us how babies were created. We were relieved to be dealing with scientific and matter-of-fact accounts. My sex education was expanded by two further finds in my parents' bedroom: a novel entitled *Brother and Sister*, about an incestuous relationship, and Van de Velde's well-known book about sexuality, which only added to my confusion.

In the fourth year, I took the entrance exam for the *Gymnasium*. One morning, Frau Huber came into our classroom and announced that she had good news: four of us, of whom I was one, had passed the exam. I had gained a place at the Municipal Grammar School for Girls in Bonn. It took me about an hour and a half to walk there, or 45 minutes by bicycle, but I didn't care. I loved the school, the warm atmosphere and the friendly classmates. I was fascinated by such new subjects as foreign languages, biology, history and geometry. My favourite subject was German. I was now in year five, did the long walk to school twice a day, and was visibly growing and developing physically. It wasn't long before I was subjected to tactless remarks – especially from the family.

Uncle Leo, my mother's brother-in-law, pursued me with brutal determination and cast a dark shadow over my childlike soul. In my fear and hatred of him, I spent many hours, even at school, devising ways of avoiding him and defending myself against his advances. But things got worse, and there was no one whom I could confide in. It was impossible to confide in Mother, and Father was completely unsuspecting, to the extent that whenever Aunt Jetta went away, I was told I could stay with Uncle Leo and sleep in their beautiful, large, four-poster bed. "Sleep at ours tonight, darling!" Aunt Jetta would insist, and I could never find an excuse. One night the monster came into my room drunk and I told him to get out immediately, otherwise I would scream and call Aunt Jetta. He did retreat but when I told Aunt Jetta the following morning, she just laughed. My school work began to deteriorate and Mother was summoned to see my class teacher. They both felt that the theatre rehearsals were taking up too much of my time. In year six, I only achieved a Grade 5 in maths and had to repeat the year, something my family found incomprehensible. I saw it as part of my tragedy. I was also plagued by recurring nightmares, one of which was my parents arranging for men in red suits to come and kill me.

One day, the French teacher noticed that I was having cramps. She sent me home, saying that Mother would explain everything to me – but Mother explained nothing. When I menstruated for the first time, all Mother said was: "That happens to all the young girls." That day, she went to help in the butcher's shop as usual and told everyone behind the counter the big news. Mother's behaviour, and her inability to understand my emotional plight, led to my increasing alienation.

School was where I felt most at ease. Now and again, I was invited to the homes of classmates from affluent families, which helped me to gain some insight into different levels of society. One such classmate was Lea Lenschner, whose family owned a furniture factory. The Lenschners, wealthy Jews, lived in an art nouveau mansion with a lift. They had several maids who wore starched white bonnets and aprons. I was impressed. Mother was pleased that I had enjoyed my time there and insisted on inviting Lea to my birthday party. I was dismayed: "We can't do that! Everything is so small here!" Nevertheless, Mother telephoned Frau Lenschner to issue the invitation. Walter promised to organise a raffle and some little pencil and paper games. The day of my party arrived. A Mercedes pulled up outside, the chauffeur rang the doorbell and escorted Lea inside. We drank cocoa and ate a variety of pastries and, at 6 o'clock, we ate frankfurters with potato salad. We played, we danced *Rosenstock, Holderblüt*, and my brother Walter organised the raffle, we had great fun and then Lea was collected. Later, the telephone rang, it was Frau Lenschner. According to Mother, "Lea thought it was the nicest birthday party she's ever been to." It gave me cause for thought.

4. Hitler Seizes Power

I read the newspapers regularly and took an interest in the dramatic events that shaped the dying years of the Weimar Republic. One day, my favourite teacher, Herr Heintke, set us an essay on the subject of Autumn. I wrote about my route to school, about the crunching of leaves under foot, and then added "...and unemployed people stand at street corners with their hands in their empty pockets." Herr Heintke called me to the front of the class, read out the entire essay and said: "A good essay, but that part about the unemployed is rather exaggerated." I insisted that I had written it the way I saw it.

For some time now, evening visits from friends had been overshadowed by the insecurity and fear caused by the economic, social and political crises. The Nazi Party had become increasingly powerful in the Reichstag. On 30 January 1933, I was woken by a knock at my door. It was Walter. "Wake up! Things are going to get really bad for us Jews now that Hitler has come to power." President von Hindenburg had appointed Hitler Reich Chancellor. I knew, immediately, that my childhood had come to an end. As indeed it had. I didn't notice much at school at first, although the Minister for Propaganda, Goebbels, immediately started spouting anti-Jewish slogans.

When Jewish friends came to visit, we spoke in hushed tones. The general view, at first, was that "we Germans surely won't allow that idiot to remain in power." A few weeks later: "The Germans surely won't let him stay in power. We give him six months." At first, we all tried to carry on as normal. Then Father took to wearing the ribbon of his Iron Cross on his jacket. He would visit his clients, but often returned home shattered, with stories of clients apologising that they were no longer able to buy from him: it had simply become too dangerous for their own businesses. Soon after, the Nazis called for the boycott of Jewish businesses. On 1 April 1933, Stormtroopers surrounded Jewish shops and daubed the windows with hate slogans, such as "*Juda verrecke*" (Let the Jew perish) or "*Kauft nicht bei Juden*" (Don't buy from the Jew). We sat round the table that day and tried to eat but were frightened and didn't know what to do. We decided to meet with our relatives from Acherstrasse. Our fears increased when we looked out of the window and saw one of the girls who came regularly to eat at our house, standing outside the front door, wearing the *BDM* uniform. But we didn't have a shop and didn't know what to make of it.

On my way to school that day, I decided that I wouldn't take part in a play called *Das Myrtenfräulein* after all, because of the boycott. The teacher was shocked because she couldn't replace me at such short notice. I, on the other hand, was indignant and would not be talked round. Desperate, the German teacher, a young student teacher I liked, pulled me into an empty classroom where she burst into tears and told me that nobody wanted me to pull out. I felt sorry for her and gave in. Later, we met our relatives in town. There was a Stormtrooper standing in front of their butcher's shop. As we tried to go into the house, an elderly couple approached us and the woman said to my uncle: "You see, Herr Grüneberg, if you, as a Jew, had closed your business every Saturday, you wouldn't have been forced to do so now!"

Discrimination against Jews did not stop at the school gate. One day, I arrived at school and Herr Heintke said: "Please tell your Jewish classmates that you are not to take part in German class today. We will be studying racial anthropology." We five Jewish girls retreated to an empty classroom. I was both frightened and angry. Otherwise very little changed. Our headmistress, Dr. Schellens, made no secret of the fact that she was not a Hitler fan. Many years later, she was disciplined by being transferred.

The highlight of the week for me was music class. We all worshipped our teacher, Herr Zumer, who believed he was a second Beethoven. His lessons were always interesting. He would, for instance, use drawing pins to turn his piano into a harpsichord. One morning, he came into class and announced that he had written a song which we must now all learn. I was horrified when I heard the words:

Germany has joyfully awoken
Sieg Heil! Sieg Heil! Sieg Heil! (Hail to the Victory)
Strong men are in power
Sieg Heil! Sieg Heil! Sieg Heil!
See the brown, the black hosts
They have dreamt of victory for fourteen years.
Gazing loyally towards their leader
All hearts beating as one for the Fatherland!
New Germany, rejoice!
Adolf Hitler leads you now!

Then the first girl to wear uniform appeared in school. I was later told by one of my school friends – the daughter of a Social Democrat lawyer – that, when challenged about the uniform, the girl had replied: "My parents thought I should learn how to hate Jews." There was one girl in my class I was particularly fond of, called Gertrud Schleimer. She lived in Wesseling, outside Bonn, and she was permitted to be late for school occasionally, because of the poor train connections. I invited her to my birthday party and, as usual, we had sausages and potato salad at six o'clock. Gertrud must have particularly enjoyed the sausages because she wanted to know where Mother had bought them. I told her that we got all our meat from Uncle Leo Grüneberg, who had a shop in Acherstrasse. She said she would recommend the shop to her mother. Years later, at a school reunion, she told me that her mother had said she couldn't possibly buy the sausages from Grüneberg's "because they're Jews!"

Jews in Germany now had to learn which public places they were allowed to frequent and where they were excluded. Both these changed almost daily. It was during that time we had a family outing to Hotel Dreesen. As usual, we sat on the Rhine terrace and, as usual, the Dreesens came to greet us. But, this time, Georg said to Father: "Herr Kober, you are a good customer and an old friend of ours, but we have to inform you that we have Hitler staying with us at the moment." Hesitantly, we got up and said goodbye and, as we skirted the hotel, there he was, standing on the steps at the entrance. To this day, I remember the overwhelming fear that overcame me at that moment. And that was our last visit to the Dreesen.

5. Zionism

I had not come into contact with Zionism until then. We had a little blue tin in our living room with the Hebrew inscription: '*Keren Kajemet le-Israel*'. The Jewish National Fund was collecting money to purchase land in Israel. But no country called Israel existed and I had no idea what it all really meant. I don't suppose Mother knew much about it either, but her winnings from her rummy afternoons found their way into that blue tin. Unbeknown to me, Uncle Sim had wanted to emigrate to Palestine with his wife and children as early as 1923, and to open a clinic in Haifa. Aunt Tilly had gone on ahead to oversee its establishment. They had to close the clinic after a year because they had too few patients. Yes, there were Jews, Arabs and German missionaries living in Haifa, but the surrounding areas were still too sparsely populated. They returned to Hamburg with their children but remained staunch Zionists. I was also unaware that, in 1932, one of my father's sisters emigrated to Palestine with her Polish husband.

My involvement with political Zionism began in the spring of 1933, whilst I was visiting my relatives in Hamburg. One day, they said: "It's Thursday afternoon, both our surgeries are closed, so we have time to go out. Would you like to come with us for a picnic on the Lüneburger Heide?" During the course of the afternoon, I realised that the outing had been 'plotted' with a view to winning me over to Zionism. Whilst we were eating our picnic, Aunt Tilly produced a book from her bag: Theodor Herzl's *Diary*. She talked about Herzl's ideas and spoke of emigration to Palestine. My spontaneous reaction was that I didn't want to live in a country where only Jews lived, but I couldn't stop thinking about it and read Herzl's book The Jewish State. The idea of having a home to go to once one is no longer welcome as a guest somewhere else sounded compelling; and this home was to be the Jewish State. The Old Testament told us about the yearning for Zion. I used it as a pretext to study Jewish history intensively.

I returned to Beuel with Karla, a distant relative I had got to know in Hamburg and liked immediately. She was to help Mother with household chores, as we no longer had a maid. Karla regarded the 'placement' as part of her preparation for emigration to Palestine. She was seven years older than me but the age gap did not matter at all, and we became close friends. Karla introduced me to Zionist thinking in more depth. In common with many of our contemporaries, she had an enthusiasm I shared and, with her help, I founded a Zionist youth group in Bonn. I had adopted many of Herzl's ideas and read books about Palestine and socialism and was busy trying to recruit new members. Through Karla, I was put in touch with Zionists in Bonn and I also talked to girls at my school who I assumed would be interested in youth group activities. My school friends heard me speak with enthusiasm about our new home: Palestine.

In those days, Germany had a great variety of Zionist organisations and alliances. My brother Walter belonged to the right-wing *Kameraden* youth organisation, for which I was still too young. I formed a group of between six and eight girls and we met for all sorts of activities, including hikes, nocturnal outings and camping trips. Even before the Hitler era, there was a strong youth movement in Germany to which I felt drawn. It was relatively apolitical, close to nature, and critical of the middle class. We were 'down-to-earth', walked in the woods, sat around campfires, sang – and despised the petit bourgeois. And so we created our own romantic adventures because the Nazis had excluded us from theirs. It was also the beginning of my dedication to the Zionist cause.

Karla and I did a lot together. She took me along to see films not accessible to my age group. After seeing *Cairo Season* starring Renate Müller and Willy Fritsch, I told Father that one day I would go to Cairo, a premonition that was later fulfilled. It was also through Karla that I came into contact with the Bonn branch of the *Hechalutz* group, an organisation that trained young Jews in agriculture and prepared them for emigration to Palestine. Many in the Jewish community were interested in our activities. Whilst Karla was still with us, we were invited by Frau Kaufmann, a friend of Mother's and a member of the women's committee of the Beuel Jewish community. After we had talked about Palestine, we were asked to dance the *hora*, the Jewish circle dance. Frau Kaufmann also asked us to sing the Zionist hymn, the *Hatikvah*, which we did with fervour. Our own vision of Palestine was strongly influenced by a Zionist film that painted the land in glowing colours.

The head of the Beuel Jewish community was a man called Goldreich. He was highly respected and exuded wisdom and kindness. Even as a child, I liked him. After I had discovered Zionism, I met him on the street one day. He told me that he, too, was a Zionist and planned to emigrate to *Erez Yisroel*, the land of Israel, with his family – indeed, many years later, I saw him again in Jerusalem.

6. The Battle for My Beliefs

The time came for Karla to go back to Hamburg. I was very sad. Matters were made worse by my having to leave my school because my parents could no longer afford the school fees. It was a terrible shock for me and one I found difficult to accept. There was no discussion and I wasn't consulted; after all, I had a roof over my head and food to eat – what else was there to discuss? I couldn't talk to my brother, who didn't understand me. I found the situation so oppressive that I ran away from home. Sadly, I only got as far as Cologne, where I stayed with members of the Alliance. However, Father came to get me and so it started all over again. Mother became more and more unapproachable and relegated me to the role of housemaid. I had to get up early, make the beds, clean the windows and do other household chores. Very often, when I had finished making the big, heavy beds in my parents' bedroom, I would collapse onto the bed, exhausted. Then Mother would hurry up the stairs: "What are you doing? Are you unwell?"

The stairs leading from the small entrance hall to the upstairs bedrooms became associated with anxiety. My bedroom was up there, too, but it was more than just a room to me. It was a sacred retreat, where I was able to read and daydream, whilst the rest of the family were downstairs in the living room. Mother often used to shout up the stairs "What are you doing up there?" Now, feeling more like a maid, my room had become even more important, and the stairs had turned into a dangerous gateway for the invasion of my refuge. I could tell by the way Mother barged up the stairs and aggressively swayed her elbows from side to side that I was about to be unfairly accused again. I also associated those stairs with another terrible event involving Mother. I had a girlfriend I used to discuss my most intimate problems with. One day, she sent me a letter that Mother proceeded to open, as if by right. To this day, I remember my fear as I stood at the top of the stairs, Mother down below holding the letter and reading words intended for no one but me. At that moment, I hated her.

32

I remember this time as one of martyrdom. My role at home had changed fundamentally – I had been demoted from daughter to maid. My shame and unhappiness was compounded by having to leave the *Oberlyzeum* and, because of my age, attend the vocational school in Beuel, where I felt completely out of place. Of course, I saw how my parents struggled to ensure that we could at least have something to eat every day and sometimes go on a little outing, meet relatives, or even go to a café or the cinema. I was often left to my own devices and visited the *Hechalutz* and met with friends. One beautiful summer's day, I was getting ready for an evening in the *Hechalutz*. The 'uniform' was white blouse, dark skirt. I had just washed my hair and used foundation for the first time. Some boys were waiting for me in the courtyard. I walked down the stairs and, as I went through the kitchen, Mother exclaimed enthusiastically "Haven't I got a beautiful daughter!" I was so very happy at that moment, receiving my mother's approbation after so long.

I always knew that my parents were good people, that they gave me a wonderful childhood with a great deal of love and freedom. They were my role models in many ways, especially in their tireless readiness to help others; this made it all the more difficult for me to cope with the tensions between us. The feeling that I simply couldn't please them and was unloved and unappreciated by them made me very unhappy. The resulting feelings of guilt have stayed with me for the rest of my life and have been made more bitter because we never had the chance to reconcile our differences.

Mother continued to work in my uncle's butcher's shop every Saturday. Business was still good because the customers appreciated quality and did not want to give up shopping there. On 10 August 1935, I went to the shop after school. Aunt Jetta had gone to Hamburg to have her heart complaint treated by Uncle Sim. The first person I saw as I entered the shop was Mother, her face as white as a sheet. She nodded towards the office where, through the glass panes, I saw two brownshirts arresting Uncle Leo. "You must go straight to the station, collect Aunt Jetta, and tell her that Uncle Leo has been arrested." I was stunned but brought my aunt the news. A week later, as I was crossing the marketplace, I heard a newspaper seller shout: "The Jewish pig butcher Grüneberg arrested for currency racketeering!" Uncle Leo had tried to protect his savings by moving them to Holland. Someone had obviously informed on him. The local newspaper, *Der Westdeutscher Beobachter*, carried the following article:

> *For many years the Jew Grüneberg has had a butcher's shop in Acherstrasse which unfortunately attracted a large clientele from the Aryan population of Bonn. Despite the many incidents occurring in Bonn's Jewish butchers and other cities, these short-sighted fellow Germans continue to buy from Jews. These customers have enabled the Jew Grüneberg to amass a fortune. Unlike German craftsmen and tradesmen whose money supports the German economy, he moved almost all of his money abroad.(...) Whilst the Jew Grüneberg smuggled*
> *the money from his German customers out of the country, he kept his business going by exploiting credit facilities which of course he had no intention of repaying.(...) And our fellow countrymen helped this criminal Jew.(...) There is no justification for this.(...) Anyone still buying from a*
> *Jew is manifesting a deliberate refusal to support the German people's fight against its biggest enemy.(...) A sizeable number of well-known Bonn personalities including high-ranking civil servants, doctors, lawyers,restaurateurs and hotel proprietors and other well-known tradesmen continue to buy from Jews. We are considering whether or not to publish their names.*

Which is what happened soon after. On 24 August 1935, Ludwig Rickert, the Mayor of Bonn, published his 'Report on the

Political Situation' listing the names of prominent customers of Jewish businesses, the same list published on 19 August by Der Westdeutscher Beobachter. Aunt Jetta was arrested shortly afterwards. The whole family was thrown into a state of desperation and insecurity. Any remnant of hope Father may have been clinging to that justice would prevail, that this could not happen to us as good Germans, especially to him, as a decorated war veteran, was destroyed. Thereafter, we heard of more political arrests; people disappeared without trace. We were not allowed to talk about them, but we knew of the existence of 'labour camps.' For fear of the consequences, the disappearance of Jewish acquaintances was euphemistically referred to as having 'gone away' (as were those who had already emigrated).

7. Hamburg

And so it was in 1935, I asked my parents to let me go and stay in Hamburg for a while. I was full of expectation as I sat on the train with Father. He looked at me with affection and sadness, unable to understand why I wanted something so different. I know he thought highly of me and believed that I would do well. He had often told me he thought I would make a good lawyer. But what would I do now? I was grateful he was letting me go to Hamburg and looked forward to being in a city so different from the small town atmosphere in which I had grown up. I had felt very much at home on my previous visits to Hamburg. The people there seemed to me to be broadminded, cultured and liberal-thinking. To me, there was also something romantic about Hamburg: in my uncle's house, people read a lot and played music. It was more free and stimulating.

Of course, I immediately joined the *Hashomer Hatzair* – the 'Young Guard' – who, again, were very different from those I had met in Bonn. This Zionist-Socialist youth movement was founded in Eastern Europe before the First World War and was especially active in Poland. It only reached Germany in 1931. Its mission was the creation of a Jewish homeland in Palestine. The organisation bore a close similarity to the scout movement, but was more political. Those I met there were unsentimental idealists of Marxist persuasion, utterly devoted to the cause. I loved it.

Aunt Tilly had found me a job with Eva von der Dunk, who owned a bookshop. She rented a room for me, which my parents grudgingly paid for. Frau von der Dunk was a widow and the daughter of the Jewish philosopher, Ernst Marcus. I was a sort of 'lady's help' for her: I made lunch and tidied up a bit. She didn't expect much but, through her, I was introduced to a new world. That included, above all, the bookshop, which was directly accessible from the flat. Whenever there was time, I would go into this paradise, help myself to the latest books and read. Many influential people came to Frau von der Dunk's bookshop, among them the Jewish philosopher, Martin

Buber. I got to know him and found him fascinating. I read his books and attended his lectures, which we also discussed in the group. I particularly remember his prophetic statements about the yet-to-be-built Jewish State.

Aunt Tilly was still in Hamburg but she was busy making arrangements for a renewed emigration to Palestine. To my great delight, I also met Karla again, who was helping Uncle Sim in his practice. Unfortunately, she already had a departure date for Palestine; I was so unhappy about this, I found it impossible to go to the station to say goodbye. Many years were to pass before I would see her again. In the meantime, Aunt Tilly had also been notified of her date for emigration. Happily for me, she arranged for me to move in with Uncle Sim after her departure. Over time, my work with the Zionists intensified and I was out a lot, recruiting new members. One such member was a sixteen-year-old girl from a Russian-Jewish family who made me very welcome, the girl and I became friends. One day, I visited her and found her in bed with 'flu. Whilst I sat with her, she became increasingly tender. I thought this was the Russian way of showing warmth at first, but alarm bells began to ring when she attempted intimacy. Not knowing how to respond, I decided that it would be wiser to keep my distance in future.

My stay in Hamburg also had a darker side. However fascinated I was by the world of this big city, I was still a child and missed love and affection. These new experiences were accompanied by a sense of loneliness, which might have been tempered had my parents been more understanding. Instead, the conflict continued and intensified. Whilst they had a good relationship with Uncle Sim and Aunt Tilly, they doubted that their liberal and intellectual influence was good for me. Added to this was the effect of their own exclusion from society and the financial consequences that had thrown them out of their familiar routine.

One day I received a letter from home, which contained the following passage from Father:

I knew it wouldn't take you long to forget us. Your parents never had a place either in your head nor your heart. And it seems that the life you're living there is unlikely to be in your future interests (...)

We have brought you up without airs and graces, and I don't want an arrogant, over-educated, loudmouthed, cheeky girl at home when you come back from Hamburg. (...)

As you know, I still have the agency for an imported product which is currently not available. Over the last few weeks I have earned 25 marks per week. That is the unvarnished truth. I can afford to pay neither rent nor an hourly rate; you will have to accept that you'll have to come home in the next few days.

So alarmed must my parents have been about my development, Mother travelled to Hamburg to check up on me. At her suggestion, we met at an elegant café on the Jungfernstieg. I turned up in my *Hashomer* 'uniform' – a velvet 'climbing' jacket and matching corduroy-velvet skirt with lots of zips. I was completely out of place and I'm sure Mother felt as embarrassed as I did! Her visit was a nightmare. I remember nothing else about it except the feelings of sadness and disappointment she communicated when we said goodbye. And I stayed on in Hamburg.

It was Christmas 1935 and the *Hashomer's* winter camp. Frau von der Dunk had given me a marvellous rucksack, and I was desperate to go. Predictably, my parents were against it. Father wrote in his birthday letter to me:

It is Mother's wish that you do not go on this trip. Your opinion is irrelevant. It is your parents' wish and you will have to comply. Right or wrong, you must leave the decision to us. You will simply have to do as you are told and if you haven't yet learnt to do so, this is the time to do so.

I was unrelenting and went anyway. The camp was a completely new adventure for me. We stayed in a primitive youth hostel. There was snow was on the ground. Everything was very basic. I was very surprised, one night, to see people pairing up in sleeping bags. Needless to say, my parents made a huge fuss when I told them I had gone after all.

I had been in Hamburg for about nine months when my uncle disclosed that, regretful though he was, my parents had urged him to send me back to Beuel. I don't remember leaving Hamburg, but I do remember my unhappiness on returning to Beuel. Mother was nervous, aloof and depressed about how we would manage financially, as Father no longer had an income. Our daily lives were ruled by arbitrary and unpredictable decisions and events. We had no option but to live from day to day.

8. Political Life

The atmosphere in Beuel and Bonn was frightening. I would lie in bed listening to the sound of Nazis marching past our house singing, and was terrified that they would soon come and get either Father or all of us. When we met others, the conversation was mainly about who had already left Germany, and where they had gone. Some countries, such as Argentina, the USA or South Africa, accepted Jews provided they had sufficient means. Some affluent Jews from Bonn had already emigrated to South Africa and Holland, others had simply disappeared. We assumed they had been taken to 'labour camps'. In those desperate times, the community developed a gallows humour.

One day, Mother and I were in the kitchen when there was a knock at the door. There stood Frau Frank: "Well, Frau Kober, look at you standing there cooking while our Führer is about to walk around the corner!" I ran to the street corner and there he was, standing in his car with his arm raised... and I was the only one there.

We talked a lot about how to obtain an entry visa to Palestine, equivalent to winning the lottery. Under the British Mandate, immigration into Palestine was strictly controlled, for political reasons. The issue of visas was limited to those with relatives already living in Palestine, or those lucky enough to reach the top of a waiting list. Most of the visas were intended for younger people. The Zionist organisations required applicants to be healthy and fit to work and to have completed two years in a field, such as agriculture. There was also the 'Capitalist Visa' for applicants who could afford to pay £1,000.

Henrietta Szold, an American who jointly founded the *Youth Aliyah* with Recha Freier, succeeded in negotiating a separate immigration visa with the British, exclusively for 14 to 18-year olds. Applying for such a visa required spending a month at an observation camp organised by the *Youth Aliyah*, who then saw to the immigration arrangements. Once in Palestine, the youngsters spent two years in a kibbutz, which was required to provide them with work and an education. Parents had to pay a contribution, and if they were unable to do so, the Zionist organisation paid on their behalf. After two years in a kibbutz, the young people were expected to form a *Garin* – a core group - and, if possible, establish a new kibbutz. Recruiting young people for immigration was *Hashomer's* main task.

After my return from Hamburg, I threw myself into its work. First, I went to the *Hechalutz* in Bonn. I wanted to start a local *Hashomer Hatzair* branch and contacted the organisation in Cologne. Herr Nussbaum, my former teacher, suggested I get in touch with one of his former students, Ulrich Rosenthal, who was interested in Zionist ideas. Ulrich and I were the same age and had many interests and aims in common so became good friends. What most attracted me to him was his intellect. We brought together young people aged 18 - 21, discussed politics – especially Socialism and Marxism – and organised outings for our new branch of *Hashomer Hatzair*. We also set up a group for the younger ones called 'Sons of the Desert' and devised a programme for them. I had been very impressed by the leading *Hashomer* activists I had met in Hamburg, and I met them again in Cologne. They advised us on how to set up our local branch and gave us practical and organisational support.

In effect, the discussion ("*Sicha*") – which followed talks given by a guest speaker or group member – was a way of educating the young members. The topics covered ranged from the practical – parenting, relationships with parents – to the latest advances in science. Naturally, the emphasis was on politics and history. We covered pacifism and liberation movements, discussed unions, read the Old Testament as Jewish history, and deliberated the question of Palestine and the founding of a kibbutz. We also talked a lot about Bolshevism, as we regarded the kolkhoz as a model for our ideas of a kibbutz. And even though we were not nationalists, we did share Herzl's ideas. Only later did I become aware of the contradiction between Herzl's nationalism and socialist ideas. One of the liberation movements we identified strongly with was the Mexican one and Zapata was one of our heroes; we even sang their song. Despite our young age – we had just turned 14 – we sensed that war was inevitable.

We set great store in cultural activities, such as theatre performances, song and literary evenings and cabarets, as well as hikes, night trips, camp fires, swimming and bicycle tours. This 'scouting' culture was essentially a legacy of the youth movement of the 1920s. We also cultivated the extreme anti-bourgeois attitude, which provoked strong reactions from the RjF, to the extent that Father had to endure reproachful questions about what his daughter was up to. They were concerned that Zionism would provide the Nazis with evidence that Judaism was not a religion but a race. I felt that it was important for the various Jewish groups to enter into dialogue and arranged a meeting between *Hashomer* representatives from Cologne and the RjF. I was pleased that this meeting led to a better, mutual understanding, and believe that Father was proud of his daughter on that occasion.

The Jewish community did not, of course, simply consist of sceptics. Some well-respected figures were sympathetic and supportive, which helped my relationship with my parents. Frau Mamlock, whose daughter was in our *Hashomer Hatzair*, introduced me to the young Rabbi Seligsohn, who held our work in high regard. I learnt even more about Jewish history through him and he visited my parents to put in a good word for me. It was, though, Herr Hammerstein, a teacher at the Jewish School in Bonn, who helped me most. 1935 saw the foundation of a Jewish school in Bonn, when Jewish children were no longer allowed to attend state schools. One day he asked Mother whether she would mind if I helped his wife around the house. Mother agreed and so I cycled to the Hammersteins every day to help with household chores and mind the children. I must have done a fairly good job because when the whole of the Jewish school went to school camp – Haus Berta – Herr Hammerstein decided I should come as a supervisor for the younger pupils. I used this opportunity to recruit some of the young girls to our *Hashomer Hatzair* branch, but I had to be discreet, as the camp belonged to the RjF and my parents had to be kept in the dark.

One day, out of the blue, Aunt Jetta was released from prison. She moved in with us almost immediately and thus began another ordeal for me. In the past, I had suffered her husband's sexual advances; now I was the object of her jealousy. She stirred my mother up against me, which resulted in a further deterioration in my relationship with Mother. I had to do more and harder housework. Ironically, Aunt Jetta had rented out one room of her now empty house in Acherstrasse to *Hashomer Hatzair*, where our group met regularly.

I suppose part of the reason our work for *Hashomer* had become so intense was that there was very little social life for us adolescents. As Jewish teenagers, we were neither able to participate in public activities, nor were we allowed into any clubs, including sports clubs. Being excluded from dances and from participating in the carnival, all that remained for us was the Italian ice cream parlour and the cinema.

Contact with our neighbours had not broken off completely and word got around that Margot Kober intended to emigrate to Palestine. Lukas, our neighbour's eldest son, heard about it, too. Unemployed and fascinated by the events in Palestine, he cycled to Palestine through Turkey. Sadly, I don't know what happened to him. As the prospects of my emigration crystallised, my parents found it increasingly difficult to come to terms with it, although we never spoke openly about it. Mother was in denial. Because of his national-conservative mindset, Father was sceptical at first, but he seemed to resign himself to my plans as the situation worsened. In the end, I had his full support.

In 1936, *Hashomer Hatzair* decided to apply for a visa for Palestine for me. They applied for Ulrich Rosenthal's visa at the same time, so we could travel together. We were sent to a *Youth Aliyah* camp in Schniebinchen, near Berlin, for four weeks, where we had to do agricultural and household work and were assessed by the Zionist leaders on suitability for emigration. I had left the parental home and all other everyday problems behind and felt very comfortable in the group. Even though it was a test phase for us, it felt more like a holiday camp to me. A month later, everyone returned home. I went to Berlin first – my first and only visit there – where I stayed with a female friend from *Hashomer*. Berlin was a sea of swastikas. My parents, by now used to the idea of my emigration, decided that I should say goodbye to some of my relatives. So I left Berlin for Leipzig to visit my paternal grandfather, who had a little delicatessen but was also the cantor in his synagogue. I loved him for his kind humour and he was genuinely pleased that his granddaughter was making her way "back to Zion."

The whole Leipzig family – Father's brother and sister and their families – had all gathered at Grandfather's. The excitement I felt about my prospective emigration, a crucial step towards my future, was mixed with the bitterness of having to say goodbye – a final farewell repeated several times in the weeks that followed.

Not much had changed at home. Mother instructed the local tailor to make some clothes for me for Palestine. The designs were influenced by a Zionist propaganda film that used music and folklore, where young girls in white headscarves harvested fruit in the orange grove and sang. Then came the day Ulrich and I received a telegram informing us of our departure date. We were also told that this was to be the last official train, organised by the Zionist organisation, from Bonn to Marseille. Even though my departure had been looming for a while, Mother was shocked. My brother, Walter, who was then working in Herford, was asked to come home. Father rushed to the town hall to get a me passport. He returned home very agitated: the registrar had told him: "Herr Kober, I know you well, but as your daughter is a Jew and has lived in Hamburg for nine months, she will need a document of compliance to prove she has done nothing wrong." Father telephoned the authorities in Hamburg immediately, explained the situation, and insisted on having the document sent to Beuel as quickly as possible. Mother, packing feverishly, was crying. "Don't go, all the drawers are empty!" In the meantime, Walter arrived home.

By Thursday, we had still not heard and I was due to travel on the following Monday. Father went back to the town hall and was told that the passport would be ready by 11:45 on Saturday morning, when he could pick it up provided the document of compliance had arrived. The photographer came the next day, 30 August 1936, and took the last family portrait. Father was constantly on the telephone, calling Hamburg. I heard him say that his daughter's future would be destroyed if the document did not arrive in time. Frau Rosenthal came to chat with Mother. I sat in my favourite chair at the window, looked at the clock, and felt sure that the document would come and I would be able to travel. I imprinted the view of the street on my memory. It felt as though the world was standing still. On Saturday afternoon, just before midday, the postman arrived with the telegram, which contained two words: No objections. Father practically tore it from his hands and ran to the town hall to get my passport. It was a beautiful Sunday in August. It being my last meal, Mother said I should choose whatever I liked. The two eggs I asked for fulfilled a childish dream. I said goodbye to Walter, who mumbled that we would probably never see each other again.

9. From Beuel to Beth Sera

Next morning we took a taxi to Bonn railway station. A group from *Hashomer Hatzair* was there to see me off. Ulrich and his family stood close by. Mother pulled me behind a bench. Holding me tight, she screamed: "I don't want anyone watching me saying goodbye to you. Don't go, don't go, I'll never see you again." Father looked like a ghost. We boarded the train and the doors slammed shut. Father ran alongside the train as it moved away and, as he disappeared from view, I laughed hysterically and cried at the same time.

Father had given me 10 *Reichsmark*. At the first stop, I went to a bookshop and bought myself a book on history of art by Hamann; I still have it to this day. The train called at many stations and more and more emigrants boarded. Similar farewell scenes were played out wherever I looked. I particularly remember an old, blind man in Strasbourg bidding an emotional farewell to his son. The train was completely overcrowded, which made the journey exhausting, but we did not mind. Two days later, as we arrived in Marseille, track workers raised their arms and clenched their fists, greeting us with cries of: "*Heil* Moscow!" They were communists who regarded us as like-minded souls. We returned the greeting.

Sitting on my suitcase in the middle of Marseille's vast harbour, surrounded by the chaos of people rushing past, cries, screams and ships' sirens, I realised I was now on my own. And then we boarded the SS *Patria*, originally a French ship, now used to carry emigrants to Palestine. We boarded: my group of twenty-five young people – six of us, girls – was led by a young woman we knew from Schniebinchen. It was too hot to sleep in the very narrow beds on the lower deck. The ship was full to capacity and more, and the food rations in our third class area were insufficient. The Zionists on board who were emigrating on 'capitalist visas' agreed to share their food with us.

After six days, Haifa came into view. Despite warnings, all the passengers rushed over to one side of the ship to catch a glimpse, and it tilted alarmingly. We sang the *Hatikvah*:

As long as the Jewish spirit is yearning deep in the heart,
With eyes turned toward the East, looking toward Zion,
Then our hope – the two-thousand-year-old hope – will not be
lost:
To be a free people in our land,
The land of Zion and Jerusalem.

All tiredness and tension vanished. It was an uplifting and highly emotional moment. We had arrived!

My first impressions after disembarking were rather sobering. It was hot, dusty and grey, and a few Arabs were going about their business. The immigration procedure took a long time. I was disappointed that Uncle Sim and Aunt Tilly weren't there to greet me and felt lost. We were greeted by Perez, the leader of our kibbutz, Beth Sera. He was German, and we liked him from the start, standing there in his work clothes, khaki trousers, blue shirt with a white cord and peaked cap. A lady came up to our group and asked for Margot Kober. Introducing herself as Henriette Szold, she came bearing greetings from my relatives, who were sorry not to be able to meet me in person. We were put on an old, dusty train, which swayed through the countryside of *Emek Yisroel*: just hills, not a tree nor a bush in sight. I don't remember how long we were travelling, but, suddenly, the train came to a halt. There was no railway station or building to be seen. As we alighted, skinny, tanned, curly-haired girls looked us up and down. One of them told me I would soon lose my flab and rosy cheeks. They were from the neighbouring kibbutz, Affikim, and had arrived from Germany six months earlier with *Youth Aliyah*.

Perez pointed to a lorry. We climbed aboard and drove a short way through banana plantations to Beth Sera. A strange noise greeted us on arrival: children were beating square buckets – '*pachim*' – with sticks.

47

We soon learned that these buckets were used during harvesting, as bird scarers. Today they served to play us welcoming music.

10. Kibbutz Life

We lived in a house with five rooms. British soldiers were camped out on the flat roof. At the back was a veranda, where, after she had welcomed us in German, a pleasant young Lithuanian woman told us: "You know there is unrest in the country. At night, we are often fired at from up there." She pointed to an Arab hilltop village on the other side of the River Jordan. "If you hear shots, please take cover under your beds. Does anyone want to volunteer to sleep on the *mechpesset* – the veranda?" I came forward with a few others and we moved into our quarters. The shooting started at midnight. We did as instructed and crawled under our beds. The British soldiers on the roof above us were fast asleep. Thus ended our first day in the Holy Land.

Beth Sera was an 'old' kibbutz that celebrated its tenth anniversary during our two-year stay. Among the kibbutzniks were Germans, members of the Socialist-Zionist *Habonim* (Builders of Freedom), and strictly Marxist Lithuanians. The kibbutz had adopted the *Hashomer Hatzair* constitution, which meant there was no external workforce. Everyone was equal, and all income was divided equally. Decisions were made democratically at meetings. I soon learned that theoretical knowledge of kibbutz life had not properly prepared us for the harsh reality. I had to leave behind my middle-class expectations and adapt to the climate and working conditions, and there were complications and embarrassments: for example, one day we went swimming in the Jordan but us girls found it embarrassing that everyone was naked. It was often a matter of trial and error, as Jehuda Wallach, a member of our group, later a military historian, expressed it.

I exchanged my German name for a Hebrew one – Miriam; Ulrich became Uri. Our day started unusually early, between five and six in the morning. Most of us took a jug of water with us when we went to the fields to work. I never did get used to the taste of that heavily chlorinated water. We worked until sunrise and then made our way to the *chadar ha-ochel* – the dining room – for breakfast at long tables. Instead of the coffee and fresh rolls we were used to, there was *deisa,* a watery porridge, and homemade *leben*, a very sour yoghurt. Then there was a big bowl of produce from our fields: hard tomatoes, woody radishes and so forth, proof that the kibbutzniks had not yet mastered the art of agriculture in those latitudes. We returned to the fields after breakfast, and continued labouring until the heat forced us into the shade and we returned to the *chadar ha-ochel*. Lunch, too, tested our Central European palates: aubergines prepared in every conceivable way. There was one table reserved for those who suffered with gastro-intestinal conditions. We called it the *bim'kom* table and dreamed of being allowed to sit there, too, and eat chicken.

After lunch, we dragged ourselves through the heat, first to the showers and then to our darkened rooms, where we lay on sheets on the stone floor. We slept and sweated until three o'clock, when we were woken. The rest of the afternoon, until shortly before supper, was spent in an extremely hot wooden hut where we gathered to learn history, sociology, Marxist theory and – above all – Hebrew. From Day One, we had been advised to only communicate in Hebrew. This was almost impossible for most of us, as we didn't know this difficult language well enough and always found ourselves reverting to German. One friend who worked in the shop tried combining both languages. She would formulate sentences like "Yesterday I took the *rakevet* (train) to Haifa to buy *tapochei adama* (potatoes) in the *marsan* (shop)." I did not want to succumb to such a mish-mash and made an effort to use either one language or the other. One boy from our group surprised us all by taking an oath never to speak German again.

Leisure activities we took for granted at home – cinemas, theatres, bars, and the like – were nonexistent. Instead, a culture committee, which I joined, organised evening events. People were asked to research a topic or person of importance and give a talk. Afterwards, it was still warm, we joined the older kibbutzniks outside and danced the *hora* and popular Russian, Rumanian and Oriental dances. The cooler it became, the wilder our dances. The music was provided by a kibbutznik, on his mouth organ. We were sustained by our solidarity, the feeling of freedom and our ideals expressed in the dances.

During our first weeks in the kibbutz, we were told that our parents could send us a crate with our belongings, as we had only been allowed to emigrate with one small suitcase. We waited for the arrival of our crates as though our lives depended on them. Then, finally, after two or three months, they arrived. My parents had had a crate made that could be used as a wardrobe. Our neighbour in Beuel, Frau Mollberg, had insisted that Mother send two pears inside the crate, carefully packed in a little basket. Of course, my leather lace-up boots, which had travelled next to the pears, did not survive the journey – they were covered in green mould.

Our first day on the banana plantation was unbearably hot. Jaakov showed us what to do. All of us, three girls and three boys, were given a type of machete to hack away dead leaves from the trees. I got to work and was snipping away at the long leaves when I heard Jaakov's voice behind me: "That's not how it's done, Miriam!" He took my machete and hacked the leaves off with one stroke. "This isn't a beauty salon." It was so oppressively hot, we jumped into the irrigation system every half hour to cool down. On another occasion, we were standing in the meadow, again with Jaakov, learning to make hay. Arabs from the neighbouring village wandered up to us. After exchanging pleasantries, they got down to business. They didn't speak Hebrew; we understood little and were a bit frightened. One of them pointed at me. I stood there like an idiot, not understanding a word. The negotiations came to an end and, as they slowly walked away from us, one of the Arabs kept looking back. "That man was desperate to buy you", Jaakov said, mischievously. I didn't feel it was a laughing matter. The following night we were fired at from that village, and so it continued: during the day we did business with each other and by night they attacked us.

Girls had to work in the kitchen for six weeks. When my turn came, I had to prepare six chickens every morning for the 'bim'kom table'. That gave me the absurd idea of slaughtering the chickens as well. Steeling myself, I held a chicken between my knees, bent its head back, and cut its throat with a long, sharp knife. I repeated this procedure six times. When I had finished, I was surrounded by headless chickens staggering around me. After this bloodthirsty episode, I was detailed to work in the chicken coop. Beth Sera was known for its poultry farming; we had several thousand birds. My job was mucking out the sheds, collecting the eggs, and repeatedly painting and disinfecting the wooden boxes. I had to separate the weak hens from the healthy ones, which wasn't easy. Surrounded by fresh brown and white eggs, we thought about how we, the group, could exploit this once-in-a-lifetime opportunity – and decided to steal. I knew a girl from Czechoslovakia who offered us her room, including a primus stove and a frying pan. We then organised a 'come sit' – a party where people 'come' and 'sit' and, most importantly, eat. We ate more and more eggs. I don't remember how many, but what I haven't forgotten is how sick we all felt afterwards. After this prank, I became seriously ill with *papadachi*, an infection with malaria-like symptoms. I asked that a cousin be informed – before her emigration to Palestine, she had married a doctor, Otto Schleier, and they had settled in Tiberias. Otto immediately came to see how he could help. I was delighted to be visited by a family member and instantly felt better. I was soon back on my feet, or should I say knees, as I was allocated to weeding duty. This was done with a *turia,* a type of hoe. It was one of the most unpleasant and exhausting jobs in the kibbutz.

Life in the kibbutz was a particular challenge for us teenagers. We were totally unprepared for life in an adult commune and the adults, in turn, had to deal with our puberty. It was a mutual learning curve. It also opened up new opportunities for the members of the group to find, and prove, ourselves. We were often surprised at the strengths and weaknesses we had developed. As the first year in the kibbutz drew to a close, we decided to organise a celebration. How thrilled I was to be rehearsing for a theatrical performance. Our Lithuanian leader wrote lyrics for different pieces, one of which I particularly remember. We were to dress as *Chassidim* (pious ones) in long, black kaftans and fur hats and dance in a circle with our heads shaking, singing: "eu, eu, eu" and "ei, ei, ei" and, while dancing, remove our kaftans and change into pioneers in work outfits. The piece would then segue into the *hora*. The idea was to show how part of the country's development was attributable to making religious immigrants into diligent workers. We didn't succeed in staging this scene because, as soon as we began dancing, we broke down in uncontrollable laughter. But we never again laughed like that.

A Jewish theatre, *Habima*, had already been established in Palestine by then. My parents had talked about it because the company had toured Europe with the well-known *Chassidic* play *Dybbuk*. One member of the ensemble was the well-known Rovina. I was delighted when I heard that *Habima* was coming to Tiberias, and that there would be a kibbutz outing to see the performance. I don't remember the title of the play. One scene dealt with soldiers who had risen from their graves. Rovina, known for her sonorous, plaintive voice, stood centre stage and called "Miriami! Miriami! – Uri! Uri!"(Miriam, my Miriam, wake up, wake up!). Naturally, I was sitting next to Uri. Some members of the audience started to giggle and glanced over to us, and the louder Rovina wailed, the louder their giggles.

May 1 approached – an important day for us all. We had planned a rally for the benefit of the neighbouring kibbutzim in Affikim. In the morning, we all marched through the fields behind a red flag, dressed in blue workers' shirts and red neckerchiefs. The groups from other kibbutzim arrived at the same time. The gathering started with the singing of the Internationale, in Hebrew of course. That was followed by speeches and socialist songs. We had a feeling of solidarity and were convinced we could realise our ideals in this country.

The first thing we had to learn, when we arrived at the kibbutz in 1936, was how to handle a gun. The only official Jewish self-defence police force allowed by the British was the *Gafirim*, a form of paramilitary unit whose numbers were strictly limited by the British. Volunteers dressed in khaki trousers and shirts and were paid a small salary. The *Gafirim* taught us how to disassemble and reassemble a rifle. Thereafter, most of us took part in guard duty. We never attacked, but were prepared to defend ourselves. The kibbutz was surrounded by a barbed wire fence and, after the British troops had been detailed, we guarded it day and night. We were attacked in our fields on several occasions by Arabs. Once, several women came back from the field in a distressed state: Arabs had tried to abduct and rape them.

The programme for newcomers included a conducted tour of the country. We went by lorry, bus and train through the scrub and still sparsely populated areas, stopping off at some kibbutzim and, of course, Josef Trumpeldor's memorial. What interested us most, however, were the cities like Jerusalem and Tel Aviv. We learnt about how the urban population lived and what to look out for. For instance, girls were not allowed to wear trousers, as that would have been considered provocative for the Arab population. One instance showed me just how small Palestine was. Our group was ambling along the Tel Aviv beach promenade. Most of the cafés were simply furnished, and patronised mainly by middle-aged guests –Hungarians, Czechs, Germans among many others. People drank coffee and ate ice cream and everything felt very Central European. And it was there that I bumped into Uncle Sim, who lived in Haifa but now here he was, in a white linen suit and Panama hat!

I also got to know another branch of my family on this trip. Father's sister, Aunt Paula, her husband and two sons had left Leipzig in 1931 to emigrate to Palestine and had settled in Petach Tikva. My uncle had a little millinery shop in nearby Tel Aviv. Their younger son was about to celebrate his *Bar mitzvah* and I was invited. I had no idea about their living conditions and was somewhat surprised to find them living in a primitively furnished wooden hut. The next morning, we went to a little synagogue. The skirt I carried with me to use in areas populated by Arabs came in handy. After the service, a big table was set up outside the wooden hut, piled high with oriental delicacies, such as *falafel* and *hummus*. There was singing and drinking, then we were joined by Arab friends from neighbouring villages. I saw Arab dances for the first time; one, similar to the *hora*, was called *dabka*. The Arabs spoke Hebrew well and their Jewish friends spoke Arabic in turn. I felt at ease and joined in the dancing enthusiastically. The return journey to Beth Sera was through the Hula swamp area, long since drained. Today, it is a beautiful, green valley, and the malaria has gone.

During my time in the kibbutz, I wrote to my parents every week, embellishing my letters with comic drawings, little poems and long and humorous descriptions of everyday life. I took special care to give my letters a positive tone. My parents were very happy and passed the letters round. After all, who knew what a kibbutz was and what went on there! I also received replies from home – from friends and relatives – one of which I have kept to this day. It is a letter from the young Rabbi Seligsohn. Amongst other things, he wrote:

My dear Margot
Just between you and me I am still using this now probably
forbidden name, if you still allow me, as I cannot picture you
properly under the new name. (…) I read all your letters at your
parents' house and it is always as though one hears from an entirely
different world. I am thoroughly convinced that
you made the best decision possible, and I believe that had I myself
known more about these matters when I chose my profession, I
would have done the same. And today I almost regret not realising
what was happening at the time. Despite loud, opposing voices you
always asserted yourself in a
victorious and energetic way and for that I admire you. I would be
so very happy if you found the time to write to me at length now
and again to tell me of your experiences, your daily routine, what
you are working on and what you do besides work. (…)
You probably know what is happening here. When I am with your
family, you are the only topic of conversation, as that is the best and
most enjoyable topic. Please send my regards to the other people from

Bonn and please accept my very best wishes for your health, work, spirit and happiness.

R. Seligsohn

❧

Then came unsettling news from home. Mother was not at all well and Father wrote, in desperation, asking me to come and visit as the doctor seemed to think this would be the best medicine. I couldn't summon up any emotional response. A return to Germany was unthinkable for me. I spoke to Perez and he agreed that such a trip would be far too dangerous. Mother mentioned in every letter that she could not wait to see me, and Father wrote that Mother's eyes had become red from all the crying.

Uri's parents had managed to immigrate to England. They promised my parents to try and help them somehow. But nothing happened. My parents were forced to sell their little house in Beuel at well below market value, because of political pressure. They took up the offer from the Jewish community in Krefeld to take on the Community's restaurant and café. The proceeds of the house sale were used to buy new coffee machines and other equipment for the café. My brother went to help. They made a success of this enterprise by dint of effort and hard work. I found it hard to think about what was happening in Germany. Even though I had managed to escape the terror there, I now had problems of my own and had little or no help.

Life in the kibbutz for young people was spartan and very routine. Of course, we all had our dreams. For me, the lifestyle was a kind of lifesaver but it brought with it the battle involved in decision-making. As a special treat, we could have unlimited amounts of coffee every Saturday morning. However, it was served at 8 o'clock and if you weren't there on the dot, there would be none left. Every Saturday, I wrestled with the decision: should I have a lie-in or should I get up and drink coffee? The coffee almost always won. I was frequently the only one in the *chadar ha-ochel*.

Then came the day we were invited to take part in the founding of a new kibbutz. The kibbutz was called En Gev and was situated on the other side of the Sea of Galilee. It was customary to invite *chaverim* – comrades – from the neighbouring kibbutzim. We drove there by night, crossed the lake – the stars shining brightly above us – and sank the first spade into the ground for the construction of a water tower.

My first year in the kibbutz was difficult. Although I was respected in the group and was one of the leaders, together with my friends Uri and Jehuda Wallach, the problem was that Uri wanted to be alone with me whenever he got the chance, but the other members of the group were neither tolerant nor sympathetic. Uri's parents had been asking him to visit them in England for a long time. His mother wasn't at all well. Now the time had come for him to go. After we had said goodbye, I became closer to the group again. Whilst Uri was still in England, I decided to apply for a job in the nursery in order to become a *metapeleth* (nursery worker). Children were considered the most important asset of a kibbutz. The group called a *sicha* to discuss this proposal and gave their assent, which is how I started my new job in the nursery. I loved working with infants. They received the best care available in a kibbutz. The children's nurse was a strict, hard-working, and skilled woman and I learned a lot from her, but the job was arduous. We had ten to twelve infants who all had to be bathed, changed, fed and cared for. I had to help the mothers when they came to breastfeed. The advanced methods of baby care practised here were impressive. The psychologist came to regularly test the children. He taught me what to look for to establish whether they were developing normally.

When Uri returned, I went to Haifa harbour to meet him. I immediately noticed things weren't right. I was under the impression that he hadn't wanted to return to Palestine. We stayed overnight with Walter and Lilli, my Hamburg cousin and his future wife, who lived on Mount Carmel, and returned to the kibbutz the following day. Uri's depression was overshadowed by the preparations for our final ceremony at first. We had been in the kibbutz for two years and our contract with the *Youth Aliyah* was coming to an end. Big celebrations were being planned, complete with a theatre performance. We had chosen Maeterlinck's *Der Blaue Vogel* and had persuaded a director from *Habima* to rehearse the piece with us. It was an Expressionist play with a socialist theme and all the members of the group took part. Josef the shepherd and I were cast in the lead roles, Myrtle and Tyrtle. We really enjoyed the rehearsals and worked hard to get our parts right. We felt nostalgic, as this was, in effect, the end of our youth in the kibbutz. We were now going to form a g*arin* and so achieve 'adult status' amongst kibbutzniks. We were asked to propose a member of the group to deliver a farewell speech, describing in detail, and honouring our work over the last two years. I volunteered and was then amazed at my own courage. In the days that followed, I spent a lot of time fine-tuning my speech. It turned into a report on the different areas of work, the topics we had covered, all the new things we had learnt, and our activities. All this was set against the background of the Marxist philosophy of the kibbutz movement. It was important to present everything we had worked on and learnt in that time, to confirm to the kibbutz that the education of the *Youth Aliyah* group had been a success. We were proud of it, too.

The ceremony, which took place in the *chadar ha-ochel*, and the theatre performance were well received. My report even won plaudits from someone we all respected: "Your speech was very good, but you did make one mistake. Instead of '*Chumash*' (the Five Books of Moses) you said '*chamesh*' (five)." Only one mistake? I was relieved.

After the final ceremony, we had to give up our rooms and move into the wooden huts. We were now real, adult kibbutzniks, had formed a *garin*, and had to wait to be allocated newly acquired land. We worked all day in the kibbutz, like the other *chaverim*. One day – it was 1938 – we were told that Beth Sera was to accommodate a new group from Berlin. On the day the group arrived, we stood at the entrance, curious to inspect the newcomers. I overheard one *chavera* tell another: "The Schmene (fat one) is the Jefefia (beautiful one)." The newcomers, who had, of course, suffered two extra years under the Nazis, looked accordingly: poorly dressed, pale and persecuted. Today, I find it strange that we did not make friends with those young people, but we were so self-absorbed and we needed all our energy to cope with our own lives.

Uri and I were given a *zrif* (hut) with two beds, two chairs and my crate-cum-wardrobe. The *zrif* had a hole in the roof and, as it was the rainy season, there was always a bucket in the middle of the room. There was no heating and we were cold. Only a few of the paths were paved; the rest of the area was muddy (*botz*). Every morning at five, I waded through the *botz* in my rubber boots to the nursery. It was warm there, thank goodness. The little ones were already sitting in their little chairs, waiting for their sweetened porridge. One day I was overcome by a thought: there sat these symbols of love, spoilt, the centre of our existence, and all they had to do was open their mouths for all the best things to be shovelled in. I stood there, myself an orphan, put my finger in the deliciously sweet porridge and licked it clean.

The children's education was free and progressive. As they lived in the countryside, sex education was taught by observing nature. No 'stork stories' as in Germany. The *metapeleth* for the four-year-olds called me into the playroom one morning and showed me how the children had placed their tricycles on top of each other. I didn't understand – nor had she, at first. But they explained to her that they wanted to have more than the three tricycles they already had. Having been exposed to the sight of a bull mounting a cow to sire a calf, they thought the same applied to their tricycles.

I began to feel isolated and unhappy in the kibbutz. Out there was a world which intrigued me and with which I was totally unfamiliar and I yearned to be part of it, to be allowed to make my own decisions. At the same time, telegrams were arriving from home: "Please apply immediately! We need a visa for Walter, too!" The group gave me permission to 'go to town' for some time. This meant living outside the kibbutz and trying to obtain an emigration certificate for my parents. Herr Knoch, the solicitor father of Marianne, my cousin-by-marriage, was to assist me with this. The thought of my parents suddenly coming back into my life filled me with anxiety. I couldn't imagine them accepting my current way of life. With hindsight, I had another reason for leaving the kibbutz. I had not found what I had been searching for: the lost parental home, with its warmth, love and feeling of security, from which I had run away. The decision not to return to the kibbutz released in me massive and enduring guilt.

11. Haifa

I left the kibbutz with my old suitcase containing little more than a well-worn coat, two or three dresses and some underwear. People in the kibbutz thought I would return. And what did I think – of course, even though I knew then that I did not want to spend the rest of my life in a kibbutz, I wasn't able to admit to myself that this would be goodbye forever. I took the Egged bus to Haifa (My cousin Joachim belonged to the renowned Egged cooperative and had invested money in this socialist initiative. He had worked as a driver, at first, and later went on to direct the company's control centre). And so began a new chapter in my life and I had no inkling of all the dramas and traumas that were in store. I had given up my ideal of living in a kibbutz community. Again, I was overcome by a feeling of loneliness. I was part of an uprooted society, whose members had brought with them the distinctiveness and culture of their mother countries but had not yet developed a collective identity.

There I stood on Mount Carmel and followed the instructions Lilly and Walter had sent me. I felt uncomfortable in my dress, which was far too short and I kept tugging at the hem, trying to pull it over my knees. I was now 19 years old and the dress had been made in Beuel. Mother probably pictured me in a straw hat or headscarf, flowery dress, skipping through the plantations with a basket in my hand, picking fruit, as portrayed in propaganda films about Palestine. My relatives had found a flat in a mansion belonging to Russian immigrants. The flat – probably originally meant for the gardener – consisted of a living room with a double bed and a teeny-tiny kitchen, as well as a shower. Lilly and Walter had a piano and a small table with some wobbly chairs. That was it. I slept on the tiled floor in the kitchen. There was no mattress but at least there was a sheet. The kibbutz sent on my grandmother's old duvet, which had worn very thin over time.

The evening after my arrival, it was decided that I should accompany Lilly the following day. She worked for an American family and had heard of a vacancy with another American family in the same house, who, incidentally, were not Jewish. Knowing barely a word of English, I learnt some important words relevant to that type of work, such as: children, washing, cleaning, and ironing. The next morning we set off to my new place of work, with the Phetteplace family. Lilly knocked on the door, which was opened by a pleasant-looking, pregnant young woman. I did not understand a word that passed between Lilly and her. It all sounded like "ouwouwouwouw". Then Lilly pushed me through the door and told me to sort out the rest with Mrs. Phetteplace. "Come upstairs to the first floor where I work if you need me," she said. I followed my new employer into the living room. She looked at me enquiringly and said: "ouwouwouwouw washing." I nodded enthusiastically, but then came a much longer "ouwouwouwouw" without a single clue. I ran upstairs to Lilly: "I have understood everything so far but now I'm stuck." Lilly came with me and spoke to Mrs. Phetteplace, who had only asked if I could start with immediate effect. And so began my career as a housemaid.

Little two-year-old Linda was adorable and we liked each other immediately. I was now living in a culture completely alien and new to me. These people had come from humble homes, were contracted to work in Palestine for two years, and earned a great deal of money. I quickly adapted to their way of life. Housework was no big problem for me. Mrs. Phetteplace often sat with me whilst I ironed and talked about the political situation. She was of the opinion that America would never meddle in a war, but I thought differently and learnt the necessary words in the evening to be able to explain certain matters to her. Soon after, she gave birth to a little boy called Georgie. Mrs. Phetteplace was fascinated to hear that my uncle was a doctor and was now practising in Kfar Ata, a little village close by. How come her maid's uncle was a doctor? It must have been confusing for her. She knew that I was fairly well informed and attended classical concerts. This was totally inconsistent with her ideas of a 'native.' Furthermore, she fell in love with my boyfriend, who often came to pick me up. He was a very good-looking, elegant Viennese who spoke good English. Whenever he came, she became quite agitated, blushed, and flirted with him. Then there was Mr. Phetteplace, a tall, slender man always dressed in khaki and with a big hat. He was shy; I hardly ever heard him speak. When we met in the morning, he would say "Good morning" and that was all I ever heard him utter.

Sleeping on Lilly and Walter's bare kitchen floor soon became unbearable. Luckily, I managed to find a room with the use of a kitchen with a Polish family in the neighbourhood. Giving up a room for financial reasons, by the way, was a typical situation for immigrants. The arrangement with Lilly and Walter was that I would give Lilly money and, in return, she would cook for us all in the evenings. One evening, I came home from work and was so tired that I lay down, immediately falling into a deep sleep but awoke suddenly and ran to have dinner. Walter was sitting at the table; I had come too late, he told me, he had already eaten my helping. I have forgiven my cousin many things – but not this!

More despairing letters arrived from my parents, including this one on their behalf from Holland:

Venlo
20 Nov 1938
Dear Fräulein Kober
On behalf of your parents and Walter I strongly implore you to take immediate action to help. The Kobers' situation is bleak. The house with all its contents has burnt down and they were unable to retrieve anything to live on including shirts or suits. Please do everything within your power to help once again, as nothing can be done from inside Germany. Please do not mention to anyone that I have written to you, as I myself am a refugee.
Kind regards
Werner David

With hindsight, their situation was hopeless, probably more so than I realised at the time. Even though I coped with my own day-to-day existence, I received no support when it came to my parents. It was as if I was paralysed, and I think my relatives felt the same. Even Uncle

Sim, whom my parents had begged for help, was not in a position to do anything. He loved his sister but was unable to help her in the end. I still found it inconceivable that I should accommodate my parents in Haifa, or indeed anywhere in Palestine. Nevertheless, I decided to make one more appointment with Knoch, the solicitor, in an attempt to get them a visa. But even he was unable to help.

Having family in Palestine gave me some stability. Uncle Sim and his family were very fond of me but saw their role as giving me moral support. They contacted me when Uncle Sim needed help or company, and when Aunt Tilly went to Tiberias to visit her daughter Ruth and then went to take the waters. I would stay with my uncle and help him in the surgery. He learned Hebrew and English assiduously and spoke both with a strong German accent. Much to Aunt Tilly's exasperation, he had many Arab patients, whom he would mostly treat for free. Aunt Tilly urged me to persuade Uncle Sim that he had to start charging, otherwise they would starve. It was no use. Uncle Sim had an Arab patient who suffered from trachoma and had already gone blind; he invited him to consider taking part in a clinical trial, of course without charge. The man was cured and the Arabs regarded my uncle as a Messiah and queued up to be treated by him. Later, Uncle Sim published an article about the successful therapy in a medical journal.

My uncle and aunt were good role models for the many assimilated Jews who had fled Germany and come to Palestine. Sometimes they despaired of ever getting on with the Eastern European Jews. Most of those living in their village were of Polish extraction and did not understand my uncle at all. Sometimes, he could be seen cycling to Arab villages to treat the sick. The Polish Jews disapproved, and his practice suffered as a result. They only consulted the crazy *Jecke* about minor complaints; otherwise, they went to the doctor in Haifa.

After I had worked for the Phetteplaces for two years, they started to prepare for their return to Ohio. Mrs Phetteplace wanted me to go with them because their children had become so used to me, but I declined. I managed to find a position as a maid with two British naval officers stationed in Haifa. The war was now in full swing and we suffered the first air raids targeting the harbour. The flat was in a newly built house in the old town, with a good view of the harbour. I undertook my work duties, cooked and tidied up. Things were going well and the pay was a bit better but, as often happened, some of my friends were jealous and tried to take advantage. They thought I should suggest that a window cleaner be employed. Unfortunately, I followed their advice. Helen came to clean the windows and charged such an extortionate sum, I was dismissed. Once again, I was looking for work. A friend of mine, Frieda, worked in a bar. She thought that might be the right thing for me, too. I was curious and introduced myself to the owner. My first thought was: what would Mother and Father say? The owner was delighted and wanted me to start immediately. Now I was selling drinks to the British and the Australians but knew I was totally out of place. An Irish soldier asked me what I was doing there. "This is no place for you" he said and, after two days, my adventures in the Haifa underworld were over.

I was now spending more time with Lilly and Walter – family bonds were very important – and Lilly's cousin, Adolf Fürstenfeld, with whom I remained friends until his life ended tragically. We often went for walks on Mount Carmel, then a wild, unspoiled landscape, and sometimes walked down the steep path into town, where there were one or two dance halls. One, 'Behal', was owned by a Hungarian couple. The atmosphere was utterly European. A small dance floor in the centre with little round tables placed around it. There were the 'respectable' girls, accompanied by 'respectable' men, but also women and girls who behaved in a way that bordered on prostitution, and they had to be ushered out discreetly by Frau Behal. Frau Behal was a capable businesswoman. She wore her platinum-coloured hair pinned up, and had a curvaceous body. She considered herself a dancer. The highlight of the evening came when the small orchestra played a drum roll, followed by a czardas, and she made her entrance dancing, dressed in Hungarian national costume. Meanwhile, I had met many young people who lived in similar circumstances to mine. Together, we went swimming, to the cinema and to coffee houses. The parents of some of them lived in Palestine, which gave them an added feeling of security.

It was not until I started living in Haifa that was I confronted with the full burden of rootlessness, something many immigrants had in common. The kibbutz had given me a sense of security, but here the battle was existential: somewhere to live, food and clothing. Even though I had contact with my family and was able to stay with my uncle or cousin whenever I needed to find a new place to live or work, they too had the same problems and insecurities and needed my help more than they were in a position to help me. I was young and inexperienced and had no one to advise me.

During this time, I visited Beth Sera several times but was given the cold shoulder and felt like a traitor. I rarely thought of Uri. When war broke out, I felt guilty that I had not been able to do more for my parents. I had no idea what had become of them. Father's brother, Uncle Martin, had sent me one last, despairing letter, in which he told me of my parents' impossible situation. He must have posted it abroad, probably in France. He was murdered in a concentration camp after the Nazis had occupied France and deported the Jews.

My flat in Massada Street had an uninterrupted view of the harbour, which is how I witnessed the tragedy played out there. It was 25 November 1940. The *Patria*, which had brought me to Haifa in 1936, was lying at anchor. This time she was carrying 1800 illegal immigrants. My friend Regi had told me she was expecting her fiancé, Moritz, who had managed to escape from a concentration camp. With the ship anchored in the harbour, and thanks to my friendship with a British soldier, I was hoping to be able to smuggle some letters on board. As I stepped onto the balcony that morning, I saw the *Patria* lying on her side, like a dead fish. Shortly afterwards, Adolf knocked at my door and told me there had been an explosion on board, causing many deaths and that he had helped to retrieve bodies and survivors from the sea. Regi's fiancé was one of the survivors. When I met him some time later, he spoke at length about the atrocities being committed in the concentration camps. Later, we heard that the Irgun haTzva'i haLe'umi beEretz Yisra'el – a Jewish underground organisation led by Menachem Begin – had hidden a bomb in the engine room, hoping to prevent the Mandate authorities from re-routing the ship to Mauritius. The passengers were instructed to come on deck at 9 a.m. on 25 November, but many did not follow these instructions, either because they did not understand them or because they were too tired or confused. 216 people lost their lives. The whole of Haifa was in shock and the fear for relatives at home grew by the day.

I had to move and find work yet again. This time I found a room with a Russian family. The husband was working for the British and had friends among the soldiers. One day, the landlord asked me if I wanted to go out with one of his British friends. I don't know if he stood to profit from this introduction but I realised instantly that 'going out' meant something different and I indignantly refused.

Again, there were enemy air raids. We sat in the kitchen with the door open and watched the low flying aircraft. We saw the pilots in their cockpits and the gunners beside them, firing at people on the street. Then I remembered Hitler's threat to destroy Tel Aviv in 20 minutes, a city the Jews had taken 20 years to build. When I left the house the following day, it felt as though the whole of Haifa had been destroyed.

When friends opened a café in Herzl Street, they offered me a job as a waitress. I enjoyed working there, juggling big trays. One day, a nice young German-speaking man came into the café. After several visits, we arranged to go out. We talked about music and literature and met at his flat quite often. One evening, he pulled me to the window, pointed at the house opposite and told me it was a brothel. He said he knew the Madame very well and was friendly with her. There was a lot of money to be made there, and he was employed, as it were, to find suitable girls. I was shocked and made it clear to him that I wasn't that kind of girl. Thereafter, he came to the café even more often, saying he enjoyed talking to me.

What I enjoyed most was swimming. I would go to the seaside and swim far out to sea. There was also a swimming pool, *beth galin*, where young people met. There was an English feel about the place, which was frequented by soldiers, although the shrill music tended to be American. Here one could listen to the latest hits, played non-stop. Then I met a Rumanian family, mother and daughter, who 'adopted' me and wanted to help me. They survived by engaging in all kinds of business activities. Although I felt at home with them, I never quite understood how they saw my role. But I was grateful to them when they found me a job in a hotel. The hotel at the end of Herzl Street was built in the oriental style and had twelve guest rooms. It belonged to Mr and Mrs Levy, who had a son my age. The Levys spoke only German and needed someone who could speak the indigenous languages. I was, in effect, an au pair. I went to see them and apparently fulfilled their criteria. I also sensed that we would get on well. We agreed that I should start by helping in the kitchen. I don't know how old they were, they had probably always looked the same. Mr Levy's hair was already white, and I suspect that he had once gone about his business wearing a suit and with a cigar in his mouth. Now he often wore polo-neck shirts and khaki trousers. He had adapted both to the local customs and to the climate but still looked like a fish out of water. He loved and admired his wife, who looked like a well-to-do German bourgeoisie.

Most of the hotel patrons were British Eighth Army soldiers and officers on leave from the desert, exhausted and hungry, and not just for food. There were also some amusing, eccentric and exotic types I found very entertaining. Two of the rather unusual guests were an Arab couple, no longer in the first flush of youth. I couldn't immediately understand what they wanted, not least because they spoke in French. They needed a room for several weeks but only for a few hours a day. It transpired that they desperately wanted a child and regularly visited a

Jewish doctor, who treated the wife with injections after which they had to 'do it'. Sadly, I don't know whether or not they were successful.

One day, the Levys asked me to take charge of the hotel over a weekend. Confidently, I accepted and looked forward to the challenge. The Rumanian chambermaid, Hadassa, was to help me. On Friday morning, a group of British soldiers arrived, tanned, exhausted and looking for somewhere to stay. They were ravenous and asked me to prepare some lunch for them. I made meatballs the way Mother had always made them, served with mashed potatoes, salads and followed by a dessert. They were thrilled. When the Levys returned, I showed them the bills. This must have given them the idea that I would make a good daughter-in-law. Their son was consulted and was not averse to winning my heart, even though I had always made it clear I wasn't interested. They then tried to trick me in a way I would never have believed them capable of: their son got into bed with me. I was outraged and threw him out.

One night, I awoke to find a strange man sitting on my bed. I wanted to scream but was so terrified I couldn't make a sound. Agitated, I told the Levys of my nocturnal visitor the following morning, but they asked me to keep quiet about it, saying it would be bad for business if word got round. My request for a key to lock my room was refused. One morning, I had a high temperature. As always, I went upstairs to the kitchen and told Frau Levy that I was ill. She was not best pleased but I went back to bed. After a while, she came to check on me and was rather angry. Then, in an unfriendly manner, she said "I suppose I'll have to get you something to eat." I asked her what there was and she replied "You'll eat what you're given." A few days later, I tried to start work again but still felt weak and had a temperature. I called Uncle Sim and, on his insistence, set off see him immediately. To add to my misery, the dry, hot desert wind – *chamsin* – had started. People were grumpy and tense; the bus was so overcrowded that I had to stand for the entire journey. When I reached Uncle Sim's flat, I was completely exhausted. He examined me and diagnosed a severe bout of Plaut-Vincent angina. After consulting a colleague, it was agreed that I was too unwell to be moved to Haifa hospital, so even though Uncle Sim and Aunt Tilly lived in one room, they looked after me for three weeks. During the day, I occupied their bed and at night I lay on the examination couch in the surgery. My aunt and uncle were with me day and night and devotedly cared for me. My condition improved slowly and, after eight days, I was able to speak again.

Much had changed for me by the time I returned to the hotel. Feeling older and wiser, I realised I had to make certain decisions, the first of which was to leave Haifa. I felt unable to continue in the hotel, deciding it was time to move on and leave behind my group of four girlfriends, all of us feeling lost in the social melting pot that was Palestine. Uschi – with her family from Poland – with her prejudices and worry that her daughter would fall for a Goy; Ohra – a loner – but intelligent and with both feet on the ground; and Regi, who was waiting for her fiancé Moritz who did indeed come. We used to go the beach together, wander through Haifa, and visit coffee houses, pretending we were enjoying ourselves. One evening I met Richie, who came from a traditional English family and wanted to marry me. The way his parents reacted to this must have been terrible for him.

12. Jerusalem

Walter and Lilly had moved to Jerusalem. I visited them and they suggested I follow them there. Adolf Fürstenfeld had joined the British Army and was in a recruitment camp. I handed in my notice at the hotel and packed my old suitcase. Walter and Lilly had written saying they looked forward to me coming but that there was so little space, we would have to share a bed. That wasn't unusual for the time; the country was very small and its limitations were set accordingly. We got used to it, huddled together, and undertook many activities, such as cooking or sleeping, in one room. Lilly and Walter lived in a small room in the attic of a large house. The double bed, some books on a shelf and a little chess table already filled the room. Then there was a tiny little room, which they called the kitchen, with a small washbasin and rusty tap, which was also used to clean vegetables. When I asked who lived in the other rooms, I was told that they were occupied by girls who were regularly visited by Australian soldiers. I didn't give it any further thought.

The following morning, I found a job in a pharmacy. The clientele was mixed; Yiddish or Hebrew-speaking Orthodox Jews came with their hordes of children. All I had to do was sell hairbrushes, toothpaste, and creams of all kinds. I brought home lots of free samples. All in all, I felt I had mastered this Babylonian situation and soon found myself socialising with interesting people. One day, Lilly came home in a state of excitement. She had seen a 'To Let' sign on an old oriental house in the Musrara district. The house was in a cul-de-sac that ended in front of the Swedish school. Right next to it was the ultra-Orthodox district of Mea Shearim. The three of us stood outside the house and Walter made energetic use of the heavy door knocker. A young, dark-skinned man with elegant features, slim and beautifully dressed in an elegant suit, opened the door. He gestured for us to come in. We stepped into a spacious courtyard and followed the mysterious man up a flight of stairs into a hall, where thick rugs covered the floor. At one end of the room stood a throne-like chair and more chairs lined the wall. The man asked if we had come about the flat. After we replied in the affirmative, he wanted to know if Lilly and I were both Walter's wives. Smiling, the man told us that we were in Princess Raskassa's throne room. Her husband was the cousin of Haile Selassie, the Emperor of Ethiopia, who was currently in Addis Ababa. After Ethiopia's defeat at the hands of Italy in 1936, the family had fled to Palestine. He himself attended on the princess and her household, which included her two sons, a cook and a maid. We walked from the main house across the courtyard to a much smaller building with two rooms on the ground floor – which we would occupy – and two on the first floor. The kitchen was in a little timber house opposite. There was a very basic shower and a toilet. In a tiny annexe lived an old Russian couple, who had come to the Holy Land for religious reasons and prayed constantly. In their little room stood a bed and a table and the walls were covered with crucifixes and devotional images. He looked like Rasputin and she looked like a Russian peasant. They did all their cooking in one pot, and there was also a kind of samovar. Conversation with them was impossible. Back in the throne room, we discussed money. Once agreement had been reached, someone fetched the princess. She was a stunningly beautiful woman and looked like Nefertiti. The man explained something to her in her language. She smiled and apparently agreed.

I continued working in the pharmacy, Walter attended university and worked part-time as a journalist, while Lilly worked as a nanny for a German-Jewish family. The family owned a large dance hall on Zion Square, where, from time to time, we would go dancing in the evenings. One day, out of the blue, we heard that Adolf, who had been at the front for some months, was coming home on leave. We were all very excited and organised a little party for him, and invited his new girlfriend, Ziporah. We had a lovely evening and Adolf commented on the fact that he had some money for the first time in a long while. I had taken the following day off and Adolf took me to a café for breakfast. He said goodbye to us and took Ziporah home before going to his hotel. The following morning, Lilly came to my room to wait for

Adolf, who had not yet arrived. At that moment, a young policeman rushed in and spoke to Lilly in Hebrew. I only understood the word 'Aharon', (Hebrew for Adolf but also for wardrobe), so I had no idea what he was saying at first. Lilly turned to me, white as a sheet, and screamed that Adolf had been shot dead. Then we heard screams and cries – it was Ziporah. Once Ziporah and Lilly had gone to the police station with the officer, I went to bed, overwhelmed by the shock. I learned what had happened later. An elderly homosexual Arab and his younger boyfriend had shot Adolf with a view to robbing him. It was a known fact that young soldiers on leave carried money with them. Poor Ziporah had run to the nearest house to get help, but Adolf was already dead. What became of his murderer's, I do not know, but the funeral was held the following day, organised by the army.

Affected by Adolf's death, I became very ill, was confined to bed with a fever and hallucinated. The community sent for an Austrian doctor who called me "you poor little thing." From time to time, Walter and Lilly brought me something to eat. It was out of sheer necessity that I started looking for work. I still had a slight temperature, but I slowly recovered, perhaps because there was no alternative. My illness was later diagnosed as typhoid. The social security people decided I needed help and supplied me with a green slip to take to a soup kitchen. I had no idea what this involved but went anyway. Sitting in a large room, at long tables, were old men with dirty beards and toothless women with headscarves and tremulous hands slurping some sort of broth. It smelt appetising and, as I was hungry, I joined the queue. The soup was very good. Then we queued again for pudding. When my turn came, someone asked me brusquely where my pink slip was; I only had a green one but, if I wanted pudding, I had to have a pink one. I fled, offended and humiliated. It seemed I wasn't poor enough to merit a pink slip.

Next, I found a job as a waitress in a café. Unfortunately, my route home took me through some very dark streets. The patrons were German immigrants and Arabs. The owners were also German and were somewhat sceptical about taking me on. My fellow waitress was a tall, portly, rather exotic-looking woman with bleached hair who appeared to be Turkish. She wore a low-cut dress, presumably to attract customers. But surprise, surprise I managed it. Despite my short stature, I was able to manoeuvre the trays between the tables and chairs. The so-called Turkish woman turned out to be German; her parents had fled with her to Palestine via Turkey.

I was happy to be living in Jerusalem. We lived close to the Damascus Gate, the entrance to the bazaar. I quickly learnt to haggle with the Arab street vendors and thought it was great fun. I visited the holy sites and the various places of worship and gradually became familiar with the Jerusalem that has been regarded as a spiritual centre for centuries. Mainly German immigrants and artists lived in the Rechavia district. The houses were shaded by trees and the courtyards were laid out with large paving stones. Despite the idyllic surroundings, there were daily reminders of the political situation. British soldiers, including Jewish ones in British uniform, were everywhere but, more particularly, the Palestinian police. Their behaviour towards arriving illegal immigrants was appalling. For example, when the *Patria* survivors arrived, the police used rubber truncheons to drive them into Atlit internment camp.

Then came the trial of Adolf's murderers. Walter, Lilly, Ziporah and I were called as witnesses. I will never forget the two defendants. The older one was a pleasant-looking man in his early 50s. He wore a conventional suit and a *kafia*, the Arab head covering. The other wore Arab dress and was between 18 and 20 years old. He looked frightened and shy. The trial was reported at length in the newspapers. The court found that this was a case of aggravated robbery, not politically motivated.

❧

I handed in my notice at Friedländer's, the café where I had been working, and applied for a job in a bakery with a restaurant attached. The boss was called Mrs Pat and everyone knew "Pat's bakery." It was patronised by everyone, from old 'aristocratic' Russians, Orthodox Jews, modern Marxists, high-ranking British civil servants, the manager of the YMCA and eccentric missionaries to little Jewish housewives. Languages spoken there were Hebrew, German, Yiddish, English and Russian. Mrs Pat directed operations from her position behind the counter – from where she never moved – with the help of wall mirrors and an ability to swivel her eyes in any direction, like a frog. With the exception of French, she understood all the languages. She knew everything that went on in her castle. She took me on because I looked like a girl from a good home. She soon found out that I had three doctors in the family, that I had gone to secondary school and could probably speak French. She spoke to me in German and Hebrew alternately. She was Russian, had lived there for a long time, had three daughters and was widowed. Not only did she have a remarkable physical presence, she also exuded an air of omniscient authority. She counted among her friends such high-profile people as the High Commissioner and the head of the British Mandate Authority. Her daughters were chubby but, unlike her, extremely spoilt, arrogant and jealous. They rarely deigned to speak to me, a mere employee. They were forever on a diet. I remember how they would greedily pick up crumbs with their well-manicured white fingers. I never saw them eat a whole slice of cake – only crumbs.

The "cake cave", as a friend called Pat's bakery, consisted of a bakery, a café next door and a restaurant in the garden. The little kitchen where the meals were prepared was directly behind the shop, presided over by a woman of indeterminate age with a slight stoop and lank, dyed blonde hair. She had small, blue, piercing eyes, always had a cold and spoke very nasally. She was devoted to Mrs Pat and nothing escaped her. I tried to get on with her because I soon realised she could be dangerous.

For weeks, a young Jewish soldier would sit at the same table in the garden and watch me. I treated him, as I did all the other guests, in a warm and friendly manner. One day his chair was empty but he had left a letter for me:

*"The name is but sound and smoke
Enshrouding heaven's glow."*

My dear Miss,

*I cannot even write your name – surely it means the world to the
one who loves you – as I do not know it. But what are names?
Empty descriptions, only created to differentiate, only valid and
justifiable for themselves. Only when they become a symbol do they
manifest their awesome power. That is why I want to give you a
name as befits a painting, as you have become, for me, an adorable
miniature and, in a certain sense, a symbol. The girl with the
radiant, beautiful, oh so treacherous eyes': this will be the name
of your picture, which will live on in my memory. Those eyes are
attempting flippantly what I hope the heart, from which they shine,
intends one day to achieve in earnest. What a deliberate game – a
dangerous one!*

*What has all this to do with you? I hope that you did not find my
presence bothersome, and I would hate my disappearance to be
thought of in the same way. Please forgive the audacity of this letter
and the cowardice of my decision. My observation showed me that
your heart was closed to me, and I lacked the courage to put it to the
painful test; after all, once bitten, twice shy.*

*One of the finest observers of mankind, a solitary poet whose
heart overflowed with love for everything human, wrote these words
with which I will bring this letter to a close:*

*"What are happiness and life! On what do they depend? What are
we ourselves, if our happiness or
unhappiness is decided by a risible carnival untruth? How are we
responsible if our reward for affection, which is joyous and devout,
is to receive ignominy and hopelessness? Who sends us such simple-
minded forms of deceit, who interferes with destructive effect in our
lives whilst they themselves dissolve like soap bubbles?" (G. Keller,*

Kleider machen Leute)
With best wishes for a happy future
G. H.

For me, this attested to a lonely, rootless man unable to come to terms with his new surroundings. I felt sorry for him and was long plagued by feelings of guilt because I felt I had neglected him.

Circumstances in the Raskassa House changed whilst I was working in the cake cave. Walter was called to a priest who had attended on the Ethiopian family. The building belonged to the church, I believe. He told Walter that the big house would become available because the Raskassas were going back to Addis Ababa. Walter saw his chance and immediately made an offer that was accepted. So he, Lilly and I moved into the big house. The two of them took the throne room and I had a smaller room. Walter let the other rooms out to friends. After our move into the Royal chambers, we were confronted with a problem that needed immediate attention: bed bugs. The city council sent professional pest controllers round and the whole flat had to be smoked out.

On Saturdays, we met our friends for coffee in the garden behind the main house. We sat underneath the fragrant citrus trees, chatted in German and philosophised for hours. We were mainly concerned with the kind of world that would await us after the war. Convinced that Palestine would be socialist, our discussions revolved around the future of socialism and the future of culture, if socialism became a reality in a world where there would be no more wars and the problems of the world would be solved peacefully. Would art still exist then? We believed that it was suffering, in particular, stimulating great artistic achievement. Of course, we also discussed the military situation. Although we were afraid of Rommel, who was already close to Alexandria, we believed in the ultimate victory of the Allies. One evening, we went for a nocturnal walk, as we used to do in Germany. We scrambled up the Mount of Olives, sat under cypress trees, looked at the lights of Jerusalem and started singing German folk songs. What a strange situation: here we were in Zion and yet yearned for the green forests back home, spoke German, read German books and really believed that we could adapt to a new life.

I enjoyed working in the bakery. One day, a tall, good-looking man in a kind of khaki uniform came into the shop. His name was Mr. Ling and he was the manager of the YMCA. He was delighted when he heard that I came from Bonn because he knew it well. It transpired that he loved classical music and organised evening concerts – albeit with gramophone records – in the YMCA. He invited me to one such event, and a friendship developed between us, but I didn't notice that he had fallen in love with me. We went to the theatre and other cultural events together. He was a father figure to me.

My colleague in the cake cave, Shulamit, was a little older than me. She came from an Orthodox family and wore a *scheitel* and a headscarf. We got on very well and she told me of her imminent marriage. Her parents had found a husband for her with the help of a marriage broker. Shulamit had met him once before and found him acceptable. They had already held hands, she told me. I was invited to the wedding, which was great fun. I remember the groom, pale and shy, being carried in on a chair surrounded by young men in black, wearing big hats. The men danced separately, shook their heads, jumped onto the tables and sang Chassidic songs. The women looked on but did not dance. The bride looked very happy, standing under the *chuppah*. Shulamit continued working as a waitress at Pat's but soon became pregnant and stopped work. She had a baby every year and whenever I saw her out shopping, she was surrounded by her ever-increasing family. Meanwhile, Walter was working part-time as a journalist writing for the review section. He was also working on a book and had founded a theatre group, which had adopted the Stanislavski method and in which I joined in with enthusiasm. Before an actor executes a movement, he is meant to analyse the character in depth. Gesture, mimic and text will then grow out of that analysis. Our first piece was Moliere's *Tartuffe*, in which I played the role of Dorine.

One day, there was a knock at my door and standing there was Mr Hammerstein, the teacher from Bonn. Even though he had aged, I recognised him immediately. He told me that his wife and children had been gassed by the Nazis in occupied Poland. He had met my brother Walter in a camp in England. Whilst my brother was sent to Canada, Hammerstein had managed to get to Palestine. He cried continuously, and I could find no words of comfort. I was very sad because I had been very fond of his family. I had already received a postcard from my brother in England, so at least knew that he had survived. Happy as I was to hear from him, I felt unable to respond at length. To this day, I feel guilty that I was incapable of showing him more love and understanding. Walter had had a terrible time. He had fled to Holland on a false passport to live with Uncle Leo and Aunt Jetta, and had worked in their new butcher's shop. But the Dutch police had arrested him after a few months and had transported him to the German border with his bicycle. There he was met by the SS and was imprisoned in Herford, the town where he had served his apprenticeship as a decorator. With a lot of luck and help, he managed to escape under cover of darkness and fled to England. The letters I received from him and Aunt Jetta in Holland accused me of heartlessness because I never wrote to my parents. I had, in fact, written regularly but the letters were returned, stamped "undeliverable."

Perhaps this is the moment to recount another incident that troubles me to this day. On 28 November 1939, I received a letter from my parents via the Red Cross. It was addressed to Uncle Sim and Aunt Jetta and was written in English:

Dear Sim and Tilly,
Today we have a large favour to ask of you. The question is our early emigration there. We want 400 $ for the passage which are to be deposited to the following address: Palestine Office, Geneva, to hands of Mr. Dr. Silberstein, for the passage of: Mr. Julius Erwin Israel Kober and Mrs. Emilie Sara Kober.
We hope that our request is not in vain, for otherwise we have no

possibility more to emigrate. We are nearly completely ready for the
emigration. We firmly rely upon you that you execute the matter
as quickly as possible. Then we can start in January. Many hearty
thanks in advance.
We remain with hearty greetings
Yours, always thankful
Erwin and Mila

The letter was typed, but I definitely recognised my parents'
signatures. I brought the letter to Uncle Sim in Kfar Ata. He looked
at me, shook his head and said: "I don't have the money." Nothing
more. To this day, I cannot understand his reaction. I simply did not
know what to think, nor did I understand what was being asked of
me. I still feel guilty, on behalf of my uncle as well, that we did not
borrow the money from someone, or at least make an attempt to find
it. The life of his beloved sister was at stake. Was he in such despair
that he didn't know which way to turn? Of course, Uncle Sim was
in a difficult position. His wife was seriously ill, he had very little
income because his practice was not doing well; he was struggling
with his feelings of rootlessness and had to fight for recognition as
a doctor. Well respected and successful in Hamburg, he was denied
recognition for his scientific contributions in Palestine. I know that I
found it difficult to imagine my parents in Palestine then, which was
attributable as much to their view of life as to my relationship with
them. But the constant battle for survival meant that I simply did not
have the strength to feel compassion. And I could find nobody in my
circle, other than my uncle, who could have helped.

My grandparents Leopold and Rosa Levy, née Kronthal

My uncle Simon Levy during the First World War

Kindergarten in Beuel,
(around 1922)

With my brother Walter
(around 1921)

*Our family home at
6 Neustrasse, Beuel*

*On Münsterplatz, in Carnival
costume (around 1927)*

Excursion to Petersberg, (around 1929). From left to right: me, Karl Grünen-
berg, Ruth Levy, Rose Levy, Henriette Grünenberg, Rosa Levy ('Omama'),
Emilie Kober, Simon Levy; behind: Walter Kober

My Hashomer Hatzair group (1933)

First excursion of the 'Chaverim'

Aged 14 (1934)

Carnival, outside Bonn City Hall (1936). My cousin Margot Levy is middle row, centre, with me on the front row, right

My last family photo (August 1936)

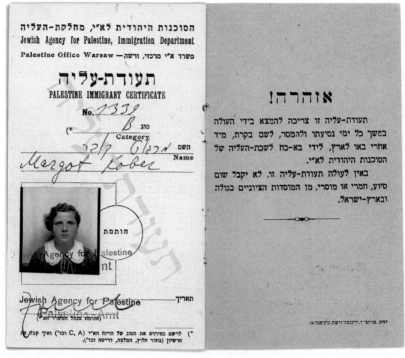

My Jewish Agency certificate of immigration to Palestine

Kibbutz Beth Sera, during a search by the British army (1936)

May Day demo. I am standing at the bottom right corner of the flag, with Ulrich Rosenthal to my left

With Yehuda Wallach and and Ulrich Rosenthal at Beth Sera (1938)

Shooting practice at the kibbutz

With Ulrich Rosenthal (Kibbutz Beth Sera, 1938)

Postcard from my parents showing the restaurant they managed in the Jewish community centre at Krefeld. (31 March 1938)

My parents Erwin Julius and Emilie Kober with my brother Walter at Krefeld (1938)

Fulda, den 20. Nov. 1938.

Sehr geehrtes Frl. Kober!

Im Auftrage Ihrer Eltern und Walter richte ich an Sie die dringende Bitte sofort von dort Massnahmen zu ergreifen, uns zu helfen.

Die Lage von Fam. Kober ist trostlos, das Haus und sämtlicher Besitz ist abgebrannt und haben keinen Pfennig Geld zum Leben retten können. Auch haben sie kein Hemd und keinen Anzug retten können.

Tuen Sie bitte nochmals alles, uns zu helfen, denn von Deutschland aus kann nichts geschehen.

Schweigen Sie bitte darüber, dass ich Ihnen geschrieben habe, denn ich bin selbst Flüchtling.

Mit freundl. Gruß

Werner David

The letter I received from Werner David (who I did not know) shortly after the 1938 pogrom, urgently asking me to help my parents

*Envelope of my last letter to my parents (November 1938), franked 'Undelivered.
Return to Sender'*

Telegram from my parents (December 1938)

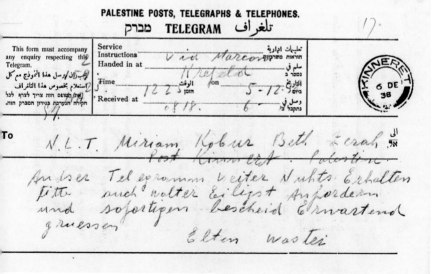

My application for Palestinian citizenship (1938) and the endorsement on the reverse (1939)

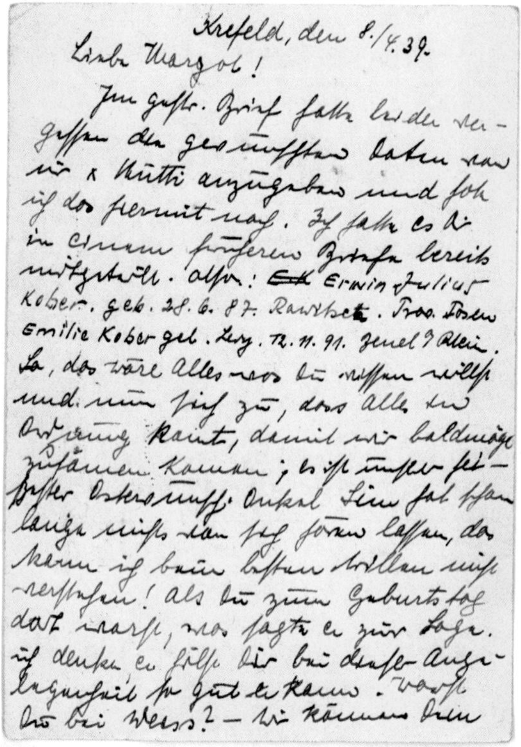

Krefeld, den 8./4.39.

Liebe Margot!

Im gestr. Brief hatte leider vergessen die gewünschten Daten von mir u. Mutti anzugeben und hole ich das hiermit nach. Ich hatte es Dir in einem früheren Briefe bereits mitgeteilt. also: ~~[illegible]~~ Erwin Julius Kober. geb. 28.6.87. [illegible]. Frau [illegible] Emilie Kober geb. Lerz. 12.11.91. [illegible]. So, das wäre alles was Du wissen willst und nun sieh zu, dass alles in Ordnung kommt, damit wir baldmögl. zusammen kommen; es ist unser sehnlichster Osterwunsch. Onkel [illegible] hat schon lange nichts von sich hören lassen, das kann ich beim besten Willen nicht verstehen! Als Du zum Geburtstag dort warst, was sagte er zur Lage. Ich denke er hilft Dir bei dieser Angelegenheit so gut er kann. [illegible] Du bei Weiss? – Wir können Dein

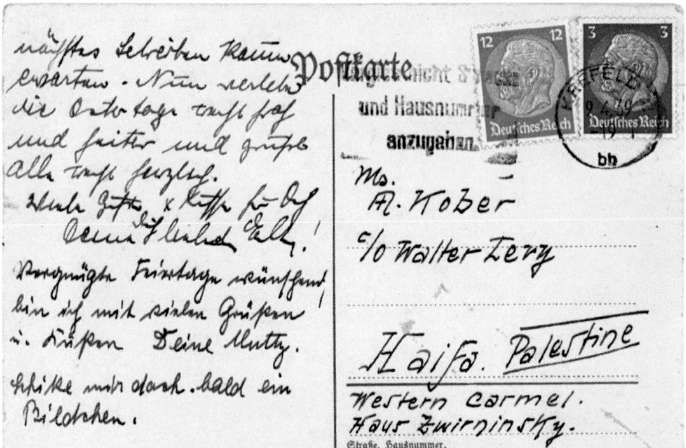

nächstes Schreiben kaum erwarten. Nun verlebe die Ostertage recht froh und heiter und grüße alle recht herzlich.

Viele Grüße u. Küsse [illegible]

Dein Dich liebender Vati!

Vergnügte Feiertage wünschend bin ich mit vielen Grüßen u. Küssen Deine Mutty.

Schicke mir doch bald ein Bildchen.

Ms.
A. Kober
c/o Walter Lerz
Haifa. Palestine
Western Carmel.
Haus Zwirninsky.

Straße, Hausnummer,
Gebäudeteil, Stockwerk

Card from my parents asking for help (8th April 1939)

Dear Sim and Tilly,

To-day we have a large favour to ask of you. The question is our early emigration there. We want 400 $ for the passage which are to be deposit to the following address: Palestine Office, Geneva, to hands of Mr. Dr. Silberstein, for the passage of: Mr. Julius Erwin Israel Kober and Mrs. Emilie Sara Kober
We hope that our Request is not in vain for otherwise we have no possibility more to emigrate We are nearly completely ready for the emigration.
We firmly rely upon you that you execut the matter as quickly as possible. Then we can start i January. Many hearty thanks in advance.
We remain with hearty greetings,

Yours always thankful

Erwin x Mila.

Letter from my parents to Uncle Simon and Aunt Tilly, requesting that they transfer mor for a sea passage to Palestine (November 1939)

Deutsches Rotes Kreuz   -4. JUL 1941 ⋆ 154354
Präsidium / Auslandsdienst
Berlin SW 61, Blücherplatz 2

ANTRAG
an die *Agence Centrale des Prisonniers de Guerre, Genf*
— Internationales Komitee vom Roten Kreuz —
auf Nachrichtenvermittlung

REQUÊTE
de la Croix-Rouge Allemande, Présidence, Service Etranger
à l'Agence Centrale des Prisonniers de Guerre, Genève
— Comité International de la Croix-Rouge —
concernant la correspondance

1. **Absender**   Erwin Israel Kober
   Expéditeur
                    Krefeld, Stadtgarten 13.

bittet, an
prie de bien vouloir faire parvenir à

2. **Empfänger**   Mirjam Kober, Haifa, Palestine
   Destinataire
              Beth Schwarz, Western Carmel

                  Scloschanah 33.

folgendes zu übermitteln / *ce qui suit:*
(Höchstzahl 25 Worte!)
(25 mots au plus!)

Immer noch keine Nachricht von Dir.

Wir sind gesund, hoffen Deinerseits Gleiches.

Was macht Onkel und Familie? Hat Walter geschr

schrieben? Schreibe ihm und uns

18 JUIL 1941

Eltern.

(Datum / date)   23.6. 41.

(Unterschrift / Signature)

3. **Empfänger antwortet umseitig**
   Destinataire répond au verso

etter from my parents (23 June 1941) sent via the Red Cross. Such letters were
llowed to contain no more than 25 words

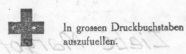

Write in Block Capitals

In grossen Druckbuchstaben auszufuellen.

From:

WAR ORGANISATION OF THE BRITISH RED CROSS AND ORDER OF ST. JOHN
Postal Message Scheme

To:
Comité International
de la Croix Rouge
Genève

046052

P.O.B. 1085,
David Building,
Jerusalem.

ENQUIRER
Fragesteller

Name **Kober**

Christian name **Margot**
Vorname

Address **c/o W. Levy, Hotel Labor,**

10 a Arlosoroffstreet, Haifa, Palestine

Relationship of Enquirer to Addressee **Tochter**
Wie ist Fragesteller mit Empfänger verwandt?

Message — Mitteilung.

(Message not to exceed 25 words, family news of strictly personal character).

(Nicht über 25 Worte, nur persönliche Familiennachrichten).

Geliebte Eltern,
Wir sind alle gesund. Von Walter gute Post.
Wir hoffen auf ein baldiges Wiedersehen.
Sorgt Euch nicht um Walter und mich.
                    Tochter Margot.

Date **15.7.41.**

ADDRESSEE
Empfänger

Name **Kober**

Christian name **Erwin**
Vorname
Address **Krefeld, Stadtgarten 13, Deutschland.**

18 AUGT 1941

10000—12.6.41—G.C.P.

Letter to my parents, sent via the Red Cross (15 July 1941)

13. Ted

I met Ted on a beautiful, sunny morning in December 1941. It had been raining but it was warm now and almost windless. It was still quite early and the cake cave was waiting for customers. There was no one there except a government official, who came daily for his breakfast. I was engrossed in conversation about the political situation with him, when two British soldiers came into the shop. They ordered cocoa and one of them asked me to ask Shulamit whether she would go dancing with him. She laughed and shook her head. Then the soldier looked at me with his impish eyes and asked if I would go out with him instead. I hesitated, but the official told me in Hebrew that he knew the soldier and that he was a nice, intelligent chap. I had no idea then that I had just met my future husband. We met that evening and, as the dance had been cancelled, went to the cinema. After that, I didn't see him for a while because Richie came to Jerusalem to visit.

1941 came to a close and Walter, Lilly and I were planning a big New Year's Eve party. None of us noticed that we were organising a typically German party, such as we were used to from home. Amongst our friends were many talented people, such as the art students who helped to design the costumes and the decorations. The entire Raskassa House was to be decorated and painted. That evening, I dressed up as a red-cheeked Dutch girl with blonde plaits, my cousin Walter became a knight in armour, complete with sword. Lilly was Puck from Shakespeare's *A Midsummer Night's Dream*. Other friends had dressed up as their favourite characters: Mahatma Gandhi, Charlie Chaplin. But there was a shortage of men who could dance, so I mentioned a nice Englishman I'd met in the cake cave. "Can he dance?" I was asked. I knew he could dance, even tap dance, and so I was instructed to invite him and to tell him to dress up. Ted arrived at the party in a genuine kilt and wearing a typical Londoner's flat cap. When I asked him about his costume, he explained that he was a 'Scottish Cockney'. We had organised a 'post office' for the party. Everyone was given a number and was able to send and receive messages. To this day, I have kept the 'telegrams' Ted sent me that evening. Ted enriched all our lives and was accepted into our group. He proved to be a brilliant entertainer, arranged games, danced, played the guitar and ukelele. And he flirted with me all evening.

Ted appeared to understand me. He approached me with great care, knowing instinctively that it would take time to win me over. What I knew about Britain was minimal. I probably knew more about the current political situation than about British history. I had done some reading, much of it when I was very young. In the kibbutz, we had learnt about British colonial policy, especially the Balfour Declaration, which, in 1917, had guaranteed the Jews the right to a national homeland in Palestine. I also knew a fair amount about the class system and the Labour Party. Ted was from an aspirational, working class family.

I read some of the letters he had received from home, admired the humour, and had a good impression of his family. Their description of the German air raids on London was understated. Ted had initially been in the Territorial Army and, when war broke out, he was conscripted and stationed in Palestine, which he enjoyed. He was to achieve the leading rank of Sergeant Major in the Pay Corps. Through him, I learnt a lot about British antisemitism, and he in turn learnt that there are many more differences amongst Jews than he had previously come across in England. He had made many Jewish friends in Palestine. Generally speaking, Jewish families welcomed British soldiers, as they weren't professional soldiers and came from all walks of life. Ted and I discovered more common ground. I told him about the founding of kibbutz En Gev, which we had taken control of one night. To my delight, Ted told me that he had been on leave there and had enjoyed it very much. Ted introduced Lilly, Walter and me to three officers. They often took part in our discussions and were also invited to our parties. However, when we came to live in London many years later and wanted to re-establish contact with them, they were reluctant in case their wives found out about their life in Jerusalem.

Then I heard that Uncle Sim was coming to visit. I was thrilled that he would meet Ted and wondered what he would make of him. To my surprise, he told me that Ted reminded him very much of Father. "You didn't know your father as a young man but I did." The coming years were to prove Uncle Sim right. The fact that Ted had passed this test gave me added confidence about our getting married. Although I sometimes had my doubts, I was very attracted to Ted, particularly his sense of humour. He was now working for a radio station broadcasting to British troops in Palestine. He also appeared in a show he had written and directed and for which he had arranged the music. All those taking part were army people and the reviews were ecstatic.

Ted was stationed in 'Schneller's orphanage', a former Syrian orphanage now used as army quarters. To get to me, he had to cross the Orthodox Jewish quarter of Mea Shearim and made friends with some of the pious residents in the process. He often played cards with Australian soldiers and usually won. He would tell the other players that he preferred to be paid in kind; after all, they had food in abundance, including tinned fruit, cheese and butter. As he passed the guards with his bulging knapsack, he was asked what it contained. Instead of lying and telling them he was carrying dirty laundry or books he replied: "What do you think, mate? Californian fruit, English cheese, butter and so on." The guard chuckled: "Once a comedian, always a comedian" and allowed him to pass.

By now we were seriously discussing marriage. I could imagine our life together, whether in England or Palestine. Ted loved Palestine and often expressed the wish to stay there. As a soldier, he had to get permission from the Army to marry. It wasn't long before he handed in his application. I had to complete a form, with some very personal questions, which had to be signed by three guarantors, one relative and two other trustworthy people who had to vouch for my good character. I later discovered that the reason for this directive, which dated back to the Boer War, was to prevent British soldiers marrying local prostitutes by sending the future groom to another posting. My three guarantors were Uncle Sim, Mr. Ling from the YMCA, and the

High Commissioner, who knew me from the "cake cave". We were confident that the endorsements of such notable people would do the trick. A few days later, Ted arrived absolutely beside himself. He had just received a transfer order to Khartoum in Sudan. Without explanation, he had been told: "You have one more week in Jerusalem and that's it." Ted was shocked and upset. He would have to give up his weekly radio programme and the shows he had been already prepared. And what about us? I had no choice but to accept the situation. I wasn't even sure whether we would ever see each other again – it was wartime after all. I had had to say goodbye to so many people in my short life and the fear it engendered never went away. And so we said goodbye and swore to be faithful. Ted wanted to continue negotiating with the military to obtain a marriage licence. Some weeks earlier, I had informed my boss of my marriage plans. One Friday, after the shop had closed, she asked me to sit down with her. She smiled, shook her head and said: "What's a girl like you, from a nice, respectable home and good family, doing planning to marry a *Goy*, a Brit? Think about it. I can see you now, out with your little children buying *challah* on a Friday afternoon, looking like a real *balabusta* (home maker)." She clearly felt compelled to save this precious Jewish soul, added to which, she didn't want to lose me.

But things didn't go the way I had imagined. I didn't feel particularly well after Ted had left. I looked pale and felt very tired and weak. I slept badly and had nightmares. I was introduced to Hans Kleinschmidt, a psychotherapist who was prepared to help me. At first, he thought I was suffering from malnutrition. It's true that I had felt starved – not just of food but of love, and had been pining for my parents and for security. And so, as well as interpreting my dreams, he gave me injections and vitamins. I had been interested in psychoanalysis for several years and was, therefore, receptive to it. I had discovered Freud when I was 14 and had read his lectures and dream interpretations. Later on, I added Jung and Adler. Their theories were of the time and very appealing to young people. One of Kleinschmidt's dream interpretations helped me a great deal. I had dreamt about my mother, but only about her very beautiful hands. He explained to me that this dream expressed the way I reproached my mother. I had punished her by ignoring her in my dream. With the help of the therapy, I soon felt much better. I understood that I had suffered as a result of the separation from my parents, from Adolf and now from Ted. It became clear to me that my depression was caused not just by my own guilt feelings, but by my relationship with my parents, with my mother in particular.

14. Joining Up

The whole country was overshadowed by the War. Daily life was punctuated by reports of attacks by Arabs and hourly news from the front, as well as reports on the activities of Haganah, which had once again rescued illegal immigrants from the sea. The streets were dominated by soldiers. We felt threatened by the Lehi, known to the British as the Stern Gang after their leader Avraham Stern, which carried out acts of sabotage against the British. Even on the bus, there were news broadcasts. The cinemas showed extensive reports from the front and the air raids on London. Rommel's army was just outside Alexandria and our pacifist philosophy became irrelevant. Looking back, my motivation to join the British army can be ascribed to the ominous situation and my need to do something. Young Palestinian Jews were joining the British Army in large numbers and I wanted to be part of it.

Whilst visiting Uncle Sim in Haifa, I met my friend Regi. We talked about joining the army. Her enthusiasm was infectious. Whilst still in Haifa, I went to the recruiting office and applied to join the RAF. I was surprised that Regi didn't turn up but later heard that Moritz, now her husband, had forbidden her to apply. My friends and cousins were astonished at my decision. My room was sub-let. My little bundle of possessions easily stored in a corner. A military lorry took a group of us young Jewish girls – all RAF recruits – to Sarafant, a recruiting camp near Tel Aviv, where we had to undergo a month-long basic training. But, above all, we had to learn how to march – 'square bashing', as it was called. I surprised myself at how easily I adapted to the daily military routine. Our female superior was the embodiment of all things British, or at least she conformed to my preconceptions. She saw it as her duty to ensure that our lives were not too easy. I don't think I ever saw her laugh. She was tall, gaunt and pale, and always had reddish curls peeping out from under her beret – two on one side and three on the other. We were taught basic military skills, ranging from roll call to survival tactics in the desert. At first, we familiarised ourselves with the different areas of work to which we might be deployed. Although we were permitted to express an interest in a particular area, allocation was by interview. I had wanted to go into air surveillance, known as Clerk Special Duties. During the interview, I was asked whether I was a baker. The officer must have seen from my papers that I had worked in a bakery. I was offended but didn't let it show. The next question came at me without a pause: how many degrees has a circle. "360", I replied. She nodded agreement: "You're in."

The bed next to mine was occupied by a recruit by the name of Molly. Already, on the first evening, she asked me whether we had met before, as she thought she knew me from somewhere. The next day she approached me with a smile: "Now I've got it!" She used to work for the military in Haifa and had gone out with a soldier called Richie. She had seen photos of me in his tent, and he had also talked about me. She seemed to know a lot about me. We had to laugh at this coincidence. And so began a friendship that has endured to this day. Molly was from Magdeburg. Her parents were originally from Poland and had a delicatessen shop in Magdeburg. Luckily for her, her family were Zionists who succeeded in obtaining an emigration visa to Palestine, applied for by her brother who had emigrated earlier. It was, however, a condition of emigration that her parents could only take one child. They had taken Molly's younger sister, leaving Molly behind. Even though she eventually managed to emigrate to Palestine, she never recovered from her parents' effective abandonment of her.

I soon felt at ease in the army. I enjoyed the company of young women. On the one hand there were '*sabras*', Jewish women born in Palestine, and on the other, young women of different nationalities, who had only recently immigrated. We all wore uniform. Life was ordered and we knew what was expected of us. I no longer had to worry about a roof over my head, food on the table, work or money. After the training month, we were transferred to a large air force garrison in Heliopolis, Egypt. The train journey through the desert took 18 hours and I was responsible for ensuring that everything went according to plan for the 14 of us female soldiers. I was to make this biblical journey by train several times whilst in Egypt. Time and again, I would recall my ancestors who had made this journey through the desert many thousands of years ago. I thought of the *Seder* evenings, when Father recited from the *Haggadah* about the exodus of the Jews from Egypt.

In Heliopolis we were quartered in barracks. On each iron bedstead lay a bundle containing underwear, socks and cotton tights, to which I had an immediate aversion. The wearing of silk stockings was strictly prohibited, but we ignored this rule when on leave. One day, I was caught red-handed by the sentry; my punishment was the cancellation of all leave for a whole week. I was outraged, as I thought I was being made an example of. In my outrage, I wrote to Ted in great detail. Naturally, my letter was censored and I was summoned before my superior. "If you are unhappy, you have the right to file a complaint with the commander," she said. "Oh, I will." And believe it or not I was given an appointment to see the commander. I stood on the massive rug in his office, in front of an equally massive desk, and saluted. He gave me a kind look and said: "I hear you are a good soldier. I do, however, have the command of thousands of soldiers so I hope you will understand that I am not able to deal with every tiny problem that might arise." I had learnt my lesson and left with my tail between my legs.

Many new tasks awaited us in Heliopolis. I was able to apply my favourite subject at school: geometry. Using pencil and compass, we calculated the movements of our aircraft and those of the enemy and transferred the result to paper. There followed a two-week training course at the FCTS, the Fighter Controller Training School. We were assigned to officers who carried out simulated operations. It was here that flight controllers and navigators were trained for their work at the front. The work demanded concentration, so we only worked from 6 in the morning until 1 in the afternoon, with three days off after each course. When the British Prime Minister, Winston Churchill, came to North Africa during the war, the Heliopolis control centre was responsible for the safety of his flight, for which he thanked us personally.

My years with the RAF were very interesting and I had a certain degree of freedom, although it was a time of much unhappiness, influenced by uncertainty about the future. We had heard that Cairo offered much that we had been deprived of in Palestine. Café Groppi, for example, offered a multiplicity of ice cream bombes, with exotic fruit and whipped cream. Molly and I soon succumbed. On our first day's leave, we took the elegant metro to town. We stood in King Solomon Street, clueless as to where this paradise might be. I approached a traffic policeman and asked in Arabic: "Where is Groppi? Aivah! Aivah!" He raised his hand, moved it to the right, pointed towards the first street, and, shaking his head, said: "Groppi lo!", pointed to the second street, shook his head and repeated: "Groppi lo!" Then, pointing to the third street, nodded fiercely and shouted: "Groppi! Groppi!" Molly and I set off – and Café Groppi became our favourite haunt. I made good use of my freedom and visited the Cairo museums. The waxwork collection made a deep impression on me. I got to know a Welshman, who invited me to explore the pyramids with him. Today the area is full of hotels, but, then, it had quite a biblical appearance. We mounted camels and allowed ourselves to be led, swaying, round the pyramids. The camel driver insisted on telling us the history of the pyramids, but nodded knowledgeably when I told him that I was familiar with it, as my ancestors had been present when they were constructed. There was a club in Cairo for the Allied troops called 'Music for All', where a number of good, and not so good, orchestras, pianists and singers performed. The club also offered classical and modern ballet and became a real place of refuge for me.

Ted sent me long love letters. He was battling against the military administration for the marriage licence with immense determination. He wrote, too, about his family, from whom I also received nice letters. My future husband assured me that his family looked forward to meeting me. "When they hear your story, they will welcome you with open arms." My replies to him were equally confident. Neither of us destroyed our correspondence from those years; it gives me an insight into the double life I was leading. On the one hand I was fascinated by my work and, on the other, I plunged myself into social life and made many male acquaintances. Then there were the Americans. They had houseboats on the Nile to which they invited us. They spoilt us with music and unfamiliar American delicacies, huge amounts of "cookies" for example. One night, they took us to a mysterious sphinx in their jeep. The night was black-blue and the sky was filled with stars. In the silence, even our normally loud American friends were speechless.

Christmas came and several comrades made preparations for a family visit to Palestine. This didn't apply to the British soldiers, which led to an ambivalent atmosphere in the barracks. On the one hand, everyone was looking forward to Christmas, on the other, it was a painful reminder to some that they could not be with their loved ones for this family festival. Molly and I often sat in the barracks recreation room dreaming of the olden days, particularly during Christmas. We dreamt of snow and going sledging and sang 'Silent Night' in German. Just then, our superior officer came in and asked who had been singing so beautifully. People pointed at us and he suggested we join a group of Egyptian Christians on Christmas Eve singing Christmas carols in the street. We thought that was going too far.

It was my birthday on Christmas Eve. I felt very lonely and drove to Cairo. There were inebriated British soldiers everywhere. I took refuge in the 'Music for All' club. People were singing Christmas carols in the great hall. The tunes were familiar and, when someone held the music in front of me, I sang my heart out.

In the summer of 1944, I received a telegram from Uncle Sim in Haifa. "Come immediately. Stop. Uncle Leo arrived. Stop. Seriously ill. Stop. Has news of your parents." I immediately ran to headquarters and presented the telegram. Although personnel from the Women's Auxiliary Air Force were not allowed to fly, an exception was made in my case and a seat was reserved for me in a Lancaster bomber. I hastily packed my kitbag, was picked up by jeep and driven to an almost empty airfield. There was no one in sight apart from one other soldier, who was also waiting. It was eerily quiet. Just as I was about to board the Lancaster, the silence was suddenly broken by a plane, which had burst into flames as it was landing! The fire brigade came to put out the blaze – and that was that.

I started talking to the other soldier, who told me he, too, wanted to fly to Palestine. He told me how unhappy he was to be posted to the land of Jews, because he hated Jews. As we took off, I saw the desert and the Suez Canal below. Two and a half hours later, we landed in Jerusalem.

I made my way by train and bus via Haifa to Uncle Sim in Kfar Ata and arrived utterly exhausted. Over coffee, I heard that Uncle Leo had been in a Dutch concentration camp, from where, together with a group of women and children, he had been sent to Palestine. They had been exchanged for Germans. Uncle Leo was seriously ill with double pneumonia in the Hadassa hospital in Haifa. He had information about my parents. The next day, we went to the Hadassa. The nurse who accompanied us to the ward suggested that next time I should wear mufti, as the uniform was likely to frighten people. Uncle Leo, whom I remembered as a tall, strong man, was lying in bed so emaciated I hardly recognised him. When he saw me, he uttered my mother's name – Mila. I visited him again the next day. This time he recognised me and told me that Father had written to him, asking if he knew where Mother was. He had lost her after they became separated. But, declared Uncle Leo, they had both definitely died. I was shocked and beside myself. I stayed with Uncle Sim and paid several more visits to Uncle Leo.

Many years later, I learned that, from early in 1944, the Nazis had transported thousands of 'exchange Jews' from the Dutch internment camp, Westerbork, as well as from other European countries, to Bergen-Belsen camp near Hanover. Among them were top-ranking Jewish officials, Jews with dual nationality, or those with important foreign connections. They were categorised as privileged and were to be exchanged for Germans interned in British sovereign territory. In actual fact, only a few hundred Jews were released. Speaking of Uncle Leo, I heard a story I didn't want to believe at the time, but which, it seems, is true. Leo Grüneberg was also interned in Westerbork, together with other members of his family, among them his sister-in-law, Berthel Grüneberg. They were told that only a few women and children were to be released, of whom she was one. As Leo held a position of trust in the camp, he had access to the lists and is said to have changed B. Grüneberg to L. Grüneberg. So Berthel's children waited in vain for their mother to arrive in Palestine; Uncle Leo came instead. I rushed back to Walter and Lilly in the Raskassa House in Jerusalem and tried to come to terms with the latest news of my parents.

There was something else. Until then, I had been utterly convinced that I had been true to my ideals and to Zionism – but now it seemed my future lay in Britain and in starting a family. I tried to console myself with the thought that my future husband wanted to stay in Palestine or, at least, return there after some time in Britain. I wandered through the streets of Jerusalem, overcome with sadness and guilt, at a loss as to what to do. The guilt was all the stronger because I had been unable to identify with any one particular group in Palestine. I felt like an orphan wanting to belong and had pinned my hopes on establishing a family of my own. I felt I had made the wrong decision, but I had committed myself to marrying Ted. I had to be true to the decision I made.

In the meantime, there had been a development. Ted had produced and directed a successful show in Khartoum, which had been seen by a general who asked to meet the director. Ted was called, and the general was full of praise. "Fabulous, dear fellow, better than anything I have seen in London. If there is anything I can do for you…?" Ted, who was quick-witted, interrupted him, saying that for a whole year, he'd been trying to marry a Palestinian WAAF. And lo and behold, three days later I was called to the office: "Kober, I have good news for you," the officer said. "Your permission to marry came through this morning." I felt relieved that a decision had finally been made. Now everything took its course. Ted's letters were cheerful. The wedding was to take place in Jerusalem. And there was the excitement of booking rooms in the Essex Hotel, two single rooms for one night and then a double room for the honeymoon – after all, Ted and I hadn't seen each other for a whole year. A week before the wedding, I accepted a friend's invitation to a sailing party on the Nile. I hadn't sailed before, but my friend insisted it was easy. It was February and rather stormy. I obediently followed his instructions and sometimes found myself hanging over the side of the boat, to the extent that I returned home wet through. Days later, I was to be uncomfortably reminded of this adventure. Ted's arrival was imminent. We had arranged that I would meet him at Cairo train station. After the train had arrived, I started searching the crowd for a dapper man in a well-fitting uniform. What I had forgotten was that, for seven days, Ted had been travelling down the Nile in the most primitive conditions and would arrive exhausted, carrying luggage and a heavy army coat. But we found each other. I had been given permission to marry in civilian dress. I had one dress and bought some silk stockings in the bazaar. On the day of the wedding, I threw myself enthusiastically into the dress and then into the silk stockings. No sooner had I pulled one stocking just above the knee when not one but a whole regiment of ladders ran up my leg. And so I married in uniform after all. Ted rushed my dress uniform to the tailor to be professionally ironed. Then we stood with our witnesses in an office in the barracks. A friendly, rotund officer said all sorts of things in English that Ted and I had to repeat, after which the witnesses added their signatures. Having been refused permission to go to Jerusalem, we had to make do with Cairo. First we went to Groppi and feasted on ice cream. In the evening, we celebrated in a smart restaurant. There was dancing and, when asked to play something for the wedding couple, the orchestra played Happy Birthday. After a great deal of laughter, they remembered the wedding waltz. Suddenly, I felt very hot and my face turned red. Everyone made fun of me and made insinuating remarks. But, when Ted put his hand on my forehead, he declared that I had a high temperature and should go straight to bed. More joking ensued but the party was brought to an end. When we came into our bedroom – it was the honeymoon suite – it was filled with flowers, fruit and sweets. The doctor diagnosed an inflammation of the middle ear, no doubt the result of my sailing adventure. I lay in the heavenly four-poster bed; Ted was very concerned and couldn't do enough for me. So I spent my honeymoon ill in bed.

Soon afterwards, our company was sent into the desert to a tented camp at El Gedida. I shared my tent with two other WAAFs. It was so hot during the day that one day I suggested frying an egg on a helmet and, believe it or not, it worked! We were introduced to the newly developed radar technology. We were told the basics and we had to operate some equipment, but we were blindfolded when we passed through the control centre on our way to our offices. We knew that the Arabs were flirting with the Nazis, and that Cairo was teeming with spies. But worst of all was how much was being stolen. Thieves broke into our tents during the day; and when we walked along the street, as like as not, the shoulder straps of our handbags would be cut with scissors and the bag removed.

One day, we were being prepared for a parade to celebrate the King of England's birthday. At first, I felt that, as an old socialist, I shouldn't march for the King. At five in the morning, we all got up, were divided into marching groups, and had to hang around the parade ground for several hours until it was our unit's turn. We marched past the King's representative and that was it. Later, we watched it all on the newsreel at the cinema. The commentator shouted: "And here come the women soldiers of the Palestinian air force. Eyes, right! Salute! The flag is being carried by a South African Jewess!" I was embarrassed and so was everyone else.

I was surprised how many of the English women were anti-semitic. One girl had worked as a domestic for an Anglo-Jewish family. She hated the family because they were so wealthy. "Weren't they nice to you?" I asked. She pondered and then said "Actually, yes they were."

She wouldn't say anything else.

Suddenly, Ted was posted from Khartoum to Jerusalem and was able to stay with me for a few days, on his way back via Cairo. We visited Giza and Gezira, the most exclusive areas of Cairo, which were full of elegant restaurants frequented by extremely rich Arabs and their glamorous wives. They mainly spoke French and moved with oriental grace. King Farouk was still on the throne. His family and entourage lived in the lap of luxury in contrast to the poor Arabs loafing around on the streets, their eyes full of flies and suffering from trachoma, begging and desperately calling 'baksheesh, baksheesh'.

Once Ted had left again, I was overwhelmed by a yearning for Palestine. I still had some unused leave and got permission to go to Jerusalem. We left around six in the evening from a dirty and dusty station full of begging children. At four in the morning, the train stopped in Kantara. Breakfast in the NAAFI tent consisted of a huge tin mug of tea and a cheese sandwich full of sand. Then on we went through the desert, the fine sand penetrating every crevice. We arrived in Gaza at 6 a.m. and then, at last, onwards to the Promised Land. It was an unforgettable moment for us Jewish girls. The sun had just risen and the irrigation sprinklers were rotating in the green fields. We started clapping our hands and singing: "*Chai! Chai! Eretz Israel.*" – Israel lives! Farm workers waved as the train passed and we waved back. During that week, which I spent with Ted in Jerusalem, we started thinking about our future and decided to stay in Palestine, if at all possible. It didn't occur to us that this would present any problems – it was only later that we were told it wouldn't be that easy. Ted would have to return to England to obtain his discharge. We were disappointed but hoped to be able to settle there at a later date.

I had to return to El Gedida after we were suddenly informed that our unit was to be redeployed to Palestine, to Haifa to be precise. Something remarkable happened to me there. We were allocated accommodation on Mount Carmel, which had been home to American refinery workers in the 1930s. Together with two other girls, I found myself in the very same house where I had worked for the

Phetteplaces. Even though the house had been converted to military quarters, I could still sense the ghost of the Phetteplaces. Ted knew nothing of my deployment to Haifa. His most recent letter told of a grand ball, which was to take place in his garrison. I knew he would be at Walter and Lilly's in the afternoon and wanted to surprise him.

Although there was public transport in Palestine, people hitchhiked a lot, if for no other reason than that it didn't cost anything. I had been told it would be difficult to get a lift on a Saturday, as it was *Shabbat*, the day of rest. This made me even more determined to try, and I went to the appointed place for hitchhikers. After a short while, a Jeep stopped. The kind Jewish officer told me they were only going as far as Sarafant, but he was sure I would find someone to take me further. I climbed over the tailgate, rucksack in hand, and sat on one of the seats running along the side, and off we went. After a while, the truck came to a halt and I thought they were stopping for me. I swung one leg over the tailgate, the other was still on the cargo area. Suddenly, the Jeep started up again. My leg dragged along the gravelled road and although I screamed: "Stop! Stop!" they didn't hear me. I desperately tried to release my leg. Finally, I managed to free myself but landed in the ditch. My grazed leg was painful and my bag was still on the Jeep. Laboriously, I clambered out of the ditch and limped along the road. Luckily, a truck stopped quite soon after and picked me up. The driver stopped at a roundabout in Sarafant to let me off. As I turned round, I saw gesticulating soldiers and a traffic policeman on the other side of the road. The nice Jewish officer was standing there, explaining to the policeman how he had given a lift to a WAAF and had then stopped briefly to allow another hitchhiker on board, who, it transpired, had wanted to go in the opposite direction. So they had continued their journey until they stopped in Sarafant to let the WAAF off, but could only see her rucksack. I limped over to the group and, amid much merriment, found out what really happened. Mind you, I didn't really feel much like laughing – my leg hurt a lot. I then took the bus to Jerusalem. I had my leg bandaged by the Red Cross and limped to the Raskassa House, where Lilly and Walter were expecting me. By the time Ted arrived, I was all dressed up for the dance, with my leg bandaged. He was very surprised and pleased to see me. Despite my injury, I went to the ball in high spirits and danced through the night. The pain had temporarily disappeared, as a fresh wound doesn't hurt that much and I absolutely adored dancing.

On Sunday, I had to return to Haifa. I was on night duty and my leg had started to hurt again. I consulted a young British doctor who had apparently come straight from university. He looked at my leg and said the wound was superficial and I could definitely go to work.

It was Aunt Tilly's birthday and she had invited the family to Kfar Ata. I was looking forward to the party and to seeing everyone again. They welcomed me warmly and said that the uniform suited me and that, altogether, I looked really well. Uncle Sim said, somewhat sceptically: "She looks a bit too well to me; red cheeks can be symptomatic of amoebic dysentery – it's very infectious and is rife in the army at the moment. How do you really feel, Margot?" Constantly tired, I told him. "So let me examine you" came his reply. "And what's the matter with your leg?" I told him what had happened and the medical advice I'd been given. "If it's not treated straight away," cried Uncle Sim "you'll get gangrene!" Back at camp, I demanded to see the doctor and reported my uncle's diagnosis. Two doctors and several telephone calls later, I was in an ambulance on my way to the military hospital in Jerusalem. In the ward, I got into a conversation with another WAAF, roughly my age. She read me a letter she had received from her mother in Tel Aviv that morning. It was full of expressions of love and caring. The next day, her mother arrived bearing all sorts of food parcels; mother and daughter hugged and kissed each other and I crawled under my bedclothes and cried as I would never again witness such maternal love.

Once it was clear that I had amoebic dysentery, I was moved to the RAF hospital in Tel Aviv. Yes, the illness was unpleasant in the extreme, but the care and attention I received did me the world of good, and would explain why I was always in good spirits. One entry in my diary reads: I have to be careful not to be too jolly. The nurses noticed it, too, because they sometimes put patients near me who were particularly depressed, in the hope that I would cheer them up. After several weeks in hospital, I was granted two weeks convalescent leave, which I spent in Jerusalem.

Soon it was Christmas 1944. Ted and I decided to spend the festive days at the YMCA hotel in Jerusalem. It was also my 25th birthday – the day we decided to start a family. Although we had no idea how and where we were going to live, we were convinced that our children would be happy wherever we were. The happy days we spent over Christmas proved to be fruitful: I became pregnant. I immediately went to see Uncle Sim in Kfar Ata, who gave me advice on what to do. I informed the RAF of my good news. I couldn't work at first because I was vomiting day and night. A not very sympathetic officer came to see me and explained that I would be dismissed, as I was, so to speak, of no use to them. I moved back to the Raskassa House in Jerusalem, settled in to my little room and was happy to be nearer Ted. In the meantime, Walter and Lilly had become parents of a little boy called Ariel, the first of this new generation. Ted and I fell in love with him and looked forward even more to our own *Wunderkind*.

During the months that followed, the atmosphere in Palestine changed. People believed in victory and prepared themselves for peacetime, even though no one knew what the future held. More and more illegal im- migrants arrived, the conflict with the Arabs continued, and attacks became more frequent. The majority of the Jewish population hoped for the partition of a Palestine and a Jewish State. I felt guilty that, at such a crucial moment, I was about to leave the country I had fought for. When I had turned my back on life in the kibbutz, my comrades had called me a traitor. Now I truly felt like one. But the prospect of motherhood and a loving family atmosphere outweighed everything. Like Ted, I had no doubts about our future in England, and Ted was convinced that his family would receive us with open arms.

The day of our departure approached. I visited Uncle Sim and Aunt Tilly in Kfar Ata one last time. My aunt, still a fiery Zionist, communicated suppressed reproach mingled with disappointment at my decision. My uncle gave me some words of advice. He thought our plans were sensible. And then he said something I had never heard from him before: "I am proud of you and what you have made of your life!"

15. My Second Promised Land

It was the end of April 1945. Ted was already in Port Said, from where we would sail to Liverpool on a luxury Dutch steamship. I took my old, battered pigskin suitcase, which could tell many a tale, and with which I identify to this day. In Port Said, it received a further sticker: NOT WANTED ON VOYAGE. You could translate this as 'Not required for the journey' or 'Not wanted for the journey', the latter, I felt, was very symbolic. As I stood with my relatives on the platform at Jerusalem station, I found myself recalling some words from a book by Jacob Wassermann: "*Nie und nimmermehr!*" (Never ever again!). Walter gave me a little bottle of sherry, and Lilly was awfully pale. Then I was on the train bound for Egypt – looking out of the window, I watched as Walter, Lilly and Ariel disappeared from view... and I wondered if I would ever see them again.

I met Ted in Port Said and we boarded the ship together. I was led to a big dormitory occupied by women and children of different nationalities. The Egyptian women spoke Arabic or French among themselves and to their children, whilst the British women lay on their beds with their books and whispered instructions to their children. The polite captain came to our table while we were eating and chatted to us in English. We had nothing to complain about, but I was reserved when he asked me about my story; I had no desire to share it in that company. Ted had been assigned to the men's quarters. We met on deck every day, talked to the other soldiers and listened to their experiences. Then we made friends with a group from ENSA – the Entertainments National Service Association – who entertained British troops at the front. They had heard about Ted's shows and were enthusiastic. They immediately started making plans for the future. I liked these brave men: they didn't baulk at the dangers of war, and were keen to brighten the lives of the soldiers.

My problems soon moved into the background, as I was now full of optimism. I had developed some curious fantasies: the war is over and I'm standing on a station platform because we've been told that lots of trains are due to arrive, carrying refugees from somewhere or other, and I suddenly see my parents. Once the media started reporting incredible stories of rescue, my fantasies intensified. Ted became more nervous by the day. Five years had passed since he had left his home as a young man to get to know the big wide world. How had his world at home changed? A young corporal walked around the ship collecting messages to send telegrams to relatives. We sent a message to Ted's mother, saying that we would be arriving home on 7 May. Until now, we hadn't been allowed to contact the family in England. The corporal collected the money and enriched himself – as we later discovered, he never did send the telegrams.

We had been at sea for some time when our daily routine was suddenly interrupted by the voice of the captain over the ship's tannoy system. "Here is important news direct from England." Then came General Montgomery's distinctive voice, announcing very clearly and with military brevity: "The war in Europe is over!" Screams erupted; soldiers and sailors threw their caps in the air. Ted and I hugged each other but I realised in an instant that I would soon have to face the dreadful reality: how many of my relatives had lost their lives and how and where? The captain said a few more words, thanked everyone for their contribution in the war, and announced that there would be free wine and beer. I was sure most of those on board could not believe the conflict had ended.

And then we saw land – my second Promised Land. This time it was Liverpool harbour. Again, it was an overwhelming moment. One solitary woman stood at the harbour, possibly a mother. Some harbour workers were walking about; otherwise, everything was grey and empty, bomb-damaged buildings in the distance. It was a forlorn scene: ahead of us was a high brick wall with an advertisement for Camp Coffee. Ted had told his family that I only drank coffee. After a while, instructions were issued via a loudspeaker. Suddenly I was a refugee again, arriving in a foreign country and having to adjust to a new situation. I knew, from my experience of arriving in Haifa in 1936, that there would be utter chaos, so I quickly pulled Ted ashore. We were the first to disembark and were directed to a vast barracks, where our luggage had been arranged in alphabetical order. My old suitcase stood there under B for Barnard. We marched off straight away and asked for directions to the train station. My first impression: grey and black, bomb-damaged, with plumes of steam everywhere. Lots of people, uniforms, and families with babies. We boarded the train to Victoria. Ted carried the heavy luggage and I carried his ukulele. We found two seats and I looked around at my new world. There was a mother changing her baby's terry towelling nappy. I was surprised, as we had used muslin and gauze nappies in the kibbutz. At first, I thought she was using a hand towel. There would be plenty more such surprises. It took me some time to digest all the new and strange things. But there was one thing I never managed to acquire the taste for: English tea.

People struck me as being noticeably pale. The women wore suit jackets with square shoulders, and a remarkably large number of them were flat-chested. Most of them had blonde, permed hair and wore a lot of make-up. I was surprised that so many people – even younger ones – already had visibly false teeth. I, on the other hand, was tanned, wore a fashionable blue dress, silk stockings, beautiful sandals and a camel hair coat. My hair was naturally curly and I wore very little make-up. That sounds rather arrogant and I wouldn't mention it, were it not for the significant part it would play in the unhappiness I was to experience in the future. But, at this stage, I had no inkling of what was to come.

We arrived at Victoria Station, another grey, damp station. Ted looked around to see if he could track down a cup of coffee for me. We saw a café, furnished in cold, white marble and with empty cake plates in the window. We went in anyway – on the servery were more empty plates covered with white paper doilies. "Could we have two cups of coffee and two sandwiches, please?" Ted asked. The 'please' spoke of his anger and frustration at not even being able to offer his wife a coffee and a sandwich in 'his' country. The café owner looked at us in surprise. "No coffee, only tea," he said. Ted was at a loss. It was a hot day in May. Where was he going to conjure up a coffee for his pregnant wife? Disappointed, we made our way to the train for Catford Bridge. Ted was heavily laden as he opened the carriage door. He groaned as he tried to manoeuvre my heavy suitcase up the narrow steps. A young man sitting in the compartment didn't move. I watched as Ted went red in the face. Then he exploded: "Of course, just sit there! I've been overseas for five years fighting and come home exhausted, overloaded and thirsty, and you can't even help me with my luggage!" The man jumped up, mumbled an apology, and helped us.

When we arrived in Catford in the late afternoon, there wasn't a soul on the station platform, apart from a boy who must have been about 15 years old. Ted asked him to find us a taxi, which was almost impossible in those days. He managed, though, and I travelled in one of the famous black cabs for the first time. For Ted, the return to his homeland was also full of drama. He was coming home after five years, with a wife of whom he was proud. And yet, I'm sure that it was during that short journey that it really dawned on him that difficulties might lie ahead after all. I, on the other hand, was confident and had no doubts whatsoever.

The taxi stopped in Firhill Street, on a council estate. Ted said: "Look, there's my mother with Mr. Philips." We got out of the cab. His mother exclaimed: "There's our Ed!" She looked as though she was in shock. It transpired that she had never received the telegram. I was introduced to Ted's mother and to Mr. Philips, an old family friend who was a local door-to-door salesman. We were standing outside a small house with a well-kept front garden. Ted's mother invited us in. The brass doorknob was gleaming. We walked into the kitchen, also gleaming. There we met a young man, who was introduced to us as Jack, the fiancé of Ted's youngest sister, Mary.

Some months previously, whilst Ted was recording a radio show, he was allowed to use the studio to cut a record, which he sent to his mother. He was accompanying himself on the ukulele and finished the song with the words: "Dear mother, because the war is on I'm not allowed to tell you when we'll be coming home, but make sure there's a shepherd's pie in the oven when we get back." Having regained her composure, his mother revealed that there was indeed a shepherd's pie in the oven. Jack went upstairs and, within half an hour, a flag was hanging out of the window: 'Welcome home, son!' What about me? I was left to sit in the living room and felt ignored. Everything was very clean and tidy, and I was pleased to see there was a piano. Then I heard Ted's voice from the kitchen: "What d'you think of her?" "All right," came the hesitant reply. Perhaps she didn't want to admit that she had expected someone entirely different. Of course, I had no idea what this family had in store for me. In my view, Ted shouldn't have asked his mother that question at that juncture... and I felt hurt.

Whilst we were sitting in the living room, Jack left to collect Mary from work. Then Ted's eldest sister, Alice, stormed into the room and confronted me. "Are you pregnant? I can't see anything," she shouted and shook her head. She clearly wasn't taken with me, either. Finally, Jack returned with Mary. Before they came in, she had asked him why they had already hung out the flag, when VE Day wasn't until tomorrow. Jack had not given anything away. Mary noticed some Turkish Delight in the kitchen and heard voices coming from the living room. "Why are we having tea in the parlour?" she asked. But then she saw her brother and threw her arms around him. I got a non-committal handshake and she didn't speak to me any further. She was young, blonde, nicely-dressed and looked very English. Then Ted's second eldest sister, Nell, appeared. She, like me, was six months pregnant but more noticeably so. She examined me critically. I was still seated and Mary and Jack sat opposite me in an armchair. Jack was smoking a pipe and was the only one who gave me a friendly look, whilst Mary remained silent and unapproachable. Now sister number four made her appearance – a tall, slim, distinguished and elegantly dressed lady. A scream: "Eddy!" Again, they embraced but nothing of the kind came in my direction. Ivy greeted me; everyone was talking at once, they were all overjoyed and hugged Ted but totally ignored me. The siblings then dispersed, leaving us with Ted's mother, who offered us the bedroom with a double bed and brown furniture. It was very tidy and I clung to the thought that Ted was with me and would stand by me. That gave me hope that everything would fall into place.

That evening, the neighbours knocked at the door. "Come on, Barnie – come and help us celebrate!" Mother-in-law turned her nose up at the idea and said it was too common for her, but Ted took me by the arm and walked me to the end of the street, where a big fire had been lit. People were dancing, especially the women, and singing *Knees up Mother Brown*. "Come on, dearie, dance with us!" they said. I sheepishly admitted that I didn't know the song. "What! Where does she come from?" Ted was asked. "From Palestine." "Where's that? Is it in Cairo?" "No. Come on – it's where Jerusalem is". "Oh yes, where our Lord walked." and they stared up into the sky.

The following day, it was decided that Ted and I should visit Ted's brother Jim and his family. They too lived in a council house in southeast London. The streets were filled with people celebrating the end of the war, and the atmosphere was euphoric. They had lived through the Blitz and were celebrating the end of the nightmare. People were standing outside their homes with their beer tankards, drinking, laughing and shouting jokes at each other. Some had even torn slats from garden fences to feed a bonfire. We boarded the overcrowded bus. At the next stop, an elderly lady got on clasping a Victorian vase filled with beer. She went from one passenger to the next offering everyone a sip. When she reached me, I declined but Ted whispered: "Just pretend." Thank goodness I followed his advice, as she would undoubtedly have taken offence. Standing at the bus stop in Croydon were three children, two girls and a boy aged between five and nine. Ted recognised his nieces and nephew from photos he had been sent. They eyed me with curiosity and we went to my new relatives' Jim and Nell's house, where, yet again, I was made to feel like an orphan being assessed for adoption. Ted also felt uncomfortable.

My brother and sister-in-law were the family eccentrics. Unlike the others, they made little effort to improve their standard of living. Jim had a good job with the post office, turning down promotion because he wanted things to stay as they were. Nell supported his lack of aspiration. The three children were doing well at school but, when their son Peter was offered an interview for a better school, they didn't attend. Nell was a pretty Irish woman with bright blue eyes and black hair. She came from a large working class family. Her father was a member of the Labour party and enjoyed talking to me.

Ted's leave was coming to an end and he had to return to the Army, so I was on my own. During this difficult time, people barely spoke to me. His mother may have wanted to get to know me, but her daughters weren't having it. Alice, who lived next door, was the first morning visitor. Before she went to work, she would pop her head round the kitchen door and then go into the living room with her mother, leaving me alone in the kitchen. I would hear whispering, doors slamming and then came the reproaches: "Why did you hang your trousers over the bath? Have you never heard of damage caused by damp?" or "Why is the bedroom window open?" or "Why isn't it open?" Not a kind word and no enquiry as to how I was feeling. Nell would ring while I was resting in the afternoon: "Where is she?" "Where do you think? In bed of course!" came the reply. My habit of taking a bath every day was another bone of contention. There was hot water in the boiler but it had to be carried up one flight of stairs to the bathroom. This was probably why people only had a bath once a week or twice a month. The family resented my wish to have a bath; they considered it not worth the effort.

Alice was married to Charlie, a butcher. The first impression of a tall, strong man turned out to be misleading. He hadn't fought in the war but had been a reluctant air raid warden on the home front. When I was introduced to him, he looked at Ted, nodded in my direction, and asked "Where's she from?" Ted was annoyed and snapped: "You can ask her yourself; she speaks good English. Her parents were gassed in a concentration camp." Charlie waved his hand dismissively. "That's all propaganda." Two days earlier, Alice had come home and had reported seeing photos showing the liberated concentration camps. Ivy was more friendly. She had different interests and wasn't at home as much as her sisters. She worked as a hostess in an American GI's club. Later, she married an American and went with him to the USA. Now, though, she had a boyfriend who had only recently returned from the war. We all gathered in the kitchen to listen to his account of his experiences at the front. He knew nothing about my background and recounted animatedly how they had stumbled across Bergen-Belsen concentration camp. We were shaken to the core to hear about the terrible things they had found there. No one thought to make a connection between those horrific images and me and my family. Gradually, I began to realise the ignorance I was dealing with. They obviously didn't know how to categorise me. First there were the Germans, their enemies. Therefore, the fact that I was from Germany made me a 'bloody German'. But I was also Jewish, so a 'bloody Jew' as well. And from Palestine to boot, "that's what it said on the uniform she was wearing in the photo our Eddie had sent from Cairo". Incomprehensible!

In the house opposite lived the Cohens, a Jewish family. Mr Cohen was a tailor, had a warm-hearted wife and four daughters. When they heard I was from Palestine, they invited me over. They gave me presents and offered to help and I enjoyed being there. But Ted's family then ticked me off as if I were a child. The Cohens were unsuitable company for me. Mr. Cohen was having it off with his daughters, and I was to stop all contact with them. But, by the same token, I noticed how Ted's family, especially Alice, kept in contact with the Cohens behind my back.

My mother-in-law and I had an ambivalent relationship. When we were alone together, she was friendly and I actually liked her because she had a sense of humour. I also respected her for the way she had worked her way up from humble beginnings. She had taught herself to read and write, and had brought up six children by herself after her husband had died in a traffic accident. But the moment her daughters were present, she had to show that she, too, was against me.

Ted came home every weekend. He was stopped by a neighbour one day, who advised him to find me somewhere else to live. "It's not good for her to live in that atmosphere, especially as she's pregnant." Ted was furious and had a huge row with his mother. When he told me we were going to apply to the SSAFA (an army welfare organisation) for alternative accommodation for me, I was relieved. On the Monday, we arrived at the SSAFA office for our appointment with Lady Lockett, who worked there as a volunteer. We were met by an elderly lady who looked like Queen Victoria; she was dressed from head to toe in black and wore a large hat. Her small blue eyes looked at us through a pince-nez and she smiled rather absent-mindedly. She sent us to an address near by. A pleasant man opened the door, asked if we had come to see the room, and took us up to a small attic room, dimly lit by a skylight. The only stick of furniture was an old gas oven. Ted turned to him and screamed: "Is my wife meant to live here with a child?" Shocked, the man replied that he had made Lady Lockett aware that the room was not suitable for a pregnant woman, who would have difficulty with the pram on the stairs, that there was running water but no bath and that the room had little natural light. Lady Lockett had apparently replied that it all depended on where one came from and what one was used to. We hurried back to Lady Lockett. Furious, Ted explained to her where his wife was from and what she was used to. I can still see her shocked expression and the pince-nez slipping off her nose. She recovered her poise and gave us a new address. We set off yet again, and yet again we found ourselves standing in front of a house on a council estate. A pale, gaunt woman opened the door and welcomed us in. From the living room, one could see through the kitchen into a small garden. Upstairs, the woman showed us three spacious bedrooms, the smallest one earmarked for me. Everything was grubby. She told us that, after her first husband had died, she had married an older man so that her children wouldn't be taken away. So this was where I was to live until the birth of my child. Ted was at a loss, but I assured him I would manage. I moved the next day, suitcase in one hand, grandmother's bedspread draped over the other arm. As I stood there, my sister-in-law Alice rode past on her bicycle. She dismounted and hastened to explain that "...we can't put you up because the council doesn't allow it." Nonsense! She felt guilty because she had a very cosy council house with a spare room but didn't want me there. I was relieved not to have to live in such an unfriendly atmosphere. It took a walk and a bus ride to reach my new home, laden with my possessions. There I was introduced to my host, a little man with thin, white hair and one solitary tooth. He worked as an errand boy on a building site. There were things about the house I found particularly repellent; for example, there was cat and dog hair everywhere. When the cat produced a litter of six kittens, they were drowned in the toilet and buried in the garden. The next day, as I was looking out of the window, I saw the dog digging up the dead kittens and playing with them. I will never forget the singular mixture of odours in that house. Ted often visited me, but never wanted to eat there.

16. David

Fortunately, even this terrible time soon passed. I received a letter from the public health authority explaining that, due to bomb damage, there were no maternity wards available in London hospitals. I was to be evacuated and should come to the hospital in Lewisham, a neighbouring district, where a bus would take me and other pregnant women elsewhere. My sister-in-law, Nell, who was also pregnant, felt sorry for me. She took me under her wing and we went to the relevant authority together and asked an official to try and accommodate me in London. "She has no family, and here in London she has us," she argued. But they were unsympathetic – there was no available space.

Once again, I had to make my own way, on foot and by bus, along streets and past bomb-damaged houses. I felt abandoned and wished that Uncle Sim could be with me. The bus was waiting outside the hospital and a few women were already sitting inside. Was this the bus to Folly Farm, I enquired. They noticed my accent immediately, and I realised that I was once again the outsider, the one who didn't belong, whom nobody talked to and who wasn't easy to categorise. I looked at my fellow passengers, some with hard, aggressive faces. They sat with their arms folded, as if ready to fight an invisible enemy at a moment's notice, and I felt threatened by their provocative stares.

Folly Farm was a mansion the Gilbey family had made available for use as a maternity hostel. They had ensured that it was technically equipped and staffed to a high standard, well organised in every respect. In comparison with my experiences in the modern infant ward of the kibbutz, and the military hospitals in Palestine, the atmosphere here was totally different. Nurses, doctors and midwives appeared very competent, but aloof and status-conscious. The matron was reserved in her contact with us; the nurses were strict and biased against me. It is possible that I was over-sensitised by previous experience, but I had no doubt that one of the nurses was an anti-semite. I shared the room with one other mother-to-be. Fortunately, we got on well, but, in general, the women were hostile towards me and didn't leave me in peace. We had to help in the kitchen, and they always tried to ensure that I ended up with an unfair share of the work. One day, as we all sat together in the living room, a young woman stormed in and started punching me. "You bloody German," she shouted hysterically, "you're responsible for my parents' death!" I later learnt that her parents had been killed during a bombing raid on London. Of course, I was now frightened and immediately asked to see the matron. I was pushed into a big office where I was received by the director sitting behind her desk. She, too, radiated a stern, Victorian attitude. "I hear you come from the Holy Land?" Oh no, not that old chestnut again, I thought. "Before the war, friends of mine went on a pilgrimage to Jerusalem and visited all the places where our Redeemer had lived and was crucified. It is my greatest wish to go there, too." It was almost impossible for me to make my complaint – she wouldn't discuss it. I had wanted to ask for a transfer because I was frightened of what the women might do. There was no danger at all, she said, in a placatory tone, as all women were good, Christian people. And, with that, I was dismissed. Now, more than ever, I felt alone and abandoned. When he visited me, Ted noticed that I didn't feel too well, but I placated him and told him not to worry.

I was looking forward to having the baby and wasn't afraid of the process of giving birth, because I knew I was in good hands. I had been having contractions for two days and two nights when the nurse asked for Ted's address. When I asked her why, I was told they needed it in case of any problems. "Tomorrow morning you'll be taken to Reading hospital; it will be a difficult birth." Another night of pain followed, without a kind or comforting word or any reassurance that all would be well. In the morning, a lorry arrived and I was put on a stretcher. A nurse accompanied me on my bumpy journey. I was brought into the hospital in a wheelchair and greeted by a nurse, who said she had some important questions. "What is your religion?" she asked. Thinking they needed to know for burial purposes, I remained silent. She reassured me, saying I needn't be frightened. They were not prejudiced and every denomination was represented in the hospital. "I'm Jewish" I whispered, and she clapped her hands, saying there were also Jewish doctors in the hospital. I was wheeled into the operating theatre. The contractions became worse and worse. A young Polish assistant doctor came to look at me: "Let's wait and see how much longer she can put up with it," I heard him say. With tears in her eyes, the nurse insisted that he call the doctor immediately, because it was obvious that this couldn't continue. She ran to the telephone and I heard her say: "Doctor, you must come at once!" I screamed and screamed and felt my strength ebbing away. An anaesthetist rushed to my bed. I remember desperately trying to rip the oxygen mask out of his hand to press it on my face and hearing him say: "Just a moment, my dear..." and then I was gone.

I awoke on 14 September 1945 at two in the morning. A nurse was bending over me smiling: "You have a healthy boy." "Has he got everything?" I whispered, fearing he might be missing a finger or a toe. She laughed: "Yes, he has everything," and I realised that she thought I had meant something else. This story made the rounds in the hospital. Finally, someone brought me the little bundle and explained that the little red dot on his forehead would disappear over time; it had been a forceps delivery. The most important thing was that I had my baby and was alive. The atmosphere around me seemed warmer and people were concerned for my wellbeing, but I was still in pain. After consulting with a colleague from the London Hospital of Tropical Diseases, the doctor diagnosed dysentery and I was moved to a single ward, where I remained for several weeks with a high temperature. Naturally, Ted came as soon as he received the telegram and was happy to see us. Meanwhile, he was walking the streets to find us somewhere to live. He saw an advertisement in a shop window in Hither Green: Room with kitchen and use of bathroom for rent – would suit single man. Ted, who was still in uniform, went inside immediately to tell the owner about our unfortunate situation. She thought the flat was too small for a family. She told me later that, whilst Ted kept trying to persuade her, she felt she really should help him, as he was a soldier who had fought for all of us. She showed Ted the flat and he was happy. He liked the young woman and assumed I would like her, too. He was right because we became good friends. The day arrived when Ted collected me and the baby. And so the three of us took our first step into family life. The first stop was 'Mum' and family. David cried the entire night and was cradled and rocked by several members of the family. The next morning we went to our first marital home. Olive, our landlady, was standing at the door. She told me later that, when she saw me with the baby in my arms, she thought "Our boys are so irresponsible – fancy bringing home such a young girl; she can't be more than sixteen." I liked the house immediately. It was on a wide road lined with big, old trees. We climbed the stairs to our room. There was nothing in it apart from a little table with two chairs, a chest of drawers and a cot. The bathroom was shared with all the occupants of the house. At the end of a long corridor was a tiny kitchen. But I was happy.

17. Early Married Life

This was the environment in which I familiarised myself with everyday life in England. Rationing was still the order of the day and entailed endless queuing, but everyone took it in their stride. Of course, there was also the black market. but it was almost irrelevant because no one was starving. Many working class families living in towns grew their own fruit and vegetables in allotments. Mothers received an extra ration of vitamin-rich fruit juices for their children. The essential things were all available but, in our case, what was missing was money. Ted's salary just covered our rent, so he had to find an evening job. Olive's husband had a second job painting lead soldiers and invited Ted to help him. The two of them sat together in the evenings, earned some money, and enjoyed the companionship. The SSAFA gave us a layette and, for very little money, we managed to get a massive old English pram. Ted spent hours polishing it until it gleamed; then he proudly took our little boy for a walk under the trees. When little David started to talk, his first word was "trees".

Wherever there was a queue, you joined it first and then asked what was on offer. Often it was bananas. Whilst I was still living with Ted's family, my mother-in-law heard that fresh coffee was available in Bromley. I set off on the long trek, found the shop and, full of expectation, joined the queue – I'd made it! The lady in front of me, with whom I'd had a pleasant chat, collected her 125-gram ration. As I assumed my place at the front of the queue, I heard: "Very sorry, I'm afraid that was the last of the coffee!"

I tried to cook familiar dishes. When David was a little older, I made his soup by cooking a small piece of meat with lots of vegetables and rice. The health visitor, who called to see how I was managing, loved my soup and passed the recipe on to other women. When my sister-in-law, Alice, called one day, she asked what I was doing. "I'm making tomato soup," I replied. "What!" she shouted, "we buy Heinz tinned tomato soup." My impression of what the post-war British housewife dished up was this: first there was the Sunday roast; on Mondays it was cold meat and mashed potatoes or bubble and squeak (left over potatoes and vegetables). The next day the remaining meat would be minced and turned into shepherd's pie. For the rest of the week, people ate corned beef, tasteless sausages, or fish, all served with either chips or baked beans.

Ted went to see his former boss, Ernest Beckett, for whom he had worked before the war, doing the bookkeeping and helping with sales. Beckett, who had a successful motorcycle business, was delighted to see Ted again and invited us over for dinner. The Becketts owned a lovely house in Eltham. And they had a TV. Ernest's wife, Pam, and I hit it off immediately and became good friends. The Becketts were my first introduction to the English middle class. Ernest asked Ted whether he would mind sorting out his books again on his weekends off. And so it was that, on Saturday mornings, we were collected by car, Ted was dropped off at the shop, and David and I were driven to Pam's beautiful house where we spent the day with Pam and her two children. For me it was a form of escape. Ernest was very pleased with Ted's work and made him an offer that, in those days, was very attractive: Ted would be branch manager; a beautiful flat and a car came with the good salary. One evening, as Ernest was driving us home and we were talking about the future, Ted said to Ernest: "Your offer is very generous but, if Maggy agrees, I'd like to stay in the Army and have the opportunity to travel." I loved the idea and agreed immediately. Ted had also been offered radio work as a comedian, but had declined that as well. Like me, he wanted to get away from England.

The window elevation of our room had been damaged by bombing, and the wind howled through the cracks. The little stove gave off insufficient heat to warm the room and Olive suggested that, when the coal merchant came, I should buy some coal. So I ran down and very politely asked for a sack of coal. But oh that wretched accent! He cracked his whip to encourage his horse to set off and shouted:

"Our women didn't have any coal in the war – you'll have to manage on your own!" Ted was beside himself when I told him what had happened and walked six miles to see his mother, who, fortunately, had some coal to spare.

ॐ

At the beginning of 1946, a letter arrived from my friend Molly in Egypt, who, meanwhile, had married George, a British soldier. They wanted to come to England to take over the care of her 3-year-old stepson, who had TB and lived with his maternal grandparents. Could they stay with us temporarily? They arrived on 2 March and our dear landlady, Olive, found a small room for them. It was terribly crowded but we all seemed to manage very well. Molly and George became involved in a custody battle – which they eventually won – because little John's grandparents wanted to keep him. All three of them moved in with George's parents, who found it very difficult to accept Molly. Molly's mother-in-law kept interfering in little John's upbringing. During one of the many arguments, she uttered the unforgettable sentence: "How can you say such a thing – a woman in your position!" It became a quotable quote.

Olive was a great support: she let me use her kitchen to wash the nappies. She also helped me to understand England and the English better. She had two young children, Robin and Michael. We babysat for each other, which meant, for example, that each of us could go to the cinema once a week. Ted found it hard to get used to our meagre existence and he wasn't much help. This normally gregarious man developed an antipathy for going out with me and socialising. I couldn't make sense of it at the time and found it frustrating. He always found a pretext for refusing invitations: the weather was bad, it was too crowded in town, and so on. Then he started bringing visitors home unannounced, which I found difficult to deal with, not least because our limited means made it difficult to extend hospitality. It seemed to me that Ted was trying to return to the lifestyle of his youth, when he was free and without responsibilities. He often played tennis with his sister Mary and went out a lot in the evenings. Perhaps he was jealous of the baby, who needed so much of our attention. One day, Olive told us there was to be dance in the neighbourhood. I bought a red silk dress on credit and was really looking forward to it. We arrived to find a wooden building in the middle of a field, from which dance music could be heard. We paid a modest entrance fee and went in, only to be confronted by the sight of an almost empty hall with some chairs along the wall and a gramophone in the corner. Deeply disappointed, we left.

The very British weather gave rise to a rather strange experience around Christmas. Ted was to appear in a cabaret at a club in Woolwich. Olive had agreed to baby-sit and, knowing the performance started at 9, we set off at 7. Friends had joined us and, despite the fog, we were all in good spirits. The station was crowded with people waiting for trains that never came, but no one made a fuss. An hour later, a train finally arrived and everyone piled in; half-an-hour later, the train left but it wasn't long before the train ground to a halt. The fog had become so dense you could almost smell it. We had to continue on foot and arrived at the club far too late. We realised that we would have to embark on the return journey straight away and I couldn't stop thinking about David, who was bound to be missing me. Very slowly, we felt our way through the dense fog. Voices, and sometimes unpleasant laughter, could be heard here and there. Suddenly, the blurred outline of a telephone box came into view. There were two girls standing inside who told us they were on their way home from a dance but had been surprised by the fog and had lost their way. They wanted to contact their parents but didn't have the right change and didn't know what to do. I took charge and telephoned one of the mothers, to tell her that we were going to take the girls home with us for the night and put them on a train the following morning. We finally arrived home at four in the morning. David was sitting on the slumbering Olive's lap and seemed happy to see me. This was my first experience of a 'London pea-souper'.

By 1947, we were still living in straitened circumstances. Everything was still rationed; clothes and other daily necessities were hard to come by. The streets were swarming with British, American and Polish soldiers and the newspapers were full of reports and photographs of the concentration camps, but – it seemed to me – no one believed them. I thought of my parents every day – I had no idea what had happened to them or any of my other relatives. I had no contact with anyone who could have helped me. My brother had sent a congratulatory telegram from Canada when David was born, but the tone was very reserved and it was obvious that he did not want a close relationship with me. It saddened me, it was only much later that I learnt the reasons for his attitude.

Despite my sobering experiences on arriving in England, I felt more confident now. I had got to know people I got on well with, but then the press started publishing distorted reports about the political situation in Palestine, and the attacks on the British Army by Jewish underground groups. I wasn't prepared to stand silently by and tried to explain the situation whenever the opportunity arose. There were few in Britain who were aware that the British Mandate policy in Palestine was not always fair. When I visited Pam and Ernest on a Saturday evening and aired my Socialist views, Ernest reacted in a typically English middle class manner. "Give a working class family a bathroom and they'll fill the bath with coal." Through him, I learnt a lot about the Conservative point of view. But, above all, I learnt that, as a guest in this country, one was not permitted to criticise. Generally, people rarely criticised. Yes, they complained in private about little injustices but my impression was that there was no desire to change anything. As for me, I felt duty bound to explain and put people right, probably because I felt guilty about turning my back on Palestine and all its problems. I was pleased when, now and again, I encountered soldiers who had been stationed there for some years, had made friends and broadened their horizons. Ted was a good example. He missed our friends, the unconventional way of life and especially the many cultural things on offer. He also longed for the 'fleshpots of Egypt'.

Even though we hadn't had that much to eat in Palestine ourselves, the country's gastronomy was varied. Ted especially loved the Viennese coffee house atmosphere, which was unknown in Britain.

During my early years in England, I had no contact with Germany, but often thought of my former school friends and neighbours. What had become of them? I dreamed about the Siebengebirge and yearned to go there. But then these images turned to blood. I still had no information about my parents. One day, something happened that touched me. I went with David, who was in a buggy by now, to visit some friends whose son Terry had been stationed in Jerusalem with Ted. While they looked after David, Terry took me sightseeing. Near Trafalgar Square, I noticed a group of German prisoners-of-war and overheard one soldier tell another "This is Trafalgar Square – you can have your boots cleaned here." It was so good to hear German being spoken, I almost blurted out: "You can speak German with me – I'm German, too." But I said nothing and watched until the group moved on. It was some time before I could make sense of what had happened.

Ted was preparing for his transfer to Gibraltar, and I looked forward to what awaited us there with anticipation. We would be separated for the first few months but I didn't mind that. After Ted's departure, I decided to look for work. Olive had grown very fond of David and was more than happy to look after him. I went to the job centre, where I was given the address of a hotel not far from our flat and applied for a post as a receptionist. Whilst I was waiting to be called in for the interview, I sat on a velvet sofa in the typically Victorian hotel and waited for the owner. Suddenly, a tall lady with a long cigarette holder was standing in front of me. She wore very long earrings and moved very seductively. "I am Madame Brown. I'm looking for someone to clean the rooms." "Oh," I said quietly, "I thought you were looking for a receptionist with language skills." She smiled. "No, I need someone like you for the rooms." I tried to convince her that

I was unsuitable, that I also had a baby, and so on, but she wouldn't take no for an answer and I eventually gave in and started life as a chambermaid. The hotel had twelve rooms. Initially, I was to work with Florence, who would train me; thereafter, each of us was to be responsible for cleaning six rooms. After a few days, Florence said she would be happy if we continued to clean the rooms together. Everyone, kitchen staff and waitresses, was amazed because, in all the years Florence had worked at the hotel, she had never expressed the wish to work with anyone else. David stayed with Olive and would jump for joy when I returned home.

Then came Ted's departure for Gibraltar. It would be six months before David and I could join him there. I knew nothing about the country and was excited. The living conditions for the families of British Army personnel were bound to be good. Olive told me that, sadly, she couldn't look after David any longer, as she herself had found a job. When I explained the situation to my boss, she suggested that I bring him along and everyone would keep an eye on him. She bought me a folding pram and so I stood at the bus stop every morning with the baby. Some years previously, Madame had adopted the child of a kitchen maid and David benefited not only from all the luxury baby clothes but also from all the delicacies prepared in the hotel kitchen. I was allowed to care for him during working hours. He would sit in his buggy in the hotel garden and when I leaned out of the window to speak to him, would gurgle enthusiastically. I was blissfully happy.

The personal touch with which the hotel was run meant that everyone felt a duty to do his or her best. One day, I told Madame that Ted had been transferred to Gibraltar and that I was hoping to be able to follow soon with the baby. She warned me not to rely on that under any circumstances. She had lived in India with her husband, and, whilst she was on holiday in England, he looked for new wife and so she felt unable to return to India. Standing there in front of me, with her long cigarette holder, her wavy hair and her long, colourful georgette dress, she seemed embittered. She had created a sort of family of her own, with employees who were dependent on her in different ways. I realised that I, too, was intended to be part of this family. The hotel world was a curious one, anyway. Among the guests were people of high standing, academics who had worked for the British Secret Service during the war – and still did. We sometimes got into conversation while I was cleaning their rooms. Florence taught me a lot about how to behave with the British. I lacked the necessary objectivity and discretion. On one occasion, Florence almost didn't forgive me for asking how much her husband earned, exclaiming "Even I wouldn't ask him that!"

By now, I often visited my mother-in-law on Sundays. It took me at least an hour and a half on foot. David would sit in his pram looking smart and I would talk to him. During the long walk, I would think about the future. One of my fantasies was that one day I would inherit enough money to prove to Ted's family that I came from a good home. I imagined us having a house and a car and, as I dreamt away, it didn't strike me how incompatible my bourgeois dreams were with my Socialist ideals. But I drew sufficient comfort and strength from them to carry on. The family's attitude towards me had changed somewhat for the better since David's birth. They commented charitably on how perfectl I looked after the baby. My mother-in-law proudly told friends and neighbours that Eddy would have had to search long and hard to find someone like me in England. Alice, who invited me for tea, gave me to understand that she would like to adopt David. She and Charles had no children. Whilst I was horrified by her suggestion, I was also pleased that she was more tolerant towards me and obviously recognised how well I was managing on my own. Nell, who also had a baby, had the support of the entire family. I think they admired me for being able to cope without Ted.

Then came another shock. Olive announced that they had decided to emigrate to Canada and were going to sell the house. Everything was going to happen rather quickly and she made me the following proposition: a friend, whose wife was in hospital with cancer, was looking for someone to keep his little house clean and share the costs with him. He lived round the corner, not far from our flat. It seemed the only solution for me, and I accepted. Olive and her family were very busy so, once again, I had to cope with the move on my own. The man in whose house I was to live was very inept and struggled to come to terms with his situation. The house was uncomfortable and very grubby. We agreed that I would start by giving it a thorough clean. I handed in my notice at the hotel and planned my move. I would sit David in the pram and fit the items to be moved around him. Curtains twitched as I moved all my worldly goods from one house to the other. Then it was the turn of the little table, two chairs and the cot. I solved this part of the exercise by carrying David and pushing the laden pram back and forth. Once the house was clean and I had unpacked, I accepted the situation, knowing it was temporary. The man was unpleasant and – thank goodness – not at home very much. My mother-in-law came to visit me with Mary and was appalled. She shook her head: "If Ted only knew!"

The ensuing six months until my departure to Gibraltar were uneventful. Sometimes Ernest and Pam picked me up and I spent a few hours with them. Pam was an attractive and remarkable woman. She was very fond of me and understood me. She thought highly of Ted and described him as brilliant. Pam had remarkable clairvoyant abilities. One day, she read my palm. In her opinion, I had turned my back on a potentially important political role in the kibbutz when I left. I also got to know her mother, who would later play a role in our life. Terry's parents very kindly agreed to look after David once more, to enable Terry to show me some more of London. As we walked past the Houses of Parliament, we were stopped by a police officer. A big, black limousine drew up, the door was opened by a man in uniform, and there in front of us stood Winston Churchill. He wore a bit of make-up, had noticeably red cheeks and a cigarillo in his mouth. He told his chauffeur to come and collect him at 6 and then disappeared into the Houses of Parliament. It was an unforgettable moment.

That evening, I went to an excellent performance of Shakespeare's *Twelfth Night* with the then famous actor, Robert Donat. Even though I was managing, I was hoping it wouldn't be long before I was able to leave the strange house. Ted's letters were very positive and kept me going. Then it was time to say goodbye to Olive. We had become good friends and wept because we believed – rightly as it transpired – that we would never see each other again. At last came the news that would release me: Ted had found a house for us on the Rock of Gibraltar.

Looking back, it is remarkable that I never held myself to account for encouraging Ted to stay in the Army. I had initially been a fervent pacifist and had hoped that, after this terrible war, the problems of the world could be solved differently. Yes, I had been involved in the war but justified it to myself as defence. What was unjustifiable, however, was to have encouraged Ted to stay in the Army. My only explanation was for the opportunity the Army offered us to escape the cramped conditions in England. There was also the sense that I was escaping from something, searching for a secure way of life for my family. And, even though I wasn't conscious of it at the time, I sensed intuitively that Ted preferred what the Army offered him – financial security and the freedom to organise his shows – to a civilian career in radio or on stage. Ted held the rank of Sergeant Major in the paymaster's office and was also troops entertainer, a dual role he felt very much at home in.

18. Gibraltar

At last, notification came that our ship to Gibraltar was to depart from Southampton on 21 November 1946. Ernest Beckett drove us there and brought his nine-year-old son along to show him the harbour. The *SS Andes* was a solid and comfortable ship and the food was good. I was prepared for the storms in the Bay of Biscay, thanks to my experience on the voyage from Egypt to England. David and I shared a cabin with an English family. With the exception of a few children, everyone, from the Captain to the ship's boy, was seasick. David and I were happy as Larry, and I proceeded to the dining room with a swarm of children trailing behind me, like the Pied Piper of Hamelin. There we were met by a solitary waiter, somewhat green around the gills, who served the meal.

Whilst on board, I was told that a certain Mrs. Elliot, whose husband was Ted's boss, wanted to make contact with me. We didn't meet, because she was terribly seasick, but we saw each other on disembarkation and arranged to meet later. Soon we reached Gibraltar; the Rock was visible from quite a distance. And then the moment came when David apparently recognised his father. As for me, I was happy that we could start our new life at last. We drove to our new home, a flat on the first floor of a big old two-storey apartment block, situated about halfway up the Rock. The sea view from the balcony was spectacular. I immediately threw myself into housework and busied myself with improving the flat. Much to my delight, we were offered a piano. Ted had already made friends with a young native family, who were very helpful. Gradually, I was able to enjoy the pleasant garrison life. There was sea, sun, beach and plentiful food. We were also able to afford a household help.

There were numerous shops in the small suburb, and the shopkeepers were very friendly and identified with England. England still had two years compulsory military service, which meant that, in addition to the professional soldiers, young men from all walks of life and all professions served in the Army, among them were artists, actors and musicians. This enhanced the cultural scene and excited Ted, because he was able to recruit plenty of young people for his shows. It wasn't long before he had gathered sufficient talent to stage his first show. I joined in, too, and had great fun because theatre was my great passion. There were some famous actors among the soldiers. One of them founded a theatre group and invited me to be the Assistant Director of a play called *The Crooked Hut*.

It wasn't long before we rented a wooden beach hut, which we reached by coach and horses. The owners, who lived nearby, were prepared to make tea and coffee for us. In the afternoons, we watched the fishermen landing their catches and enjoyed buying fresh fish. In the evenings, we drove home exhausted but happy.

It was some time before we crossed the border into Spain for the first time. The first town after the border crossing is La Linea. It was close of business, and some Spanish workers were waiting at the checkpoint. Children were milling about, then came closer to inspect us. "Lacki Striki?" they asked, offering us American cigarettes. We found a little café where there were only men seated at tables, watching the new arrivals. The waiter dashed over. As my Spanish was still rather basic, I raised two fingers and ordered "dos café" and – something else I had learnt – "con leche." The waiter nodded, "Si, si" and returned with coffee and milk. Ted, convinced I was a walking foreign language dictionary, asked me to ask the waiter what kind of milk it was, as he had heard that goat's milk, which he didn't like, was often served. "My Spanish doesn't run to that", I told him, but still tried to work out how to find out. Looking deep into the waiter's eyes, I pointed to the jug of milk and, with all eyes in the café on us, asked: "Mooh, mooh or baah, baah?" The waiter laughed: "Mooh, mooh!" and, amid gales of laughter, everyone repeated: "Mooh, mooh!" We became regulars there and each time we arrived, we were greeted with a chorus of "Mooh, mooh!"

Like all other British families, we employed a Spanish maid. When Josefa introduced herself, she deluged me with a tidal wave of Spanish, most of which I pretended to, but didn't really, understand. She was married with children and came from a very poor background. She was hard working and told me a lot about her life. She was not a supporter of General Franco and animatedly told me how she would hide the red flag under the bed when the police came. It was quite hard to distinguish between fact and fiction but at least I learnt a great deal of Spanish from her. After she had been with us for a while, I noticed that coffee and sugar was going missing. One day, when she thought she was alone, I watched Josefa lift her skirt with lightning speed and hide something underneath it. I confronted her and discovered that she wore a second skirt under her dress. The skirt had several little pockets sewn into it, which she obviously often filled whilst in our home. She tried to explain with words and gestures and, knowing how poor she was, I forgave her. But then we discovered that she was stealing our son's toys. She had developed an ingenious method that took us a while to work out. At first, things would disappear. When we noticed and asked her about them, she helped us search for them and found them in the most unlikely places. If we didn't miss them, they disappeared for good after a while. The final straw came when we discovered that she was using the same method to steal food. Ted liked to shave in the kitchen and one day, looking in the mirror, he noticed a half-pound packet of butter under the fridge, obviously an intermediate staging post. Sad though I was, we were left with no choice but to dismiss her. I didn't employ any more maids, but I found a gem of a seamstress who could sew anything: curtains, little suits for David, dresses for me. In the meantime, my Spanish had improved so I listened to her stories and learned a great deal about life in Spain. Because I spoke Spanish, I was sometimes asked by some of the soldiers' wives to act as interpreter, and I had some interesting problems to deal with. For example, Spanish maids confided in me that their English employers emptied their chamber pots down the kitchen sink. The English women, on the other hand, wanted me to ask their maids, as diplomatically as possible, to eat less garlic.

I wanted to acquire a sewing machine, which wasn't easy. Because I got on well with the greengrocer, who appreciated me both as a customer and as an interpreter, I decided to consult him on where I could buy one. He gave me an address on the Spanish side. I went across, bought a good quality sewing machine, and then the greengrocer smuggled it by donkey, concealed under his wares. Both my linguistic skills and David came in useful for my own smuggling. We heard that Ted's sister, Mary, was getting married. Rationing was still in force in England, so I crossed the border with David in his buggy and bought fabric for a wedding dress, handbag, shoes – in fact, everything necessary for the happy event. I stowed it all in the buggy, sat David on top of it, and crossed the border again without being checked. The customs officials were so taken with David, they didn't notice all the layers he was sitting on! I gradually acquired a reputation as an expert smuggler, but felt rather uncomfortable about the whole thing, so limited myself.

One day, Ted brought home a soldier who had started work in his office. Bob had recently been liberated, after four years as a Japanese prisoner-of-war, and Ted wanted to take him under his wing. A long friendship was to develop between Bob and the two of us. That first evening, Bob told us the difficulties he had in finding his feet again after the hardship and suffering at the hands of the Japanese. He came from a coal-mining family in Durham. After leaving school, he had worked in a grocer's shop. At 17, he ran away from home and, lying about his age, he volunteered for the army. After his release from the Japanese prison camp, he had returned to his home town to recuperate and, on the spur of the moment, married a 17-year-old, whose arrival in Gibraltar was imminent. The young woman regarded our friendship with distrust and it was because of her that, sadly, our friendship suffered. So we concentrated all our energies on the rehearsals for Ted's show.

Life in Gibraltar was particularly instructive for me because, for the first time, I met families from different parts of the British Isles. I found the snobbishness of officers' families difficult to deal with, and had to learn how best to get on with them. Mrs. Elliot, whom I had met on the ship, invited me over. David enjoyed playing with her little daughter. On one occasion, she answered the door and I heard her whispering: "I can't at the moment, one of my soldiers' wives is here." I was rather shocked, and was more cautious after that. I joined the literature and discussion club, which organised interesting cultural events. The speakers were sent by the government in London. One day, the topic was Palestine. Curious and expectant, I sat there ready to react forcefully to the usual distortions. The speaker had travelled through Palestine and spoke about his observations and experiences objectively, in my view. "Any questions?" One hand went up: "Can you tell me about the relationship between the kibbutz people and the Arabs?" The speaker shook his head: " I spent too little time in the kibbutzim I visited to express an opinion." I raised my hand: "I'm from Palestine and lived in a kibbutz for some time, so I can tell you a lot about it." The speaker smiled. "Please do join me up here and tell us." I was happy to oblige and it ended up being a very interesting evening. There were lots of questions, which gave me the opportunity to set the record straight by contrasting the distorted accounts in the media with my own experiences, altogether very therapeutic! There were two British captains in the audience, highly educated and very interested in Palestine and the Middle East. I invited them home on more than one occasion, and we had many an interesting discussion – including the future of Jews and Arabs in Palestine – while their ships were at anchor. They gave me Arthur Koestler's *Thieves in the Night*, one of the best books about the British Mandate in Palestine.

One day, I went to the hairdresser's, where I was welcomed by a pretty, plumpish and lovely young lady. Her name was Fortuna and it transpired that she belonged to a large, Jewish family, which had probably fled to Gibraltar before the Spanish Inquisition. She invited me to her home to celebrate the beginning of the Sabbath. It was an unforgettable evening. The family was *Sephardi* – Jews of Spanish-Portuguese – origin whose customs differ from those of the Ashkenazi Jews indigenous to Central and Eastern Europe. The entire family had gathered to meet me. They were particularly interested in me because I came from Palestine. First the introductions: mother and father, siblings and their fiancés/fiancées, grandparents from both sides of the family, and aunts and uncles. They all stood in a long line, and I was kissed twice by each one, not to mention all the handshakes and hugs. At the end of this ordeal, I collapsed into a chair and thought I could not possibly do this all over again. After a wonderful meal, I attempted to abbreviate the ritual, hoping to get away with one kiss per person. But that was out of the question. Fortuna's fiancé lived in Tangiers, and Ted and I were invited to visit her there. We sailed to Tangiers, where the couple met us and took us to a tapas bar – we assumed this was lunch. The food reminded us of what we used to eat in Palestine and we tucked in. Alcohol accompanied the meal and we were feeling replete when Fortuna suggested we should make our way to the hotel, where the meal had been booked. This came as something of a surprise and we asked if we could postpone lunch by a few hours. Fortunately, they both sympathised. In any event, Ted and I had planned to go to the bazaar to buy me a watch. We loved the oriental atmosphere and were in our element. In one of the displays I saw the watch I had always wanted. "Speak English?" I asked the no longer young salesman. "No." "Français?" "Un peu." Laughing, I said to Ted: "I wonder if he speaks German or even Hebrew?" "Yes, yes, I speak Ivrit! I am from Jerusalem." It was smiles all round, and I got the longed-for watch for a bargain price. We met up with Fortuna and her fiancé for the huge meal, most of which ended up inside the bellies of fish on the return trip!

Ted's show was a huge success. He had added a couple of new numbers to the programme, which were well received. He had also managed to recruit some new talent, including a very good local singer. The company had grown, which had implications for me, as Ted had started to invite everyone back to our home on a regular basis. He would sometimes come home at ten in the evening with twelve people in tow. "Maggy, can you rustle up something to eat?" Of course, it would turn out to be a jolly evening and, initially, I enjoyed it. After a while, though, it became very onerous – financially, too – and our hospitality was never reciprocated. Not only was Ted oblivious to all this, but it didn't occur to him that I desperately needed his help around the house. One of the people involved with the show – a young electrician responsible for the lighting – also supervised the cinema for the soldiers and their families. He always got the latest films from England and it was decided that the screenings should be in our home. A sheet was draped across the wall and 20 to 30 people would turn up to watch. In the interval, I would serve sandwiches, cake and coffee. At the end of one such evening, arrangements for the next film evening were being discussed and I realised I'd had enough. "If you want to come here again, then, at the very least, you should contribute to the food. It's been annoying me for some time that none of you ever reciprocates our hospitality. I feel exploited. Not for nothing are we known as the 'running buffet'." Then I looked at one particular couple: "Why have you never invited us?" There was a deathly hush; seldom had I seen Ted so lost for words. This direct confrontation – not something the English were accustomed to – had the desired effect. The next time, they all arrived with sandwiches, coffee and even sugar. Unfortunately, it didn't last long. This was one of the problems in our marriage: I was repeatedly expected to house, feed and entertain people I had no connection with, who never reciprocated, and most of whom I never saw again. Ted never helped with housework, but was extremely demanding. I ended up doing everything and, regrettably, didn't teach my son to help with the housework. Ted became ill while we were still living in Gibraltar. He had choleric attacks, which were initially attributed to high blood pressure. Only later did the doctors diagnose heart disease, the cause of his early death.

As our time in Gibraltar came to an end, we often discussed

moving back to England. Where would we live? Ted suggested that we start by moving in with his mother. "Oh yes," I said, "that might work for about two weeks, and then we'll have the jealousy issues again. Your sisters will behave as they always do – why should it be any different this time? You'll be in the garrison, away from it all. When you come home, you'll find me out on the street with the child. Then you'll phone Pam and Ernie and ask them to put me up and that will be the end of a beautiful friendship." And, sadly, that's exactly what happened.

Meanwhile, ships started mooring in Gibraltar harbour, carrying hundreds of former concentration camp prisoners; survivors with terrible physical and emotional scars. Many of us collected some clothes together and took them to the harbour. The migrants were on their way to the Holy Land, full of hope. I had heard from my cousin, Walter. His wife and children had remained in Palestine while he first visited his home town, Hamburg, and then came to London, hoping to find work. I still had no links with Germany. I only knew that my parents and relatives had all died in concentration camps, but one heard extraordinary stories about people who had managed to escape and suddenly resurface. These reports stirred up all sorts of emotions in me, and I found myself dreaming that it would happen to me, too. Next door to us lived a family with a small child. One morning, the mother appeared on the communal balcony with a playpen. "I hope my baby won't feel as if he's in Bergen-Belsen, locked up." I was deeply affected by this glib remark.

19. Nottingham

We slowly started preparing for our move back to England. We bought a few items still rationed there, including soap, sugar and silk stockings. Ted would come back every day with stories about people paying large amounts of duty on entering the UK. I had to repack our boxes several times and try different ways of hiding things. Another sea voyage, another journey into an uncertain future. We arrived in Southampton. Ted was nervous because the customs officials were undertaking thorough checks on each passenger. I was holding David, who was now almost four. He was fidgeting and chose just the right moment to start crying. "Please go through with the child – or have you something to declare?" I shook my head with conviction and we sailed through. Once in England, everything happened just as I had predicted. We lived with mother-in-law, but not for long. Even though she liked to take her handsome grandson shopping, to show him off, the old jealousy reared its ugly head again and I was soon driven out.

In the meantime, my cousin Walter had arrived in London and wanted to see me. I decided that we should meet at Piccadilly Circus. David was left with his grandmother. There I stood, in Piccadilly Circus, wondering why middle-aged men wearing floppy hats were circling round me, whilst 'ladies' gave me hostile looks. Thank goodness Walter soon arrived. We hugged, happy to see each other, and when I told him about my observations, he laughed out loud. It seemed that everyone, apart from me, knew what kind of a place this was. We were delighted to be reunited once again and that Lilly would soon be joining us. When I arrived back home, Ted's youngest sister snapped: "How can you leave a woman in her sixties alone with a baby!" I knew the time had come, and ,once again, I was homeless. Ted was home for the weekend and, when he realised how things stood, he looked at me and then called Pam and Ernie to ask if I could stay with them for a while. Of course, they said yes. Then it transpired that Pam's mother had a spare bedroom to let in her small ground-floor flat. David had to sleep in the tiny, shared living room. It was very cramped and I felt somewhat uncomfortable. I also had the feeling that Pam's mother wanted to use me for her own ends. When that failed, she started to scheme against me and destroyed my friendship with Pam. I did try again and again to get on with her, so we just about managed.

❧

In 1948, Ted was transferred to Nottingham. I only saw him infrequently but sensed that he was unhappy and unable to cope with life. Maybe he still couldn't accept that he had family responsibilities. He wrote to me from Nottingham, saying that he wanted a divorce. I clung to the hope that he might change his mind. I felt lonely and was glad to have David. In the meantime, Lilly and five-year-old Ariel had managed to get to the UK. War had broken out in Palestine and she, too, had been threatened by Arabs. Ariel was happy to see me again, perhaps because he was able to speak to me in Hebrew. And so we all met again in England. Walter was fortunate enough to have found a job as a translator with the BBC.

Ted came home unannounced and we reconciled. The Army had found us temporary lodgings with full board with a family in Nottingham. Once again, I had no idea what was in store. Nottingham in those days was an industrial town and the family we would be lodging with was working class. The husband had already retired. He had worked in a cigarette factory but became ill and had a permanent tremor. His wife was an alcoholic and the pub was her second home. Even when relatives came to visit, it was straight off to the pub. On one occasion, she told us that she and her husband were going to 'convalesce' for a week in notorious Blackpool, which was not known for its refinement or sophistication. I hardly recognised them when they returned. They had obviously had a seven-day rehabilitation in a pub.

Our next home was a spacious council house. We had been allocated two rooms – one bedroom for Ted and me and a small room for David. Despite the full board arrangement, we didn't see much food. The whole thing was a nightmare. Our landlords were narrow-minded: Ted was 'one of us' whilst I was from a different planet. They took the view that I belonged to a different social class, which was ill disposed towards them, and they treated me accordingly. Of course, they were careful not to alienate us because, had we complained, they would have had to wave goodbye to their income. When I saw that they had grown fond of David, I decided to find work to earn some extra money. Their daughter-in-law told me that there was a job in the factory where she worked, in the ice-lollies and ice cream packaging department. Yes, I thought, I'll give that a try! And so I stumbled into a world I knew absolutely nothing about. My much younger colleagues showed me how to wrap the precious goods and, after a while, they started to quiz me: Where are you from? Are you married? Do you have children? I thought nothing of it and told them I was from Palestine. Silence. But the inquisition continued over the next few days and I felt compelled to answer their questions. "Where did you live in Palestine? And what did you do there?" "I lived with my uncle, a doctor, and helped in his surgery" I replied. They looked at each other as though they had caught me out lying. Soon I had given them enough material to force me out.

I managed to get an office job at Boots the Chemist. I was pregnant again, so the work suited me. And, having learnt my lesson, I kept quiet. I was subjected to the same kind of jokes as in the ice cream factory but was able to endure them because I knew that, at heart, the women liked me. One day, I started feeling sick at work and realised I was in danger of losing the baby. I went to see the office manager who called a doctor and an ambulance and informed my landlords. The doctor sent me to hospital, where I was instructed to have complete bedrest for a week. I was treated very well both medically and personally and returned home fully recovered.

In November, we moved to Chillwell, an estate for army personnel and their families. The house had a small living room with an open fireplace, a very small kitchen, a bathroom and two bedrooms. It was pouring with rain on the day we moved. The flatbed lorry, normally used to transport coal, was covered with a layer of black dust and was totally unsuitable for use as a removal vehicle. Our belongings became ingrained with coal dust – it took me weeks to get them clean. And so I sat in a primitive house with David, no telephone, no friends. I knitted and cleaned, and looked after David, who was a great help. At the time, I didn't recognise my repetitive behavioural pattern – a legacy of my childhood where I was always trying to please my parents. I wanted to be the well-behaved, dutiful child that does everything correctly and expects to be rewarded. Of course, I also found it gratifying because I managed to make Ted feel a little bit guilty.

20. Stephen

When I went to pregnancy check-ups and heard the women next to me sing their husband's praises, I lied and told everyone about all the things my husband did for me. I felt well and, as the due date approached, I started to think about how I would call the ambulance when the time came. I saw very little of Ted and hoped I could avail myself of the neighbours. But it never came to that. One day, around lunchtime, the butcher was at the door taking my weekend order. No sooner had we finished when my (second) son announced his arrival. Laughing, I shouted to the butcher that I would be away for a little while. He understood. I was just about to go over to the neighbours when Ted arrived unexpectedly and immediately called the ambulance. The hospital was small and intended for more complex cases. Accordingly, one got more individual attention, and my experience of this birth was good. Stephen weighed almost ten pounds. The nurses wrote the name of a well-known heavyweight boxer, Bruce Woodcock, on the card above his bed. Unfortunately, there were complications, as he didn't want to drink. In those days, it wasn't considered important for babies to be fed breast milk, but I insisted. Although I was concerned, I also had the feeling that the nurses wanted to get rid of me and so I was discharged with a note informing my doctor to undertake an immediate examination of the baby. I was standing in the entrance hall with Stephen in my arms when Ted and David came to collect me. David came towards me, and I laid the baby in his outstretched arms – it was a beautiful moment, during which the older brother must have somehow been aware that this baby belonged to him, too, and he felt pride and responsibility. Their relationship was born in that moment, and it has endured.

Back home, it was immediately obvious that the heating was insufficient for a baby. I went to the accommodation office and was promised something better. We moved in February. Then it transpired that little Stephen was suffering from gastro-enteritis, which was widespread in those days. There followed six difficult months during which, every other day, an ambulance took Stephen and me to a hospital two hours' drive away for treatment. During this time, he gained almost no weight and, because he was so weak, he developed bronchitis and then pneumonia. We were frightened that Stephen wouldn't survive and then, to cap it all, David's tonsils had to be removed. Slowly, Stephen's condition improved. One day, as I was telling our young Scottish doctor about both boys' health, he interrupted me suddenly: "And what about you?" My exhaustion had not gone unnoticed. "You really should get away for a few days." It had never occurred to me. Having spoken to Ted, we decided that I should spend a weekend with my relatives in London. Naturally, I prepared everything very carefully, down to ironed nappies and notes about feeding times and portion sizes, and left reluctantly, wondering how Ted would manage. It had been a long time since I had been to the theatre and conversed with interesting people. And I was able to catch up on some sleep. On my return, Ted, exhausted and weary, informed me that from now on he would help in the house. "How do you manage?" he asked. To my amusement, he found nappy changing particularly difficult.

It was 1950 and rationing was still in force. The kitchen gadgets that make a housewife's life easier hardly existed. I had to boil the washing in a tub, which I had to heave onto the rusty gas stove. We didn't possess a vacuum cleaner. The living room had an open fire that only warmed the person sitting in front of it, so we stood a small electric heater at the back of the room. The room was reasonably warm by the time we went to bed and the following morning, the same procedure started all over again. It was impossible to heat the bedrooms. I had made friends with the neighbours. As always with the army, I was surrounded by people from a variety of backgrounds, who interested me as much as I interested them. On our right was a family from Nottingham. The husband had been in the army a long time and his wife had completely adapted to army life. They lived fairly separate lives. "As long as she's home before midnight, I'm not worried" he said. She came out with some very funny expressions. During a conversation about the relationship between men and women, she suddenly pronounced: "A rising cock has no conscience." One day, she lent me her electric washtub, saying my need was probably greater than hers. The neighbours on our left were a family from Wales. The husband looked after the kitchen and grocery shopping. This meant that all sorts of things found their way into the house. His wife told me, one day, that they had received another meat parcel from her uncle in Cardiff. "He sends it in a box filled with ice, so it stays fresh," she said. "How kind of him," I replied, giving the impression that I believed every word.

David was now at school and had made friends with Roger. Roger's mother belonged to what was referred to as the 'backbone of English society' or 'salt of the earth'. It was only much later that I realised that such people were, generally speaking, not only anti-semitic but prejudiced against anyone and anything of non-British origin. We had settled in and the children were healthy. Daily life had become easier. There was a lot of laughter because, despite his occasional choleric outbursts, Ted was a humorous and witty man. Nottingham offered 'cultural events' that were completely new to me and were connected with the well-known British passion for betting. Very popular, especially among the working class, was greyhound racing. Ted often went to the races and won small amounts. One evening, he came home with a brown paper bag. "I spent the winnings on some expensive pears," he said. The bag lay there until the following morning; when I went to unpack 'the pears' I discovered that the bag was full of bank notes. On another occasion, his response to my question about how he had fared (expressed in that inimitable Jewish way "Nu?"), he pointed to the apricot design round the edge of the carpet, where he had placed a half-crown on each of the apricots. "The money's yours", he said, "but the price is that I watch you go on all fours to collect it."

Sundays in Chillwell were unbearable. In the morning, the men – Ted included – usually went to the pub for a pint and a game of darts or billiards, while the wives stayed at home to cook Sunday lunch. After lunch, one read the papers and snoozed. Then came the promenade through the manicured parks, with the children in tow, dressed in their Sunday best. "Careful, don't get dirty!" wafted permanently in the ether. The children's playgrounds were unimaginatively equipped. Where were the coffee houses with the exquisite cakes, the Siebengebirge hills where one could scramble or go donkey riding? Where was the lido or the snow with its sledge runs? It was deadly boring here. One day, Ted suggested that I take the children to the seaside. He bought tickets to the well-known seaside resort of Skegness. We packed the usual beach equipment and set off early. Stephen suffered from travel sickness, the neighbouring passengers grumbled and Stephen cried. The journey was long and unpleasant and, when we arrived at the beach, we couldn't see the sea because the tide was out. Nevertheless, the children had fun playing in the sand. After a snack at a fish-and-chip shop, we took the bus back home, utterly exhausted. I struggled up the hill to Chillwell, Stephen on my arm, David in the pram and the beach things piled on top of him.

I joined an army theatre group, whose members were both amateurs and professional actors serving their two-year compulsory military service. David Webb, later a well-known television actor, was a member. The group entered a competition organised by the army. Our play was set in Victorian England. I played the role of a strange, mad old woman who believed she was Queen Victoria; I was in my element. We made it to the finals, which took place over the course of three days in a large cinema in York. Martin Browne, a well known director, was the adjudicator. After the performances, we were all on tenterhooks waiting for Martin Browne's decision. After talking in general terms, he said: "The best performance was that of Margot Barnard, especially because of her timing and diction." Maybe I fainted, but I didn't hear the rest of what he said. We were called onto the stage where Lady Hamilton presented each of us five actors with a medal. I was introduced to Martin Browne and heard myself thinking: "You have no idea how happy you've made me, to be told I have good English diction – me, a bloody foreigner!" When I arrived home at four in the morning, I woke Ted and showed him my medal. He was very proud of me and told everyone about it. Many years later, whenever we had visitors, my children would jump up and down until they were allowed to tell the story of how their mother had won a medal.

Ted's youngest sister Mary had written to say she would be spending Easter with mother in Catford, and that it would be lovely if we came, too. I hoped this was a sign that our relationship would improve. Ted's mother was pleased to see us. We went to the station together to meet Mary and her husband Jack, but nothing had changed. She either ignored me or gave me hostile looks. Sister Nell and her children arrived a little later. Sister Alice, who lived next door, invited us over for dinner. As soon as we entered the house, she started issuing orders: "Sit here, mind Stephen doesn't tear my curtains! David! Sit further back on the sofa otherwise it'll wear out too much at the front!" Ted tried to make conversation and told them about the theatre competition. Alice turned scarlet and there issued forth what can only be described as a tirade: "How can a mother neglect household and children to go on the stage? Surely she had more important things to do than acting." Ted was shocked and gave up. The next day, the whole thing started all over again: "Is it true you didn't have the children baptised?" I don't remember my response. I had had enough and was glad when we left.

Out of the blue, Ted was unexpectedly notified that he was to be transferred to Greece on war office special deployment. We were offered a house by the sea and household staff. But the political situation changed suddenly and the mission came to nothing. Then came a visit from a high-ranking officer, who had a lengthy discussion with Ted. By the time he left, we knew that the next move would take us to Nigeria. As before, Ted was to fly out on his own and only when he had found accommodation for us would we follow. Once again, the familiar situation: transfer to an unfamiliar country, separation for a minimum of six months, a move (with all that entailed) and the eager anticipation of being reunited and of new experiences. I was full of ideas about how I would organise with my life in the meantime. I had met a woman in Chillwell, whose husband was also serving in Nigeria. She was very maternal and agreed to look after Stephen should I find work. David was at school until 4 in the afternoon and so

I answered an advertisement: Nottingham University was looking for a temporary library assistant with a knowledge of foreign languages. At the interview, it transpired that the job, which I was to share with a young Lithuanian woman, actually entailed cleaning the rooms of female students. I got to know some of the students, one of whom was a ravishingly beautiful Nigerian woman who told me a fair amount about what I could expect when I moved to Lagos. She came from a distinguished family and was proud and even a little arrogant. She regarded me as an educated, white woman but remained reserved towards me. I later got to know the black upper class in Lagos; they chose not to socialise with the British.

My day started at six in the morning. After washing nappies, putting David on the school bus and taking Stephen to the babysitter, I made the long trek on foot and by bus to the university in Nottingham. After work, I collected Stephen, David came home from school and I fell into bed exhausted. One Sunday afternoon after lunch, I was sitting in front of the fire. David was playing with his toys and Stephen was asleep in his cot. I must have fallen asleep because I awoke screaming, with a severe pain in my foot. The red hot poker had fallen on my foot. David ran to a neighbour who called a doctor. When the doctor changed the dressing the next day, he looked thoughtful and suggested that I was overdoing things. If I didn't stop working immediately, he wouldn't be in a position to approve the trip to Nigeria.

Ted's letters sounded very positive. He wrote that, on his way to Lagos, he was thrilled to have met our old friend Bob from Gibraltar, who had also been transferred to Nigeria. He was still searching for a house for us. He too felt I shouldn't overdo the work but, at the same time, said that he needed money to buy furniture for our new home. So I carried on working until the day came when Ted had found a house. As I started preparations for the move, there were shipping crates everywhere. By now I knew that the good crockery was best protected from damage by packing it between nappies and clothes. Moving seemed to have become a way of life. I was still lugging my old books from Germany from place to place. But the most unpleasant part of the whole procedure – the handover of the house and contents to the army administration – was still to come. Every item was listed using sometimes incomprehensible military terminology. Everything had to be laid out and checked against an inventory. Experience had taught me that there were always discrepancies. By noon on the day of departure, I had cleaned the house, lined up all the items with military precision, packed the suitcases and prepared a bag with nappies, milk and food. Three funereal-looking men in hats arrived and started to check the inventory. I was asked to explain the alleged soiling of one of the mattresses. I protested that we had never used them.

I had arranged for a taxi to take us to the station. The neighbours stood outside their houses and waved, some with tears in their eyes. We travelled to Catford to spend one night with Ted's mother, who accompanied us to Gower Street the following day, from where the army bus took us to the airport. "This is my daughter-in-law", she proudly told the taxi driver, "she's flying to Africa all on her own with the children." Flights like this were still quite unusual at the time – it was, after all, only 1951. It was also my first long-haul flight – three days and two nights on various propeller-driven planes with neither air conditioning nor food. I didn't mind, but the children and other passengers suffered from the turbulence. The first intermediate landing was Bordeaux, and Stephen needed a great deal of persuasion before he would board the plane for the next leg of the journey. He screamed from take-off until we landed in Gibraltar; a doctor travelling on the plane took pity on me and gave Stephen a tranquilliser. There was an overnight stopover in Gibraltar and all the stewardesses threw themselves into the familiar nightlife with unfortunate consequences for their ability to carry out their duties. From Gibraltar, the flight continued over the Algerian desert. Some of the stewardesses were as white as a sheet and incapable of work. It was so hot, pregnant women were on the point of fainting. It transpired that the supply of water had run out because the water containers had not been re-filled in Gibraltar, thanks to the activities of the previous night. The pilot decided to land on an airstrip in the desert. Palm trees were visible from afar, it looked like an oasis. We took water on board and continued our flight. The next stopover was in Kano, in northern Nigeria, where we spent the night in a bungalow. I felt uncomfortably hot and not at all well. The doctor who had been on the plane established that I had a high temperature, which he attributed to over-exertion; he gave me sleeping pills to enable me to get some rest. Things had righted themselves by the morning and Stephen had calmed down. The flight from Kano to Lagos was without incident and, as we disembarked, we saw Ted and Bob standing by the gangway. The children hurled themselves at their father.

21. Lagos

Africa positively overwhelmed us as we travelled to our new home. Even the climate was unusually humid. Although the sun was hiding behind a layer of grey cloud, there was a harshness about the light. Our house, which Ted had rented from a Nigerian Muslim, was spacious and occupied two floors. We shared it with a British officer and his wife. The house was on an unmetalled road, at the end of which was a nightclub. On the opposite side were clay huts where indigenous families lived. The properties on our side of the road were built of stone and were probably rented out to foreigners by wealthy Nigerians – in this case, Syrians, Lebanese, Jordanians and Egyptians.

Ted had bought lounge and dining room furniture but there were no wardrobes, so we hung our clothes on stands. The kitchen and bedrooms were minimally furnished. There was a walled garden that bordered on forest, and a veranda from where we were able to observe the comings and goings on the street. The simple furnishings belied the fairly luxurious life we led, as we had two black servants, Herbert and Paul. Although Paul was the more intelligent of the two, the hierarchy decreed that Herbert – being the older – was the superior in rank. Ted was well paid by the war office and was driven to his office.

In the mornings, we could hear the calls of the women inviting men on their way to work to buy their fried bananas with a kind of rice pudding. It sounded like "reisovalombeeo!" We often heard women arguing in front of their houses some distance away. We called it the 'boolovoolo-language' because that's what it sounded like. Sometimes groups of young women walked past our house, singing and swaying. They all wore similar clothes and carried their babies on their backs. Most of all, we enjoyed watching the children on their way to school, each balancing small inkwells on their heads. Old, rickety buses regularly drove past, full to bursting with women on their way to market. Larger department stores sold a wide range of products, some from Britain and the rest produced in Nigeria, or were imported from neighbouring countries. The market was geared to the needs of foreign residents but also to middle and upper class Nigerians. There was a large variety of groceries – lots of fruit and vegetables but not much meat. Ingredients used in European cooking were not always available, so we had to adapt the menus. For instance, we found the white bread inedible, so I learnt how to bake my own from a Yorkshirewoman. It needed a special type of flour, which I hadn't come across in Britain. Many foreigners, certainly all the British officers, had African cooks.

❧

One of the unpleasant features of our house was the toilet – a hole-in-the-ground latrine. Two men would come every evening at six to empty it. One day – we were awaiting the arrival of an officer's family – the latrine men were on strike. Ted, who was very fussy about such things, had suddenly disappeared. I found him in the dressing room with a horrified look on his face. As we were expecting visitors, he had decided to empty the containers over the garden wall but he had spilled some of the contents on himself. Our houseboys did not use the outdoor toilet, but availed themselves of the forest. They called it "go for bush". Paul was often nowhere to be found; when he reappeared, and I asked him where he had been, he would only say "go for bush". I asked him to give me advance warning when he went "for bush" in future. He took me at my word one afternoon, whilst I had visitors for coffee, suddenly appearing carrying a stack of newspapers and shouting: "Madam, I go for bush!"

Looking back, it is remarkable how quickly we adapted to the new lifestyle. An anti-malarial tablet, Paludrin, was an integral breakfast ingredient. Naturally, we sweated a lot and tired easily. I tried to help with the housework but was soon exhausted. Even my political convictions had to take a back seat. Nigeria was a British colony, where black and white knew their immutable social place. There was an almost unbridgeable chasm between us and the indigenous population, and no organisation existed to challenge this type of apartheid. Added to this was the tension between the Ibo and Yoruba tribes, which eventually led to armed conflict. Being identified with the colonial power, we were advised not to get involved in politics.

For the first eighteen months, we lived in a villa belonging to a Muslim Haussa, who came to collect the rent every month. He was a rich man about whom we knew very little, except that he expressed his wealth through the number of houses and wives he had. One evening, we heard his voice from far away: "Master, Master, come here, I want to show you my new wife!" With great ceremony, Ted, the children and I went to the front of the house. Ted handed him the cheque and our landlord introduced his sixth wife. After we acknowledged her beauty, Ted asked him "And what do you do on Sundays?" Our landlord burst into uncontrollable laughter and kept repeating: "What do you do on Sundays?" We thought he had a good sense of humour.

Next door to us, a Syrian family lived in a big house with a roof terrace. They introduced themselves and invited us over. The wife had married at 14 and was almost illiterate. The husband was often away on business, or busy with one of his countless girlfriends. The children attended expensive private schools in Switzerland. They had numerous black servants, who were never referred to by name, only as 'boy'. We spent a whole evening there just eating – we were served innumerable courses, one more delicious than the next. Conversation consisted of the few Arab words I knew and used in differing combinations. Poor Ted was at pains to converse in pidgin English. It was agonising, and we hoped this would be the first and last time. But these neighbours did little by way of entertainment, and their life seemed to consist of boasting to other foreign families that they were friendly with English people. We often left the house in darkness, to give the impression that we were out. We didn't respond to the neighbour's desperate calls of: "Missi Barnard, chop, chop, pass time!"

When Ted had once again directed a very successful show, our neighbours insisted that it be performed on their roof terrace. Ted invented all sorts of excuses and, as a last resort, told them that the show couldn't take place without a piano. "Oh! That's no problem, we'll have one brought up," they said. Believe it or not, the next day

– to the accompaniment of a great deal of noise – we watched, open-mouthed, as a piano was winched onto the roof terrace. The piano was tuned and, having run out of excuses, we resigned ourselves to the idea. In honour of the event, many chickens lost their lives and all sorts of meat, exotic fruit, Arabian tapas and other delicacies were imported. Cooks were employed, but the lady of the house did her share of cooking, mixing and pureeing. She was in her element. We were allowed to taste beforehand, and everything seemed to be in order. The evening came, our troupe gathered, and the high society of Lagos arrived in their convertibles. The roof terrace had been converted into a fairytale pavilion, magnificently lit, with a specially built stage. It was a very successful evening. Our Syrian neighbours were thrilled to have achieved what none of their rivals had ever managed. The following day, we heard a loud bang. Alarmed, we ran outside and there, surrounded by labourers laughing hysterically, lay the piano, shattered into a thousand pieces, the little hammers still bouncing noisily on the strings. Unperturbed, our Syrian neighbour maintained that it didn't matter, he would pay for it and, in any event, it had been worth it.

There were other reasons to leave the house in darkness – to prevent social invasions. We had got to know a middle-aged Cairo Arab, who treated us to an exquisite dinner in an elegant hotel. This time, the conversation centered on food. I don't recall how many courses there were, but each course was punctuated by a reviving cigarette. We found the whole thing rather dull. I repeatedly dragged out my limited Arabic and our host understood a little French and English. We philosophised at length about humus, and he promised to obtain a supply of this oriental hors d'oeuvre for us. One evening, he appeared with a little package. Of course, I assumed it was the promised humus and asked Paul to put it in the fridge. Some days later, I remembered the gift, unwrapped it, and found to my astonishment that the package contained not humus but some beautiful blue taffeta, the significance of which I was soon to discover. One day, I was home on my own when there was a knock at the door. There stood our Arab friend with his car. From the look he gave me, there was no mistaking his intentions. "Come for a ride in the car with me; we'll go down to the beach and get some fresh air." I was not a little scared and slammed the door shut. For some time after, we kept the house in darkness in the evenings.

We saw our first Elvis Presley film in the romantic setting of the open-air cinema. We sat down in front of a row of young men, who, we assumed, were Greek sailors. Before we had even settled in our seats, I heard – to my great surprise – Hebrew being spoken behind me. I turned round spontaneously: "Gam ani bat Yisroel!" – I too am a daughter of Israel. That's how poetically one expresses oneself in Hebrew. We were amazed to have met in Africa, so far from everything we called home. After all, the State of Israel had only been in existence since 1948, so the feelings for this homeland were particularly strong. One never heard Hebrew spoken, let alone in Africa. We learnt that the ship that brought these Israeli sailors to Lagos was there to collect timber. We invited them home and they reciprocated by showing us round the ship. Through them, we met two Persian Jews, the younger of whom had left Persia and gone to Palestine after his father died in the 1920s. Later, he and his friend moved to Lagos, where they appeared to have a successful business trading in fabrics. Even though they were Jews, I had very little in common with them. Added to which, I disliked their reactionary attitude towards women. But once I had made my views clear, they treated me with respect. They might have even learnt a thing or two from me. They invited us to their home, where we tucked into a delicious (kosher) feast. There were twelve courses to get through, most of which involved some part of the chicken, whether chopped, stuffed, marinaded or fried. Salads and accompaniments were served with each course, as were the best wines. There were even special delicacies for the children. When it came to reciprocating, I agonised over how to cater for everyone, not least because of the requirement that the food had to be kosher. I finally managed to produce four kosher courses. The family enjoyed my cooking, but I suspect that it was a little too primitive for our guests.

Ted must have sensed my disappointment because he brought out his guitar. He sang *Old MacDonald Had a Farm* and each of us imitated one of the farm animals. When it was the turn of the pig, the squealing could barely be heard for laughter. The evening was great fun and our guests maintained that they had never enjoyed themselves so much.

We observed that many of our compatriots behaved completely differently in Nigeria than at home. Apparently, life in Africa had a strange influence on their behaviour. Many found it hard to cope with the climate and living conditions and were sent home. We met the same people again and again, whether on the beach, at bingo, or at dances. People got to know each other more intimately and there was an erotic feel to the atmosphere. Thus we discovered why the husband of Stephen's nanny was unable to find accommodation for his family; like many other married men, he had a girlfriend. Some men behaved totally irrationally. They disappeared into the forest with black girls and were never seen again.

We, however, enjoyed our family life. And, when his wife decided to return to England with their children because she was unhappy, our friendship with Bob became closer. The children loved Bob, and we went on many outings together.

One day, one of our acquaintances, a British civil engineer, proposed an outing into the forest. Not being aware of any danger, we saw no cause for concern. In the middle of the forest, we suddenly heard music and saw some of the native population sitting at tables. Standing on a platform, singing and stamping their feet, were six black men, painted and adorned with feathers, wearing grass skirts and armed with spears. Although my instinct told me we should leave, we sat down and ordered some beer. The singing and stamping was now accompanied by inarticulate sounds and cries, and we saw that we were being stared at with rolling eyes. We jumped up and raced to the car, pursued by the dancers, and drove off without stopping to look round. We later learned that the troupe had probably been under the influence of drugs. The next escapade was my idea. Black women had their own means of transport, and I saw no reason why

I, too, shouldn't use the bus they called *mummi wagon*. This was also my way of showing my disapproval of apartheid. The bus arrived and I climbed in, much to the astonishment of others waiting at the bus stop. The women stared at me, pushed their turbans further into their faces, and talked in their guttural language, presumably about me. I felt utterly ridiculous and soon got off again. Shortly after, I discovered a colony of lice on a certain part of my body. Ted took one look at me and started laughing. Then he got out his razor and relieved me of this evil.

There were some amusing episodes involving our black servants. One day, I asked Paul to go and buy some steak. If he couldn't get steak, he should buy sausages instead. I had written on his shopping list 'steaks or sausages instead.' He returned empty-handed. When I asked him whether there had been nothing at all, he replied: "Yes, they had sausages – but not sausages-instead!" Our night guard was a Muslim, who prayed three times a day and took Muslim fast days and religious holidays off. Noting this, Paul approached me one day, having had time off over Christmas and Easter, and said he had now converted to Islam and needed time to fast and pray. He was surprised when I told him he could only belong to one religion, at least as far as the holidays were concerned. One of the boys who worked for us for a while was called Henson. He had attended a missionary school and we liked him very much. One day, I asked him to scrape, rather than peel, the new potatoes. When I examined the now shrunken potatoes, he said: "I'm sorry but the potatoes didn't agree to being scraped."

We spent most weekends at the beach. One could take a little boat over to an island, which had huts offering overnight accommodation for the British. We all, especially the children, enjoyed the convivial atmosphere, but we also experienced rather less pleasant things. For example, the beaches teemed with crabs of all sizes. They didn't do any harm, but there were some young men who evidently felt the need to release their aggression and went 'crab beating' with sticks.

❧

After eighteen months in Lagos, we prepared for a three-month home visit. Lilly and Walter had booked rooms for us in a guesthouse right next to their home in London. We were looking forward to being in England, meeting old friends and going to the theatre. We were also curious to see how things had changed. We arrived in England in February, to the same cold and inadequate heating as before, and had to buy warm clothing. My old coat needed a new belt, so I went to Selfridges and explained to the shop assistant what I needed. She looked me up and down and then said snootily: "Madam, we only have leather belts here, the plastic belts are over there." So not much had changed!

We had stayed in touch with the friends in Chillwell, whose son Roger was a friend of David's. Roger's father had accepted a job in the newly-built nuclear power station in Aldermaston. When they invited us to their new home, they implied that they had planned a surprise for us. We were intrigued. This reunion was particularly important for David and Roger. The surprise was to be delivered that Saturday afternoon. Then came a phone call to say that the delivery had to be postponed. Roger's mother reacted hysterically. The surprise in question was a television set, the recent acquisition of which she had arranged for our benefit, because we came, so to speak, from the back of beyond and would have probably never come across such a thing. She went on to tell us that all the foreigners here were lowering the standards. When she heard that my cousin Walter worked for the BBC, as a translator, she said: "Yes, that only confirms it: foreigners take the best jobs from us British." We couldn't get away from this inhospitable home fast enough.

Both boys attended a Catholic convent school in Lagos, which had a good reputation and was better than the army school. They learnt well and were happy there. We were pleased that they had been given good school reports to take to the London school they would attend for three months. They were allowed to talk about Africa at length. Ted was also asked to come to the school and answer the children's many questions. In London, we went to concerts, operas and the theatre. Ted had some good luck on the horses, which boosted our spending power. But, one day, Ted disclosed that even the slightest exertion caused him to have palpitations. He was immediately examined at the army hospital and we also consulted a heart specialist, who explained to Ted that he had a hole in the heart that was not life-threatening. This was the start of Ted's long-term illness, which would lead to him having Britain's first open-heart surgery. Shortly after, our namesake, Dr. Barnard, performed the first successful heart transplant in South Africa. I wrote to Uncle Sim, who gave me good dietary advice for Ted. Three holiday months turned into four, as there were no flights to Africa.

A new home awaited us on our return to Lagos, a well-equipped, spacious, modern bungalow in an British neighbourhood. There was even a swimming pool with a diving board on the estate. Ted had returned from England full of new ideas and threw himself enthusiastically into preparations for the new show. He had found new talent, and, when most people in Africa were having their afternoon nap, we were rehearsing tirelessly. When we learned that other camps also wanted to see the show, the whole troupe travelled to Abeokuta. The children came, too. We were given a warm welcome, a stage had already been constructed, and everything was well organised. The premiere was an out-and-out success. The shows always took place outdoors, but we were unaware of how much depended on the direction of the wind. There was a large audience for the second performance, including a number of Nigerians. The air of expectation was palpable. We began the opening chorus and, whilst I was singing enthusiastically, I looked at the children, who were in the front row, and saw the horrified look on David's face. It was then that I realised the audience couldn't hear a sound, as the wind was blowing towards the stage. We carried on, as many members of the audience had already seen the previous performance and remembered enough of it to laugh and applaud in the appropriate places. Although an uncomfortable experience for us, it was, fortunately, the first and only time it happened.

One day, a nightclub owner asked Ted whether we would perform our show for his black patrons. We doubted whether a native audience would understand the sketches and punch lines, as they dealt with social situations in Britain. And, although I was pretty uninhibited, I felt slightly uncomfortable about this performance. Ted, on the other hand, had no reservations whatsoever. I discussed it with Bob, who was also involved, and we both agreed to do it out of love for Ted. This evening, too, was a great success. Ted had barely altered the programme, he cracked his jokes and people laughed in the right places. The sketches Ted and I performed together dealt with a particular working class environment and seemed to go down well. The audience jumped on their chairs and were bent double with laughter. Once again, I was learning from experience. It was in one of these nightclubs that we were introduced to a dance called 'Highlife'. We sat at wooden tables, set out in the middle of the bush, lit by little coloured lamps, whilst, on the dance floor, colourfully dressed, hip-swaying people enjoyed themselves. We liked the music very much and were totally involved. Suddenly, a tall, black man came to our table, turned to Ted and asked: "May I dance with your wife?" To my surprise, Ted said: "But of course" and gave me a little push. I had no choice but to accompany this giant onto the dance floor. There I stood, stiff as a board, and tried a few clumsy steps, managing to trample on the man's feet. As a result of this embarrassing episode, we learnt the dance properly and took it back to England with us. Soon after, the newspapers were full of photos of Princess Marina dancing the 'Highlife' during the independence celebrations in Lagos.

Entertainment was also the responsibility of the officers' messes, where people partied, drank and, of course, played bingo. Our trio was very popular, because Ted always livened things up. Although we didn't play much, we did occasionally play bingo and usually won something. Every regiment had its own mess, and people played over a particular period until a large sum of money had accumulated, the amount then being made public. One day, Bob, Ted and I went to play bingo, knowing that there was a fairly large sum at stake. There was already tension in the air when we joined the game, and the hostility towards us was palpable – after all, we hadn't contributed to the jackpot. Bob bought the tickets, the numbers were called out and, when the main prize-winning number was announced, Bob croaked: "Bingo!" A loud clamour erupted, people turned to us with fists shaking, shouting: "Not fair! Not fair!" As Bob walked to the front to collect his winnings, we feared for our safety. One of the organisers quickly got us out through the back entrance on to the street, where we hid until a taxi took us home.

Our African adventure was gradually drawing to a close after three years. Ted, especially, was sad, because he felt very much at home there and was popular at the office. The Nigerian staff would come to him for advice with their personal problems partly because Ted had a certain charm, but also because he was not just regarded as the white boss but also as a wise man. One day, one of the employees said to him: " Master, come outside please, I want to introduce you to my wife 'with the shop'." Ted did not understand but followed him anyway. Outside stood a woman with several rolls of fabric balanced on her head – that was her drapery. "And I have two more wives," the man told Ted proudly, "one of them looks after the children and the other cooks and does the housework. Now I'm looking for a younger woman for sex." Ted expressed his surprise at this division of labour, but the man reassured him that they all got along very well.

During our time in Africa, I tried – unsuccessfully – to have closer contact with the black population. I probably knew too little about their culture. Much remained a mystery to me, how people dealt with death, for example. When someone died, the corpse was carried from house to house. If the deceased had been elderly, people sang and danced; if death had been premature, the grieving took place in silence. There were many things I found disconcerting. We had a houseboy whom Ted caught stealing. When Ted sacked him, the boy responded in a dead pan manner: "I'll send my older brother – he'll beat you up. And I know when your wife is on her own at home." We reported this incident to the police. But, ultimately, Africa held a special magic for us. There was the primeval forest with its unfamiliar sounds, the drums, which could be heard every night, the chirping of the crickets at night and the evening rains that announced their impending arrival with thunder and lightning and, even after a downpour, didn't refresh. Africa was a journey of discovery. Our children had made good friends at school and were sad to have to bid them farewell.

22. Return to London

The news from London was not good. My mother-in-law had been diagnosed with stomach cancer. Ted was granted permission to return ahead of us, by ship. He had a damaged eardrum, and aeroplanes in those days did not have pressurised cabins. He went straight to his mother's and the children and I followed by air. Initially, we were able to stay with Ted's brother, and, after a while, Ted and I moved to stay with my mother-in-law whilst the children stayed with Ted's brother, where they felt at home. Ted's mother was pleased that she was being cared for by her son and also to have me there. We stayed with her until she died. We had hoped to be able to take over the tenancy, but in vain. There were, of course, strict rules and waiting lists, but we believed that, as relatives, there would be no problems. To this day, I find it incomprehensible that Ted's brother wrote to the local authority maintaining that we had no right to live there. Eventually, we were offered an army flat in Woolwich, a suburb that hardly seemed to have changed since the Boer War. Not only did the houses have a neglected air, so did the grubby children playing outside. We entered a courtyard surrounded by old, unpainted buildings. Our flat was on the first floor. The front door had been temporarily repaired with wooden slats. The living room stank of urine, and cornflakes had been trodden into the carpet. There was a rusty cooker in the kitchen and the bathroom was unusable. I stormed into the one of the army offices without an appointment and, in full flood, raged: "It's outrageous to expect families of His Majesty's Army to live like this. I've seen cowsheds cleaner than this flat. If the whole flat is not cleaned and repainted immediately, I'm going straight to Buckingham Palace to take over one of the rooms. I've heard that there are 360 empty rooms there!" Within a fortnight, the flat was renovated and unrecognisable. The children's school was close by and Ted had an easy journey to the office.

During our last home visit, I had gone to visit UNRRA, the United Nations Relief and Rehabilitation Administration, in London. I had heard that the West German government wanted to pay 'restitution' to relatives of Nazi victims. After the first meeting, I was told to not expect anything. I decided to wait and see what happened once the lawyers became involved. I constantly thought about my parents and still had no idea what had happened to them.

❧

In 1955, as I mentioned at the outset, I received a letter from Uncle Sim, who had returned to Germany. His wife, Tilly, had died and he had remarried. He had never really settled in Israel and, at the age of 70, had returned to Hamburg to start a new medical practice. He wrote that 18 Siegburger Strasse, where my cousin Fritz had had his butcher's shop, had been restored to the heirs and that my brother and I were to receive a share. The house had been confiscated by the Nazis, and my cousin Fritz had been sent to a concentration camp, where he was murdered. He had been accused of 'racial defilement' (*Rassenschande*) because he lived with an 'Aryan' woman. Uncle Sim also wrote that Aunt Martha, his and my mother's cousin, had survived the Nazi era in Oberdollendorf. Furthermore, Dr. Meier, the lawyer, had survived the concentration camp and had re-opened his office in Bonn. I was deeply touched that, once again, my uncle and I were in closer contact, and that Aunt Martha was still alive. His letter triggered something else in me: I suddenly felt an urgency to go to Germany and confront the past and the present. Ted agreed and was supportive. In the meantime, the English had become better informed about the horrific events in Nazi Germany. The dreadful pictures from concentration camps and the media coverage of refugees' accounts ensured that there was public awareness. At every social event, I was asked: "Where are you from? Italy, France, Scotland or Wales?" I would reply that I was from Israel, but originally from Germany, which enabled people to understand who I was.

Ted took me to the station. My mind was racing. Yes, I had a British passport, but I found myself imagining situations where I might be sent back. I knew I was returning to a different Germany.

But what was it like? Would it match my childhood memories? Would the woods and neighbours from those days still be there? I travelled by ferry to Ostend and, from there, by train to Bonn via Cologne. In the compartment was a student from Wales. After listening to my story, he asked if I would show him Bonn University and the city itself. I was relieved not to have to arrive there on my own. I took the young man to the market square. The short walk there was familiar to me and my thoughts were all over the place. It was as if my throat was tightly knotted. I pointed out the old town hall and the Metropol cinema, then suggested we go to the Kaiserplatz and the university. But first we booked two rooms at a hotel on the market square. As we rounded the corner, so to speak, I quipped: "Here stands our Kaiser Wilhelm." But he was no longer there and, nowadays, he's standing, barely visible, in front of the Café Bristol. The next morning, the student left Bonn with a favourable impression. For me, it was a new start. I was beginning to see the painful past with different eyes, and it was with these thoughts that I returned to London. On the train, I met Grete Borgmann, who was on her way to an international women's conference in London. When her eldest son, Albert, who was also in London at the time, met her at Victoria Station, I invited them both to Woolwich. We had no idea that fate would bring us closer together, when Ted was transferred to Germany. We lived in Woolwich for a year. Socially, it was a good time for us. It wasn't far from central London, the children went to school there, made new friends and settled in well. David developed a talent for acting, which was even mentioned in his school report. A few weeks before Christmas, I started working in the toy department of a big department store. I had great fun advising young parents on what to buy. The head of department took pleasure in informing me that I had achieved the highest sales figures and asked if I wanted to stay on. They were even prepared to give me Fridays off to look after my family and go shopping. Having convinced my reluctant husband that it would be good for our finances, I was there in the new year, working as a shop assistant in the hat department.

❦

In 1956 came the news that Ted was to be transferred to Hanover. I could hardly believe it – I would be living in Germany again, this time as a foreigner. But it meant that I would be on the spot to search for my parents. Of course, I was asked whether I would find it difficult to return to Germany – a legitimate question to which I had no ready-made answer. When I met with Jewish survivors and listened to their tales of horror, I suffered with them and was angry that such things could have happened, and that it was the Germans who had perpetrated them – but I felt no hatred towards the Germans. I was deeply saddened when I thought about the victims, especially my parents and relatives, all of whom had been murdered. When, in later years, I spoke with women in Germany who had lost husbands or sons in the war, I felt sympathy for them.

Once again, after Ted's transfer to Hanover, the children and I had to wait until accommodation had been found for us. As always, I packed the crates and, since the army was storing any goods we didn't want to take to Germany, I left my books behind, those irreplaceable links to Germany that had accompanied me wherever I went. When I later heard that my books had been damaged or destroyed in floods in Woolwich, it took me many years to come to terms with their loss.

23. Hanover

At last we left for Hanover. Ted was waiting to meet us at the station, accompanied by a friend who presented me with an enormous bouquet of flowers. Having lived in Germany for some time, he was – he told me – putting into practice the German custom of welcoming someone with flowers. I was highly delighted. The house we had been allocated was a 1930s mansion, which had belonged to a doctor, but had been requisitioned by the British army. I began to feel rather uneasy in the house, as did Ted. I didn't know then that the properties confiscated had mainly belonged to Nazis. The previous owners visited us several times. We got on with them well enough but were relieved to be able to move into an army house. We got to know the German family who rented the attic flat. Herr Beck worked for the British, in administration. He had a sense of humour and was a little eccentric. He felt at ease with the British because he found their attitude to work more relaxed than that of the Germans. When he subsequently returned to work in a German company, he would regale us with comparisons. Start work at 8 a.m. sharp, shake hands with everyone, no tea, no friendly "How are you?", a constant eye on the clock. We often took the Becks with us on outings. Our family still quotes a phrase coined by Herr Beck. At weekends, when the weather was good, he would appear at our door, rub his hands and say in his inimitable English: "I wonder me, I wonder me, are you taking a trip to the Harz today?" We quite often obliged.

We liked Hanover. The prosperity of its inhabitants, then and now, was expressed through its buildings. One glorious spring afternoon, the smell of coffee wafting through the air, I went onto the rear balcony, which overlooked the neighbouring garden, and observed the domestic scene: an elderly couple were sitting at a little table laid with cheesecake served on expensive Rosenthal china, for all the world as if there had never been a war or gas chambers: it could have been my parents sitting there. I started to sob, powerless to cope with the emotions. What I really wanted to do was scream at those people.

The children attended a British school and adapted well. I had never discussed the past with them; all they knew was that there had been a war and that we had won. I had engaged an 18-year-old German girl to help around the house. Christa was a country girl and was still influenced by Nazi ideology. Her view was that Hitler had been a great man, a great leader. Then she told me about her mentally handicapped brother, who had been sent to a home. I asked her where he was now and she replied "... they gave him an injection and then we were told he was dead." Shocked, I asked her what she thought about that. "We think it was for the best," she replied.

Soon after, I travelled to Bonn to consult Dr. Meier. He remembered my family well, as, like my father, he had been in the RjF. He said he was willing to represent my and my brother's interests in the restitution proceedings. In passing, he told me that my rosy cheeks made me look like a girl from the Moselle. I didn't let on that it was probably my make-up. I went on to visit Martha Steeg, my mother's cousin. She was waiting for me at Bonn station and, despite the passage of time, we recognised each other instantly and she was delighted when I spoke in the Rhenish dialect. We would meet several times thereafter. Aunt Martha was amazed at how much I remembered, for example, an occasion when she whispered something in Mother's ear. Although only ten years old, I knew immediately that they were talking about a pregnancy. Her son, Günther, must, therefore, have been ten years younger than me.

We moved yet again, this time to a small house on a British Army estate, a strange situation for me because here I was, in Germany, living as if I was in England. When I went shopping in town, I spoke German and nobody had any idea that I was a British citizen and Jewish. I had some extremely unpleasant encounters with post-war West German society. Although I often restrained myself, there were times when I had to explain my background.

The four years we spent in Germany were some of the most important in my life. The rest of the world thought the war against Nazi Germany had been won and that Germany had been humiliated and was free of Nazis. Not so! Of the Germans I met, only a few were willing to confront the reality of the Nazi past. Many had learnt nothing and suppressed, or even denied, the fact that their fellow citizens had been murdered, tortured and gassed. There were also those who had allegedly known nothing and others who even approved of the genocide of the Jews. Some believed, or persuaded themselves, that they had been forced into certain things. When they discovered I was Jewish, they were quick to emphasise that they had known nothing and, in any event, had been powerless. When I talked about the murder of six million Jews, they covered their faces with both hands and shook their heads in disbelief, as though they were hearing the appalling truth for the first time. I thought it extraordinary that so many young Germans didn't face up to the appalling crimes their country had committed. They didn't know any Jews and, possibly for that reason, they felt no guilt. I was all the more pleased to meet Germans like Grete Borgmann's family, who had helped Jews trying to flee and had provided them with a hiding place from their persecutors.

One day, while we were settling into our new home, I met the neighbour who lived to our right, a portly German woman married to a British soldier. I couldn't quite make her out because she repeatedly used innuendo. One morning, I looked out of my bedroom window at the moment she appeared at hers. She held up an old-fashioned, worn out and very large corset and exclaimed: "This would suit you!" Peter was one of the two boys' friends, who they often played with in the Eilenriede, Hanover's urban woodland. Having not seen him for a while, I asked David what had happened to him, only to be told that our neighbour had told him not to play with David and Stephen, as we were Jews and devils. Soon afterwards, I noticed that food was disappearing from the kitchen. Christa's behaviour towards us suddenly changed. Whilst I was out shopping, she played records and damaged the gramophone, the records and other things instead of working. When I challenged her, she insisted that the neighbours had incited her, arguing that, as we were Jews, she should steal and damage as much as possible. The neighbour's husband happened to be working in the garden when I told Ted, who immediately demanded an explanation. Next day, they had both disappeared. Ted pressed charges against them and it transpired that the wife had been a guard in a women's concentration camp in Poland and her husband was a fan of Oswald Mosley, the founder of the anti-semitic British Union of Fascists. We assumed that they would be dealt with by the courts. Fortunately, the children didn't think too much about it, and Peter came back to play.

We got on well with the new neighbours. Margret was also German, married to an Englishman. She told us that she had been a leader in the *BDM*, but had not thought anything of it until now. Mind you, she once expressed the view that Germany would have won the war if it had entered into an alliance with the Russians. I also met Margret's parents. They were kind people I remained friendly with until their death. They told me about the day their Jewish neighbours were taken away. It had saddened them because they were nice people, but they had done nothing about it. Margret also told me that, during the last days of the war, her mother had gone out onto the street and invited the recently conscripted *Hitler Youth* boys into her home, otherwise they would have beeen shot by the Americans. After the arrival of the Allied forces, her father had to help restore order to the Jewish cemetery. None of this affected our friendship, and I started to think about how I would have behaved in such circumstances.

I often visited Dr. Meier and my aunt in Bonn. I also went to Krefeld, to find out more about my parents' fate. Both had been deported from Krefeld to Izbica in Poland in 1942 and, from there, had been taken either to Sobibor or Belzec extermination camps. Dr. Meier helped me with my restitution claim. I was constantly expected to provide the authorities with documentary evidence. Sometimes they went to extremes, requiring me to obtain documents relating to Father's Dresdner Bank account, for example, even though the bank had long since destroyed its Jewish customers' papers. I found all this difficult to cope with emotionally. I wrote to my brother Walter in Canada, telling him I had instructed Dr. Meier and asked him to let me know his thoughts. He replied, rather brusquely, that he had already instructed a lawyer and would have various files and documents sent to me – but nothing ever came.

David was now twelve years old and, in common with other British children, had to go to a British boarding school in Plön, Schleswig-Holstein. He was not enamoured with the prospect of leaving home. One day, he came home from football with a swollen foot. The young doctor that examined him omitted to x-ray it. The poor boy was in considerable pain, but, as is often the case with young, ambitious parents, we put it down to the prospect of boarding school. I took David to Plön and will never forget the sadness in his eyes as we said good-bye. As Hamburg was on my way home, I stayed overnight with Uncle Sim and told him about David's foot. A few days later, the school telephoned to tell us that David was in hospital. The injury to his foot had its origin in tuberculosis. I called Uncle Sim immediately, who agreed there and then to come with me to Plön. On the way there, he speculated that it might be something else. He was right: David was suffering from an inflammation of the bone marrow and was transferred to an excellent hospital in Hanover.

24. A Flying Visit to North America

Some weeks before, I had decided to visit my brother in Canada. We had 'inherited' a little money from Uncle Karl. Karl's butcher's shop in Beuel had been confiscated by the Nazis and the property had been transferred, but we were to receive a restitution payment. My brother had waived his share in my favour, so I decided to spend the money on the fare to Canada. I hoped this would bring us closer and clear up some misunderstandings. But now that David was in hospital, even though he was making progress, I was unsure whether it was right to go. I talked to David's specialist and his doctor, both of whom agreed that he was well on the way to a complete recovery. David himself told me that, were he to stop me from going, he would never be able to forgive himself. So I was finally going to see my brother again. I was excited, as I also intended to visit my sister-in-law Ivy in Michigan, and my father's sister Aunt Else and her son Fredi in New York. Everything had been well prepared: Ted took time off to look after Stephen and visit David, and we employed a woman to do the housework. Just in case, I made a big pot of goulash that was repeatedly 'stretched' by a friend in the neighbourhood. I was rather apprehensive, having heard nothing from my brother, but, thankfully his wife sent a telegram shortly before my departure to say I was welcome.

The day of departure arrived. David had recovered to the extent that we were able to collect him that morning and take him to the airport with us. The aeroplane was luxuriously appointed for those days. It was the first flight where warm food was served. The long flight gave me time to prepare for the reunion after more than 20 years. At Montreal airport, then small and old, I looked around at the small number of people who were there and instantly recognised my brother. He had hardly changed and greeted me in English. On the phone to his wife, Ruth, I heard him say: "She might as well be a stranger." He stood there, apparently finding our meeting embarrassing, and couldn't bring himself to give me a hug. I, too, felt paralysed. We were even separated by language: my brother did not want to speak German with me, so we were unable to voice the names we used to call our parents: *Mutti* and *Vati*. He could not or would not speak about the past, whether in German or English.

Walter's car was big, so we sat quite far apart. I don't remember any conversation on the way home, but the atmosphere improved slightly when my sister-in-law, Ruth, opened the door and gave me a warm welcome. Relieved, I kissed my nephew Gary, whom I took to immediately. I also met Ruth's father, who had been widowed and whose second wife was also from Poland. They were devout Jews and also treated me with kindness. Only my brother remained reserved. He worked as a window dresser, was popular, and had a lot to do. He took one day off to spend time with me in the beautiful Laurentian Mountains. Walter talked about his work and the people he had got to know. And he joked. Not a word was mentioned about our childhood or about the time he spent with our parents after I had left for Palestine. I sensed – and was saddened by – his anger towards me. He was convinced that I had abandoned our parents to live in the land of milk and honey. I wanted to tell him about Palestine, the difficult years, illness and hunger, about daily life, about all the things that had prevented me from communicating with him. I couldn't even discuss his false picture of me. His wife confessed that she had imagined her sister-in-law to be a pale, bespectacled, blue-stockinged communist. What surprised me was the similarity between Walter and David. Movements, gestures, his whole demeanour reminiscent of my son, even though the two had never met. I hoped our relationship would improve over time.

From there, I went to visit Ted's sister Ivy in Holland, Michigan. Like many British women, Ivy had adapted to the American way of life. She was 'the English rose from the old country' and her in-laws were proud of that. Ivy had a lot of kitchen gadgets she had written home about, and with which she could show off. Her cuisine was entirely American. One day, we were strolling through the town when a beautiful, large road cruiser stopped alongside us. Inside sat an elegantly dressed lady. Ivy spoke to her briefly and then said: "See you

166

on Friday." It was her cleaner!

Ted reported from Hanover that David was well, the goulash was almost finished, and that he was looking forward to having me back home soon. But, first, I flew to New York to visit Aunt Else and her son Fredi. Aunt Else had emigrated in 1946, from Leipzig via Great Britain to the USA, and now lived in a Jewish area. I felt rather uncomfortable when I arrived at Idlewild Airport on the Friday evening. I promptly got lost and tried to telephone my aunt – being an observant Jew, she wouldn't have been able to meet me at the airport on the Sabbath. A young American man came to my aid and led me through the airport labyrinth to the bus, which got me to the Hilton Hotel, chosen for me by Ivy's husband, Frank. They had reserved a suite – bedroom, dressing room and bathroom – in this huge skyscraper with over 2,000 rooms. As it was terribly hot, I ordered a Coca Cola from room service. "One glass or two?" enquired the Irish waiter and, naively, I asked for just one. Well – he locked the door on the inside. Armed with the bottle, I managed to force him out of the room.

At my aunt's suggestion, I took a taxi to her apartment. The taxi driver asked me, in a loud voice, where I was from. Israel didn't surprise him. "Yeah, I have family in Israel. And where do you live now?" In England. "Yeah, I was stationed in England during the war." And so it continued. "Where have you just come from?" From Germany. "Yeah, I lost a lot of family in the concentration camps." The questions kept on coming. I told him I had lived in Palestine, in a kibbutz. "Oh yeah, I'll be going there soon." Nothing surprised him. He had either already seen or experienced everything, or was about to. I'd have loved to give him a 100-dollar tip when I got out of the taxi and tell him I'd won the jackpot. Maybe that would have surprised him! In my aunt's home, the candlesticks were on the table and the wine and *challah* were ready for the Sabbath. She talked about the Jewish community and gave me the impression that she was worried she might not be leading a sufficiently orthodox life. She worked in a factory, Fredi had become an engineer. He was completely under his mother's thumb and would never have dared to get married. After a bit of sightseeing in New York over the next few days, I flew back to Germany. I was looking forward to seeing my family again.

಄

David had recovered and started life at the King Alfred School in Plön. Overlooking a beautiful lake, the atmosphere was calm and melancholic. We went to visit him often, as it wasn't easy for me to let go. Stephen, too, missed him very much. Ted didn't seem well; he was more nervous than usual and looked out of sorts, so we drove to Hamburg to see Uncle Sim. We booked ourselves into a small, friendly guesthouse and enjoyed spending time with him and his Hungarian wife. Having examined Ted, Uncle Sim explained to me that Ted had aged more rapidly than normal because of the hole in his heart. He could give him injections, which would improve his condition. So we drove to Hamburg regularly and Ted improved visibly. One day, my Uncle Sim expressed the wish to go to Bergen-Belsen. He had the feeling that friends of his had died in the concentration camp. Looking around, not only did we come across mass graves, but also individual ones, and Uncle Sim actually found the grave of a friend. He was very deeply moved. And I was relieved to leave this place where, yes, there were a few trees but no birdsong. Despite his advancing years, Uncle Sim continued to run a successful medical practice. Former patients consulted him. He had developed a cancer treatment that, for some of his patients, had resulted in a cure. During our time in Germany, we had a warm and close relationship. The children liked him and he came to visit us often, as did other family members from England and Israel.

಄

We celebrated our first Christmas in Germany in 1956, in Freiburg with Grete Borgmann, whom I had stayed in touch with since we first met on the train to Ostend. We were met at the station by her eldest son, Albert, and loved the snowscape. The Borgmanns lived in a fairly new house, and we loved the cheerful, cosy atmosphere. In the living room stood a large Christmas tree, with a number of promising parcels underneath it. It was 24 December and everyone seemed to be aware it was my birthday. While we were sitting together at breakfast, Grete's husband Karl went over to the piano and they all sang Happy Birthday, after which, I was presented with a box of chocolates. Of course, the chocolates have long been consumed but I have kept the box to this day. Before handing out presents, Karl read from the Christmas Gospel and we sang those familiar songs. Shortly before midnight, we woke the children and set off to midnight mass in the cathedral. The town was utterly still, as if under a spell. When we got back to the house, we had cocoa and cake. The festivities continued the next day: At ten o'clock in the morning, we all went to communion mass in the cathedral. The choir and orchestra were rehearsing Mozart's *Coronation Mass*. There was a buzz of eager expectation. The archbishop entered with his retinue and the mass began. For me, this was the highlight.

The following days were spent skiing, sledging and with snowball fights. Grete's children, Albert, Rainer and Margrit, took us to the Schauinsland, Freiburg's 'local mountain', where the snow was even deeper. In the evenings, we sang English folksongs with the children, with Ted accompanying us on the guitar. It was the beginning of a long friendship with Grete and her family, which has lasted to this day. When it was time to go, Grete said: "Do look out of the window when your train passes our house." We did and and saw a member of the family waving from every window. None of us would ever forget the 'waving house'.

With my past, living in Germany in the late 1950's was far from easy. In effect, I had three personas: I was still German and Jewish – in itself a problematic combination – but, in the meantime, I had become a British citizen, and was thus a member of the occupying power. I was able to reconcile these three personas and they coexisted happily enough, but there were times when I was oversensitive. On one occasion, I went shopping in Hanover market. I had just bought some bananas when a woman and her child came up behind me. The stall holder gave the child a banana and the mother told him, in English, to say thank you. The stall holder turned to me and whispered: "If I'd known they were English, I wouldn't have given the child a banana." Boiling over with rage, I threw my bananas on the stall: "Keep your bananas – I'm English, too!" I later regretted this outburst.

Ted received a surprise transfer to Herford, a small town where we lived alongside other British army families. I missed my friend Margret, but soon made new friends. Stephen had to get used to a new school and David, too, had to change schools because the boarding school premises in Plön had been handed back to the German Navy. Like all the other British children, he now had to attend a boarding school in Hamm. At the beginning of the new school year, we took David to the station. He was twelve and cut a fine figure in his new school blazer. We then didn't see each other for three months – a long time for a mother, probably also for a son. At last, he came home for the autumn holidays. Ted collected him from the station and, when I heard the car outside, I ran to the door to give my little boy a hug. But standing in front of me was a tall, spindly young man in a blazer that hadn't kept up with him. In my astonishment, I called out his name and heard an unfamiliar, deep and rather gruff voice: "Hello, Mum!"

One of our neighbours was a young German woman married to a British soldier. We were familiar with such marriages from our time in Hanover. Over time, she started to trust me. When I mentioned that I was Jewish, she asked me about my family. I told her my parents had died in a concentration camp; her response was unexpected. She had lived with an SS man during the war. "We lived opposite a compound secured by barbed wire. I used to hear terrible screams, especially at night. I didn't want to think about what was going on there, and I didn't want to ask him either, even though I knew he worked there."

25. Restitution

The restitution procedure was causing ripples. In the course of an appointment with Dr. Meier, I mentioned our former maid, Gretchen, who had married a man called Borst and, prior to my emigration, had lived in Dottendorf. It transpired that they were neighbours of Dr Meier's secretary. I arranged to visit Gretchen, by now an old woman, but she had hardly changed. It was a difficult reunion; she obviously knew what had become of my parents. Covering her kitchen table was a white damask tablecloth embroidered with the letters M.K., my mother's initials. I also noticed a familiar silver candlestick. I stood there transfixed, whilst Gretchen told me my mother had given them to her. I needed her signature for my restitution claim – to confirm our circumstances at the time – which she willingly gave.

I visited Aunt Martha and Uncle Fritz fairly regularly. Their son Günther and his wife lived with them. Fritz was once again working in the Didier brickworks in Oberkassel. He had been sacked during the Nazi era, for refusing to divorce his Jewish wife. Fritz was always nice to me but, that evening, they were expecting visitors, who were not to find out that I had emigrated to Palestine. I was annoyed at first, but said nothing. There was lively conversation, during the course of which, in the heat of the moment, I blurted out that we had lived in what was then Palestine. After the guests had left, I heard Fritz scream: "She's not coming here ever again!" The next day, I told Aunt Martha that I had to get back to husband and children without delay and, what is more, I would never deny my roots. My aunt replied: "But you don't have to shout it from the rooftops." I was speechless, and it was some considerable time before I visited them again. Fritz was rather subdued in my presence, but the incident was never mentioned again.

❧

What Ted enjoyed most was driving our Opel on the motorway. He could plan itineraries, knowing that there would be no, or few, holdups and that we would reach our destination quickly. We travelled around Germany, but also went to Denmark, Italy and Austria. The children loved the mountains, the sea and the beaches, and they experienced other cultures and ways of life. I was pleased that David and Stephen grew up without prejudices. In the summer of 1958, we drove to Freiburg via Bonn. It was important to me that my family should see where I grew up. I showed them Beethoven's House, my school and, in particular, my route to school. They looked at the Rhine Bridge in disbelief and were glad to be sitting in the car rather than having to walk all that way. As we drove along the Rhine, I pointed out the Siebengebirge and the various places where I had played as a child. Arriving in Freiburg, both the weather and the welcome was warm. On Grete's recommendation, we drove on to Überlingen on Lake Constance. First we stayed in a small hotel but soon moved to a guesthouse directly overlooking the lake. We loved the local food, roast saddle of venison with cranberries or *spaetzle*, for example. Tanned and in good spirits, we were driving back through the Frankenwald when, out of the blue, Ted said: "Maggy – what d'you think about staying a couple of days longer? There's a bit of money left." I agreed that it was a wonderful idea and, at that moment, we saw a little forest track with a signpost "To the Trout Pond – accommodation." Without a moment's hesitation, Ted turned the car round and we drove through the forest until we reached a clearing. There stood an enchanting little farmhouse surrounded by meadows. Excited, we knocked at the door. The young woman who came to the door told us that the rooms were all taken by a group of miners, who were regular annual visitors, but when she saw how disappointed we were, she offered that we could sleep in the attic. She and her Polish husband had fled East Prussia, had bought the smallholding, and had started a trout farm. That evening, we met the miners from Duisburg – four men and four women – who were seated at a long table. We greeted each other and I added a few words in German, because I thought they might be somewhat confused by hearing us speaking English amongst ourselves. Alcohol increased the volume and we started exchanging witty banter. The miners began singing: *In einem kühlen Grunde* and I sang along happily. Ted went and got his guitar and accompanied the singers as best he could. Then it was our turn. The boys sang *Hang down your head, Tom Dooley* and, finally, we all sang *My bonnie lies over the ocean.* The young woman and her Polish husband soon joined in.

Next day, the farmer took David and Stephen with him to the fields. They happily sat on the trailer, after which we saw very little of them. Ted and I walked for hours through the woods, in glorious weather. It had been a long time since we had felt so relaxed. All too soon, we had to leave this paradise, but not before our hostess told us her story. During the war, she had been raped by Russian soldiers and, with many others, had trudged westwards through ice and snow without food or warm clothing. While on the run, she had given birth to a child who had died of cold and malnutrition.

26. Barton Stacey

It was now the beginning of 1960. After four years in Germany, we wanted to get back to England. Ted's military career was nearing its end, and my restitution claim had been reasonably successful. We often talked about planning our future. I felt that we should try and gain a foothold in London, buy an old block of flats and live off the rental income and possibly go on to buy our own family home. Thinking about it now, I was probably striving to achieve a way of life subconsciously modelled on my parents. Still politically left-wing, in practice, I was living a middle-class life. In the eventful years of my youth as a member of the *Bund*, I had learned that one should use the wisdom of one's parents as a springboard. I had done that, but had landed in a different place to the one I had expected. It was this dichotomy that probably caused my clash with the kibbutz. The radical ideas of the kibbutz movement – for example, the communal upbringing of children – had led me back to values my parents had espoused. Even then, I knew, instinctively, that I wouldn't want my children to be brought up by the community. I had been called a traitor, but kibbutz life today is different. I now had to let go of Germany, but was pleased to have established a link with Aunt Martha, and to have made new friends, who had become very important to me. We knew that Ted would leave the army with good references, which would enable him to find a remunerative position in 'civvie street', but he still had two more years in the army and had to be prepared to be transferred anywhere.

This time, it was Barton Stacey, a small town in Hampshire. I had never been to Hampshire, known for its extensive woods, and was looking forward to being back in England again. Yet again, I had to pack, and, yet again, we had to decide where to live temporarily. With a great fanfare, Ted's sister Alice offered that we spend the first ten days with her. We were rather apprehensive about it, knowing what we were letting ourselves in for. Stephen and I took the ferry to Dover and then the train to Catford; Ted and David crossed the Channel in our fully laden car. Ted had to ensure that the car was parked plumb outside his sister's house, so that everyone knew which house the beautiful red car belonged to. We exchanged this for army accommodation, which turned out to be even worse. It was winter, it was cold, and it had been snowing. On our arrival from London, we were taken to a room with a double and two single beds. The room was unheated and freezing cold. There was a damp patch on one wall. We were offered the use of a dining room of sorts, with a table and four chairs. There was a barely noticeable tiny open fireplace, which gave off very little heat. We sat down, shivering, and each of us was given a plate of mincemeat swimming in OXO gravy and some potatoes. With OXO, an important universal ingredient, nothing could possibly go wrong in the British kitchen. The great humourist Peter Ustinov, once related how, on her first visit to Britain, his mother – who spoke not a word of English – travelled through several railway stations before arriving at Victoria Station where, impressed, she exclaimed: "That's a huge OXO!" Having eaten, we were at a loss as to where to go. All the rooms were either cold, damp or both, and there was no shower in the bathroom. There was nothing to do in Barton Stacey, so we wandered through the streets peering through windows and seeing cosy living rooms. We drove to the nearest larger market town, Andover, where there was a tearoom that served sandwiches and scones. Of course, you can't spend more than an hour over tea, so, having warmed up a bit, we left. The children never grumbled, but David caught bronchitis. Our 'hosts' pretended not to notice us, although they accepted good money from the army. It was a relief when the ordeal was over and we moved into a lovely, spacious house on an army estate in the middle of a wood.

Stephen attended the local primary school and we were pleased that David was accepted at the grammar school in Andover, a short cycle ride away. It was good to live normally again and to take stock. I was alone in the house all day and felt quite isolated, but that didn't last long. The extended family soon found out that we lived in countryside, surrounded by beautiful woodland, where you could pick berries and go for wonderful walks, not to mention that we lived rent free and were even served hot meals. So they came on a Friday and left on a Sunday, and I spent the intervening week shopping, cooking and washing in preparation for the next weekend invasion. One morning, I was in the living room with the vacuum cleaner when I suddenly had the feeling that someone was staring at me. I turned to the open window and saw the head of a cow dribbling onto the carpet. That was it! When Ted came home, I broke it to him that I couldn't bear the loneliness any longer. Why didn't we buy a house in one of the small towns? "D'you think we can afford it?" was his response. "We have £400 in the bank," I said. "We need £200 as a deposit and £200 to buy furniture." "If you think you can do it, then I'm in favour," said Ted.

But first I decided to track down Molly, whom I hadn't seen for seven years. I knew that George worked for the railway, so I asked a railway official in Andover whether he knew George. To my surprise, I learnt that George was working at the freight terminal in Andover. At that moment a train arrived. "If you take this train, it will take you directly to Mr. Sheraton. He works in the office." I did as he suggested and soon found myself in a small Dickensian office, with smoke pouring from the old-fashioned stove in the corner. Then George appeared. "Where have you come from, how did you manage to find me?" he asked. "We've often talked about you, and Molly has really missed you. We live in Tidworth but she's in Andover today. Come on, let's go now!" Excited, we walked to the house Molly was visiting and George called out: "Molly, there's someone to see you!" I walked into the living room; Molly jumped out of the chair and went pale. "I knew you'd be back one day," she said. And so we renewed our friendship, which has endured to this day.

My vision of a house of our own was realistic and modest. Ted was surprised how confidently I approached the project. We found a small, typically English semi-detached house with a garage and, as advertised, a well-kept vegetable garden. The house had three bedrooms, a lounge-cum-dining room, and a small kitchen, all in good condition, with a purchase price of £2,000, towards which we paid a £200 deposit. It was my first time at a furniture auction with Ted and he looked on as I haggled over every penny to scrape together the furnishings. It wasn't long before we were sitting in our first, very own house.

Soon after, Stephen had to take the dreaded 11-plus, which would determine what secondary school he would go to. Matters were made more difficult because he was a product of the post-war baby boom, which reduced his chances of making it to a grammar school on the first attempt. When I made enquiries of the headmaster, he told me that, in Stephen's case, it was particularly unlikely, given that he had only been in the school for a couple of months and, of the 50 pupils in his class, only two or three stood a chance. This came as a shock to us, but our little boy was unperturbed. Come the morning of the exam, some of his friends, very nervous, called for him. Stephen appeared unaffected. A few days later, he came home for lunch waving a piece of paper, which confirmed that he had gained a place at the grammar school. We all hugged each other and danced all over the house. But then he decided that he would prefer to go to boarding school, like his brother had done. Ted enquired whether a scholarship was available for the Duke of York Military Academy in Dover, which mainly took war orphans. It was possible to acquire extra points if, having passed the 11-plus, one sat one more exam. Stephen passed this one, too, and we then drove to Dover, where, over the course of two days, he went to classes and took further tests. I was shaken by Stephen's decision to go to boarding school but didn't want to stand in his way. He was now in a completely new environment, presumably not what he was expecting, added to which, the school's expectations of its pupils were unsuited to Stephen's family background and upbringing. I missed him very much and had to resist going and fetching him home. When he had been at the school for some months, we were allowed to visit him. We asked him what he missed most and our 13-year old son replied, in a firm voice: "Women!" We had no idea just how unhappy Stephen was at the school. He had to put up with a great deal of harassment from the teachers. In common with almost every English boarding school, the emphasis was on sport, whereas we, his parents, set more store in academic achievement. Stephen had always been a good student, but it was at this school that he discovered he was also good at sport. It had become apparent in Hanover that he had a talent for boxing. The school encouraged this, because he was seen as important in maintaining the school's sporting prestige. After he had won a school boxing championship, which was even televised, boxing in schools was banned; but he soon showed excellence in other sports.

Unquestionably, our life in Andover had advantages and stood in marked contrast to our previous experience as army tenants. We now had our own house, which we called 'Shalom' – peace. We enjoyed being close to the countryside, in one of the most beautiful parts of England. The garden had been laid out in an exemplary fashion by the previous owner, and we managed to consume all the vegetables we grew in the two years we lived there. I enjoyed being a housewife and mother, and it was really the first time, for many years, that we were able to settle. But there was also a dark side. It was a period of self-examination; terrible thoughts about my parents, a mixture of haunting perceptions and guilt, which intensified in this environment. I sometimes became almost obsessive about my parents' fate, and my imagination filled any gaps created by the lack of information about what happened to them. Every morning, I effectively forced myself to relive my parents' journey to the concentration camp. I kept all this from my family, but, when it got worse, I confided in a friend, who was involved in spiritualism. She explained that my mother's soul was still earthbound and an influence on me. I should pray. I don't remember what I did, exactly, but I worked very hard on it and, after a while, the feelings stopped.

This experience reminded me that, from early childhood, I sometimes had dark premonitions that meant little to me as a child but later came to pass. For example, on one occasion, I remember standing on the Rhine Bridge in Bonn with Ulrich Rosenthal, discussing the political situation. Suddenly and briefly, I had a clear vision of war and fire. Later, I was often aware that my premonitions proved correct. I had just become interested in parapsychological phenomena when friends from Hanover took me to a spiritualist church. This was a sect that had come to the UK from the USA in the 19th century and had attracted many followers. In essence, they believed that humans retained their personality after death and that communication with them was, therefore, possible through a medium. It was my first time and I was excited and curious. The medium looked at the congregation for a while, then pointed to me and described my background in astonishing detail and told me that my parents had found peace. Later on, I took part in some séances, once with the author Fay Weldon, but distanced myself from them because there was something uncanny about them. Fay Weldon, however, encouraged me to buy Tarot cards and it transpired that I had a gift for fortune-telling. Over the years, I gained a reputation for this ability and many of my friends made use of it. Later Fay and I became good friends.

An affliction of an entirely different kind was the extended family. As we lived in such a beautiful area, and had more space, their unwelcome visits increased. If I tried to explain that it was inconvenient, I was completely ignored. Ted even had to drive to London to collect his sister and her husband. On one occasion, the relatives arrived while we were out. They forced open the little pantry window and then pushed their youngest child through, so he could open the door from the inside. He had the misfortune to fall into a bucket of soapy water, which I had kept to scrub the front yard. These invasions also put a strain on our budget. It got so bad, I couldn't sleep at night and had asthma attacks. In the end, I was in hospital in Andover for a week.

We had agreed that we didn't want to stay in Andover in the long term; we always felt that real life was going on elsewhere. In any event, we had always dreamt of living in London. After retiring from the army, Ted was offered two good jobs, one in St. Andrews in Scotland, the home of the famous golf course where famous Hollywood stars came to play golf. What was on offer was the post of manager at the golf club, bringing with it a good salary and a house. The other job offer was a well-paid administrative post with the City & Guilds Institute in London. With Stephen at school in Dover, we decided on the London job and started looking for a house between London and Dover. While Ted looked for temporary accommodation, I organised the sale of the Andover house. Our search for a new home ended when we found a house in Bexleyheath, close to the station, as Ted had to commute to Central London every day. When we had settled in, I became aware that my dreams had been fulfilled: two lovely children, a husband with a good job, a house in London, and a smart car. And I enjoyed good health. But, in time, those dreams were to be thwarted.

In June 1963, we drove from London to Dover for the first time to attend the annual garden party held by the Duke of York's Royal Military School. We booked a room in a traditional English guesthouse, drank a whisky with the owner, and told him that we had come to visit our son at the military school. Little did we know that, some hours later, our old friend Bob, whom we hadn't seen for six years, would book himself into the same guesthouse and get into conversation with the owner. Hearing about the recently arrived guests, Bob sneaked a look at the guest book and saw our names. He knew that, like him, we had a son at the military school and that he would be seeing us at the party. And so when we met Bob brought us up to date. Coincidentally, he, too, was to have been transferred to Herford shortly after us. But because his wife was determined to avoid a renewal of our friendship, she made successful representations to Bob's superior, which resulted in the reversal of the transfer to Germany. They stayed in England, but the marriage broke down. Bob had also left the army and was looking for a job in London. He was over the moon to have found us again. His son, Robby, who was a little older than Stephen, was at the boarding school and his 13-year-old daughter Eileen still lived with her mother. Bob was to play a significant part in the next phase of our lives. As he had nowhere to live, he and his daughter moved in with us at the same time as I started work as a shop assistant. I found the combination of the new job and catering for a larger household a considerable strain. When the boys came home in the holidays, there were seven of us. We had neither a washing machine nor a dishwasher, and it wasn't customary for the husband to help in the home after a day's work. I no longer had any time to myself; I went shopping in my lunch break and, after work, Bob picked me up and took me home, where there was more to do – it was all too much. It was a relief to all of us when we helped Bob buy a house nearby – and so our friendship continued.

Lilly and Walter lived in a large house, which they partly sublet. At the time, Walter was writing articles for the political and review sections of the *Frankfurter Allgemeine Zeitung*, under the pseudonym 'Peter Munk'. He often took me along to cultural events. Lilly and Walter's New Year's Eve party proved to be an occasion I would never forget. Their parties – offering us a glimpse into some of London's glamorous circles – were unconventional. There was no dress code, still a novelty for us. Ted, Bob and I marvelled at this colourful, eccentric collection of young actors, writers, painters and journalists, many of whom later became well known. I particularly remember a gay couple: a beautiful young South African Indian and his English boyfriend, a butcher. Actually, it was here that I first met Fay Weldon.

Having done well in his exams at grammar school, David successfully applied to Esso, for a grant that enabled him to attend college in Enfield. He came home at weekends. In general, I enjoyed my job as a shop assistant, not least because of the friendly working environment. I felt I fitted in well. But then I made two mistakes, which brought my career to an abrupt end. Our department manager liked me, but attached great importance to her place in the hierarchy. One day, she talked about her holiday in Tangier. This prompted me to relate how I had often travelled from Gibraltar to Tangier. She withdrew in a pique and didn't speak to me again. Things got worse. Christmas sales figures had been very good. Our manager came to see me and announced, for all to hear: "Mrs. Barnard, you had the best sales figures, I will introduce you to our general manager." I had not reckoned with collegial envy; it became impossible for me to continue working there.

Liebe Margot!

Hoch erfreut durch umseitige Nachricht. Wir sind gesund. Was ist Deine Beschäftigung? Dir, Onkel und Kindern Grüsse Küsse Walter schreibt regelmässig Deine treuen Eltern

Datum. 1. Oktober 1941

Letter from my parents via the Red Cross (October 1941)

*With Royal Air Force friends
(Heliopolis, 1942)*

In Egypt (1942)

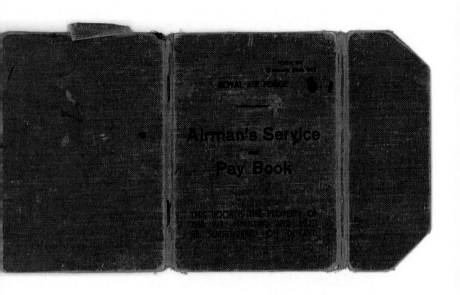

My Royal Air Force pay book and identity card

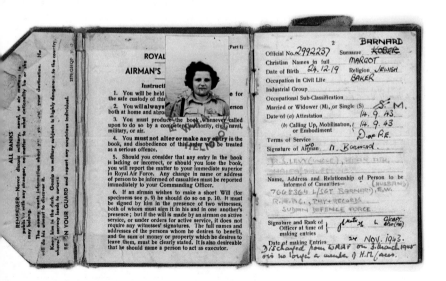

ROYAL

AIRMAN'S

Instructi

1. You will be held   e for
the safe custody of this

2. You will always   erson
both at home and abro

3. You must produce the book whenever called
upon to do so by a competent authority, civil, naval,
military, or air.

4. You must not alter or make any entry in the
book, and disobedience of this order will be treated
as a serious offence.

5. Should you consider that any entry in the book
is lacking or incorrect, or should you lose the book,
you will report the matter to your immediate superior
in Royal Air Force. Any change in name or address
of person to be informed of casualties must be reported
immediately to your Commanding Officer.

6. If an airman wishes to make a short Will (for
specimens see p. 9) he should do so on p. 10. It must
be signed by him in the presence of two witnesses,
both of whom must sign it in his and in one another's
presence ; but if the will is made by an airman on active
service, or under orders for active service, it does not
require any witnesses' signatures. The full names and
addresses of the persons whom he desires to benefit,
and the sum of money or property which he desires to
leave them, must be clearly stated. It is also desireable
that he should name a person to act as executor.

(Part 1)

2   BARNARD

Official No. 2992237   Surname KOBER

Christian Names in full MARGOT

Date of Birth 24.12.19   Religion JEWISH

Occupation in Civil Life BAKER

Industrial Group

Occupational Sub-Classification

Married or Widower (M), or Single (S)   S. M.

Date of (a) Attestation   14.9.43

(b) Calling Up, Mobilisation,   14.9.43
or Embodiment   D. of P.E.

Terms of Service

Signature of Airman   M. Barnard.

R.S. LEVY (UNCLE) NEAR RTH.

Name, Address and Relationship of Person to be
informed of Casualties :-   (HUSBAND)

7665369 L/SGT. BARNARD, E.W.
R.A.P.C., PAY RECORDS
SUDAN DEFENCE FORCE

Signature and Rank of
Officer at time of
making entries

Date of making Entries   24 NOV. 1943.

Discharged from WAAF on 3 March 1945
was no longer a member of H.M. forces.

ALL RANKS

REMEMBER—Never discuss military, naval, or air matters in
public with any stranger, no matter to what nationality he or she
may belong.

The enemy wants information about you and your destination. He
will do his utmost to discover it.

Keep him in the dark. Gossip on military subjects is highly dangerous to the country,
where secrecy leads to sureness.

BE ON YOUR GUARD and report any suspicious individual.

Instruction at the Royal Air Force Fighter Controller Training School, 1943

stand at ease! and easy

In Royal Air Force uniform (Cairo 1943)

*Time off during
a Royal Air Force
exercise in the
Egyptian desert
(1944)*

*With Ted in Cairo shortly
after our wedding (1944)*

With Ted and David in Gibraltar (1948)

With Ted, David and Stephen in Nigeria, (1954)

SYNAGOGENGEMEINDE KREFELD

Bescheinigung
================

Hiermit bescheinigen wir, daß Herr Erwin Kober, früher Krefeld, Südwall
11 ab 1. September 1941 Sternträger im Sinne des Gesetzes gewesen ist.
Herr Kober wurde am 20. April 1942 nach Izbicka/Polen deportiert.

Synagogengemeinde Krefeld

Krefeld, den 15. August 1955

Fritz Leven

ertificates issued by the Krefeld Synagogue Community Centre (dated 1955)
ncerning the fate of my parents who were deported to Izbica in Poland on 20 April
942

SYNAGOGENGEMEINDE KREFELD

Bescheinigung
================

Hiermit bescheinigen wir, daß Frau Erwin Kober, Emilie geborene Levy,
geb. am 12. November 1891 in Beuel, letzte Wohnung Krefeld, Südwall 11,
am 20. April 1942 nach Izbicka/Polen deportiert wurde. Da bis heute von
Frau Kober kein Lebenszeichen eingegangen ist, muß man leider annehmen,
daß sie den Tod gefunden hat.

Synagogengemeinde Krefeld

Krefeld, den 15. August 1955

Fritz Leven

Krefeld, den *5* . *8* . 195*5*

Aufenthaltsbescheinigung

De*m Erwin Kober*

geboren am *28 . 6 . 87*   zu *Raxitsch*

Kreis: ....   Land: *Posen*

wird hierdurch bescheinigt, daß er / sie seit dem

15 . 10 . 37 - 20. 4. 42 in Krefeld   *Südwall 11*

gemeldet ist. *war*-

Im Auftrag:

Gebühr: 0.50 DM

Gebührenfrei

Stadtobersekretär

Certificate attesting to my parents' last address in Krefeld, between 1937 and 1942

Ehefrau Emilie Kober geb. Ivery
12.11.91 in Beuel
v. 15.10.37 - 20.4.42 gemeldet Südwall 11

London, February (1968)

Welcoming party at Freiburg railway station (around 1976): Judy Grosch with Juli Alexander Albickar, myself and Grete Borgmann

Reunion of my former fellow pupils from Bonn on a trip to Windsor (1985). Stephen is standing to my right

Presentation by pupils and teachers at Medinghoven school. (1996)

Der Verein der Freunde und Förderer

der

Realschule Medinghoven

ernennt

Frau Margot Barnard

in Anerkennung ihrer Verdienste um die Schülerinnen und Schüler
der Realschule Medinghoven

zum Ehrenmitglied

Seit nunmehr acht Jahren informiert Frau Barnard als Zeitzeugin
Schüler und Schülerinnen am Beispiel des eigenen über das
Schicksal jüdischer Mitbürger in der Zeit des Naziregimes. Mit
großem Engagement und Einfühlungsvermögen unterstützt sie damit ganz wesentlich das Anliegen von Eltern und Lehrern unserer
Schule, heutigen Jugendlichen die Notwendigkeit von Toleranz und
gegenseitigem Verständnis begreif- und nachvollziehbar zu
machen.

Bonn, den 4. September 1996

Karanis

Vorsitzende

*Certificate of honorary member-
ship of the Association of friends
and sponsors of Medinghoven
School (1996)*

'Begegnungswoche' (Reunion week, 2006). Bonn Town Hall reception. Left to right – Gerda Wiener (died 2008), former Mayor Hans Daniels, Mayoress Bärbel Dieckmann and myself

Giving the lecture 'Bonn-Palestine-England: The search for a new homeland' at the Haus der Geschichte (House of History, 2007)

27. Open Heart Surgery

I began to notice how pale and exhausted Ted looked. He came home after a thorough examination and said: "You know about the hole in my heart? That's the bad news. The good news is that it's now operable." I was convinced that an operation would be the right thing and encouraged him to agree to it. The doctors invited me to come and discuss it. Today, I know I was only given part of the picture. Had Uncle Sim been alive at the time, I would have been better prepared. I was also unaware that Ted's operation would be the first time open-heart surgery had been performed in Britain. So I was confident and planned a post-operative convalescent holiday. I was now 45 and had never felt better. Ted preferred to be on his own. It so happened that Bob had to go to Germany, in the course of his work for a vintner. Ted suggested that I accompany Bob as an interpreter, whilst he himself would go to Dover for a few days, to visit Stephen. On our return, Ted went into hospital. I tried hard to cheer him up and be a positive influence, but, for him, this was a terrible time. I was still optimistic on the morning of the operation. I walked round our garden enjoying the beautiful flowers Ted had planted. The neighbours came and asked after him. Then came a telephone call from the hospital. Even though the operation was over and Ted had opened his eyes, he wasn't well and I should come immediately. I raced to the hospital in a taxi and was taken to the intensive care unit. Ted was lying there motionless, tubes everywhere. I was ushered into a small room and a young doctor came to talk to me. As I stared out of the window, my eyes burning, I heard him say: "It's a pity the operation was unsuccessful, but your husband had, at most, only two more years. He would have been aware that he was getting weaker and weaker." My mind went blank – there was nothing but this terrible horror. How should I tell David and Stephen that their father was dead? I remember praying: Dear God, you can have my arm, even my right arm, if I can be spared having to tell the boys. Bob arrived in tears. The matron came, also in tears, and told us how Ted had entertained the whole ward in the days before his operation. Bob drove me home. David asked: "Has father gone?" After all these years, I can still hear those sad words. The boys never got over the loss of their father. Bob supported me over the next few days. He had already sold his house and was living with us while waiting for a council house. My cousin Walter was beside himself, railing angrily against the doctors. "You should insist on a post-mortem and sue for compensation; something must have gone wrong." I begged him to calm down. Ted's eldest brother, who never visited us, despite often driving past the house, told me that he couldn't come to the funeral as he was working that day. He did come in the end, but only after I had appealed to his conscience. I couldn't picture the funeral, but still managed to organise everything with great care. I went to the dress shop I had been to with Ted only two months earlier. The shop assistant remembered how impressed she had been when, with my indecision between two dresses, Ted had insisted we buy both. Friends and family came to the funeral. As I was getting into the taxi with the two boys, David asked whether I would be going back to Israel now. I assured him that I wouldn't even consider it. I was deeply touched that it was a cemetery worker, a young black Nigerian, who threw the first three spades of earth into Ted's grave.

On the day Ted was buried, I was already given a foretaste of what the future held. Some friends neither came to the funeral nor apologised for not coming. Later, someone explained to me that women didn't socialise with widows because they posed a threat to their husbands. I often experienced this kind of jealousy, but I was not prepared for the isolation that accompanied it. Sometimes the rejection was discreet, sometimes less so. I noticed the same behaviour amongst my relatives. One day, in desperation, I telephoned a cousin and asked if I could come and visit her. Her response: "Yes, you can come but you can't talk about anything personal because we have friends here."

The problems confronting me were entirely different now. David had left college, played his guitar ceaselessly, and seemed to have lost his way. Shortly before Ted's death, he had told his father that he would rather go on stage than go to college. Ted had advised him to finish his studies first. "After that," he said, "we'll see what I can do for you." I was very worried about David, who didn't seem to be coping. Stephen wanted to leave boarding school. He complained about the way his teachers treated him and begged to be allowed to come home. I refused, as my own situation was uncertain and I felt he would be better off at boarding school. Then there was Bob, who was pestering me to marry him. Everyone who knew us thought it was predetermined. But even if I had wanted to, it was far too soon. Bob had, it seems, always loved me, and Ted had apparently suspected it. We had been a well-rehearsed and harmonious team, but things were different now. However much I appreciated Bob's support, I felt under constant pressure from him. I was still grieving, and marriage was the last thing on my mind.

I found a job in a ladies dress shop. The owner was Jewish and roughly my age. His wife was young and blonde and had a child from her first marriage. There were two more employees apart from me. I really enjoyed advising customers, who felt that I understood their needs and so were prepared to buy. My boss was, of course, very pleased. It turned out that he, too, had been in the RAF during the war and, like me, had been stationed in Heliopolis. We sometimes exchanged little comments harking back to the war – as war veterans do. I also noticed that the more dresses I sold, the ruder his wife was to me. One day, a customer bought six dresses at once. The boss's wife screamed at me that this was not a good way to sell. "She'll only come back tomorrow to return the dresses and ask for her money back." Of course, the customer did not come back. Despite this sort of harassment, I stayed on.

❧

When Stephen did well in his exams, I began to think about a holiday. A travel agency had recently opened opposite the dress shop and, for the first time, I heard about package holidays, which seemed practical and affordable. Stephen was all in favour and looked forward to it. We plumped for Gabicci Mare in Italy – and it turned out to be a great success. On the first evening, I knew I would have to rack my brain to think of how to introduce Stephen to this colourful world. We walked along the garishly lit promenade and then went to a café, where I noticed a very pretty Italian girl sitting at a table with her grandmother. Without hesitation, I made directly for them, bumping clumsily into their table. I said in English: "Oh, sorry." And the beautiful Italian girl replied, in perfect English. "Are these seats taken? May we sit here?" The grandmother encouraged us to join them. And so Stephen began a romantic friendship. The young Italian girl was a student and introduced Stephen to her fellow students, from then on I saw very little of him. He was busy with picnics on the beach and drank alcohol for the first time in his life and at other times he was intoxicated by the sea, the sun and freedom. After winning first prize in a competition dancing the 'fashionable' dance, the Shake, he acquired the nickname 'the Shaker'. One evening, the grandmother, her granddaughter, Stephen and I all went to a lovely restaurant, where one could also dance. My son wasn't best pleased the first time his mother was asked to dance and liked it no better the second time – but he learnt that his mother had a different side. I, too, found the company congenial and made friends with a German couple from Munich, who I went on a few excursions with. I also enjoyed the attentions of an attractive Frenchman. It was good that Stephen and I were able to relax and enjoy ourselves after the difficult time we had had.

David, meanwhile, had 'dropped out' altogether and was giving me cause for concern. He hung around Bournemouth, living off the proceeds of casual work, but, above all, played his guitar. He returned to London and turned up one day with a pretty young girlfriend. They both had long hair. David was busking on the streets of London with his guitar, accompanied by an Irishman on the violin. This was the early days of 'swinging London' and the buskers – a British tradition – were an integral part of it: musicians playing in the street, in pubs and wherever the opportunity presented itself. Although I considered myself broadminded where my children were concerned, I was unhappy about David's activities. I had to resist the expectations of a Jewish mother, who wanted her son to be a surgeon, at the very least – I didn't quite manage it.

I continued working in the dress shop and took every Wednesday afternoon off. One Wednesday, I dressed up and went into town. From Marble Arch – where a new pedestrian underpass linked both sides of Oxford Street – came the sound of distant music. Turning the next corner, I saw David, his face covered by his long hair, with a cap on the ground in front of him. He sang raptly and sounded really good. All of a sudden, I was standing in front of him. Sweeping his hair away from his face, he said, in a deep voice: "Hello Mum, I knew you'd come one day." I put on a relaxed front and suggested going for a cup of tea somewhere. He was delighted and we were able to talk.

Bob and his children were still living with me in Bexleyheath, which I found difficult, even though both his son and Stephen were at boarding school. His daughter wanted her father all to herself whilst at the same time wanting to exploit my good nature. The time came when I decided that I would not, under any circumstances, marry Bob. He showed his disappointment by avoiding me and, having been allocated a council house, he moved out and we didn't see each other again. Our lovely home in Bexleyheath was no longer the same after Ted's death – it had died with Ted, so to speak. The few acquaintances in Bexleyheath weren't enough to keep me going and so I decided to move to London. The question was, where? I asked my cousin Walter to advise me. "You're on your own," was his reply. At that time, it was almost impossible to find anything but, using my instinct and with God's help, I managed to find the right needle in this haystack. And the house in Bexleyheath went on the market. Among the potential buyers was a charming Indian family with four well brought up daughters. When they came to view the house, the children sat round the table like organ pipes. I would have liked to sell the house to them but they were unable to pay the asking price. Then the neighbours stopped speaking to me. In the end, I sold to a man with an ice cream business, whose ice cream vans returned at night playing their jingles. When I called to say goodbye and asked about their strange behaviour towards me, I was told that my intention to sell to "blacks" had been unacceptable, because it devalued their property. Instead, my bigoted neighbours ended up with the irritating noise of the ice cream jingles!

As a temporary solution, I found a small but adequate flat. But not before being the victim of "gazumping". I asked Walter what I should do and he advised me to go ahead. I knew I could raise the extra couple of hundred pounds, but I was disappointed when I saw the flat in Gloucester Avenue for the first time. It was one of a number of converted flats in a street that was scruffy and neglected at one end and upwardly mobile at the other, Primrose Hill, end. A few well-known people had already settled there and the trend continued, thus – happily for me – ensuring that the value of my flat increased.

8. Life in London

It didn't take me long to adapt to my new surroundings, and I soon felt at home in the metropolis. I knew it wouldn't be easy to find a circle of people who would be interested in me. After all, I didn't have the right entry ticket and just being a nice person was probably not enough. At the time I moved to Gloucester Avenue, my cousin was in adult education, teaching politics and German drama. I attended his, and other, lectures and was very taken with them. At last I was re-surfacing after the shock of losing my husband. There were new friends who helped me and old ones who disappointed me. Maybe my expectations were too high.

Stephen now had the opportunity to get to know London nightlife during the holidays. The friends he brought home felt at ease in our little flat. As often as not, coming from a conservative, English middle-class background, they enjoyed the somewhat unconventional environment I provided. At night, they went to cellar bars to listen to jazz and ended up falling asleep there. Things were still difficult with David; he was living with a girlfriend and still played, but rejected any attempts to interest him in other things. All I could do was help where possible.

My time in Gloucester Avenue was intended as a springboard, but, above all, I needed money to support my family, hence the idea of letting one of the three rooms, preferably to a German student. I discussed it with my cousin Walter, who agreed that one should offer one's hand to Germany's younger generation, to show them that they were not held responsible for the terrible past. I steeled myself against the hostility I knew I would encounter from many in the émigré community. There was a busy German butcher's on the corner, where many young foreigners did their shopping. I asked the butcher if he knew of a German student who was looking to rent a room. Shortly after, he sent a young man we nicknamed 'Kaiser Wilhelm'. He was small and wore a smart suit with a loud tie. Hans-Jürgen was a law student who had a six month internship with a solicitor. He had a sense of humour and was easy-going. When he left, his friend Theo took over the room. Theo came from Aumühle, a small village near Hamburg, and was training in the hotel and catering trade. He had previously worked in a big hotel in France, whilst studying French at university. Thereafter, he worked at the Hilton in Madrid, where he specialised in gastronomy. It was there that he met his future wife, Rosie, a beautiful Spanish woman. Now he was working at the Hilton in London. His father had died in a British prisoner-of-war camp. Theo knew I was Jewish. He became a friend of the family and stayed for about two years. When Stephen came home from boarding school, we would talk late into the night. On one occasion, I drew back the curtains and was astonished to see that we had talked all night!

Whilst visiting a friend in Hamburg, she suggested that we go to Aumühle for the day because it was lovely there. "Excellent!" I exclaimed, enthusiastically, "I can visit Theo's mother and bring greetings from her son!" In Aumühle, I stopped someone in the street and asked if she knew Theo's family. Not only did she know where his mother lived, but also knew that she was visiting her daughter, who owned a shoe shop. As it was Sunday and the shop was closed, I knocked at the door and the daughter opened it rather indignantly. She invited me in and introduced me to her mother, an elderly white-haired lady, who was sitting in the kitchen. She reacted somewhat coldly, and I realised that, for some reason, I was not welcome. The sister had a sad look about her, but she and her husband were pleased to have met me. Theo was surprised that I had visited his family, but seemed pleased.

Theo and Rosie married and bought a house in Marbella, where Theo again worked at the Hilton. I visited them several times, latterly as a guest in their home, where I spent many happy hours. They had three children and eventually moved back to Germany, where I often visited them. Rosie learned German, which deepened our level of communication and brought us closer. The German magazine *Der Spiegel* was Theo's bible. He was well-informed and it was interesting to hear the opinions of a young German, born after the war, of his country and its politics. He had left Germany to avoid conscription. He rejected Nazi ideology but knew it had influenced his parents.

Of all major cities, London must have the most parks. I lived close to Primrose Hill and Regent's Park and took advantage of both, often going for walks with friends and also with Stephen. It was then that we had the opportunity to discuss problems. I was pre-occupied with my uncertain future, whilst at the same time trying to come to terms with my complexes – which included being socially accepted. One Sunday, Fay Weldon invited me over for drinks. On arrival, I was introduced to my fellow guests with the words: "This is Margot Barnard – but she is very nice!" The room was full of well-known actors and other celebrities. I felt like I didn't really belong but I tried, somehow, to hold my own and sometimes succeeded.

I had started to work at Boots again; it was 1967 and the year of the Israeli Six-Day War. People congratulated me daily on the Israeli victory, but I had mixed memories of Palestine. After the Arab defeat, Stephen was treated like a hero at school, whereupon he wrote to the Israeli government offering his services. Fortunately, I persuaded him to adopt a pacifist approach. We often joke about it even now.

Having given up my job as a shop assistant because standing for long hours was not good for me, I decided it was high time I visited my relatives in Israel – after all, I hadn't seen them for over twenty years. I booked my passage on two luxury Israeli steamers: on the outward journey, I sailed from Venice to Haifa on the *Moledet* and returned on the *Dan* to Marseille, from where I went to Paris to visit Uncle Sim's second wife. It was an unforgettable trip. While I was in the travel agency in Venice, confirming the booking, a woman asked me, in Hebrew, if I, too, was going to Israel. "Why don't we combine forces," she suggested. "The ship doesn't sail until tomorrow so we have time to explore Venice." She knew a good, inexpensive guesthouse where we could stay the night. She introduced herself as Dr. Anna Wildikann, a Jewish doctor from Lithuania who had worked for many years with Albert Schweitzer in his Lambarene forest hospital. She had stood by him and forcefully defended his work when it was alleged that the hospital fell short of acceptable standards of hygiene. She had left Lambarene because she had diabetes and now practised as a paediatrician in Jerusalem, where I subsequently often visited her. We used the time before our departure to visit the most important sights of Venice. Anna also came to visit me in London. She looked as she was: a domineering spinster. She wore her hair in an impressive plait around her head and her piercing blue eyes missed nothing. When she stayed with me, she started, already over breakfast, relating her experiences – mainly about her life in the forest.

But back to Venice. We boarded in bright sunshine and were in good spirits. There was a real mix of passengers, and the atmosphere was happy and relaxed. The entertainment was enjoyable and the food was excellent. There was dancing in the evenings. After a few days at sea, the MC came onto the dance floor. "We have a genuine *chaluza* on board – one of the many pioneers who helped build our country." People stood up and applauded. I was pushed onto the dance floor, people formed a circle round me and we danced the *hora*. I often found myself surrounded by some of the many young Israelis on board, asking me to tell them about my time in Palestine. I saw them as representative of Israel's new generation – free of prejudice, open-minded, and proud of their country. They compensated for my dread of being accused of deserting Israel.

We docked both in Greece and Turkey, which gave us the opportunity to do some sightseeing. And then, at last – amidst much rejoicing – we arrived in the port of Haifa, where my cousin Ruth was waiting to take me to Marianne and Joachim in Bialik. Marianne's parents, Mr and Mrs Knoch, had emigrated from Breslau (now Wroclaw) to Palestine in 1931 and had built one of the first houses in Bialik, a settlement between Haifa and Akko. Built in the Bauhaus style, it was reminiscent of all things German. Even the garden – laid out by Mrs Knoch – had something European about it. Although convinced that the Jews must have their own country, they neither could, nor would, give up their German culture. Frau Knoch refused to learn Hebrew. Marianne's appearance and lifestyle also remained completely German, despite having gone to school in Bialik. They belonged to the '*Jeckes*', German Jews who had immigrated in the 1920s and 1930s and who exercised considerable social influence at the time. Marianne and Joachim clung to this way of life. When I visited, we spoke German; if one of the children joined us, we spoke Hebrew. Whenever I visited Israel, I usually stayed with Marianne and Joachim, who, in the meantime, had moved to Mount Carmel. They lived in a modern flat with the heirloom Biedermeier furniture and bookcases full of Goethe, Schiller and Rilke. I always looked forward to the German cuisine. A dip in the sea and an afternoon nap were followed by coffee and home-made cake, especially cheese cake. Joachim would put on a record, usually Beethoven, and we watched as the lights in Haifa gradually came on.

The country had changed a great deal, but so had I. I went on guided tours, just like a tourist, but also visited my old kibbutz, Beth Sera – it was unrecognisable. My first port of call was the large dining room, where there was now a cold lemonade fountain and a large selection of salads. I asked after our former leader, Perez, who had been on my mind so often. I was told he was almost blind. The elderly man walking up the path looked just as he did back then, with his peaked cap, his working trousers and blue shirt. "Perez!" I called, in a tremulous voice. And he – I could hardly believe it – replied: "Miriam!" He recognised my voice after all these years. We fell into each other's arms and then he took me to his house. He was pleased that I was still able to converse so well in Hebrew and I spent several hours with him. Happy hours! Only then did I realise how fond he was of me. We were able to set the record straight in many respects. I was overjoyed when he told me that he didn't consider me a 'traitor'. He was sad that

I had left but understood why. I asked him what had become of the old comrades. Joseph, our shepherd, still lived in Beth Sera. He had a family and was still working as a shepherd. "Oh, so I can go and see him," I exclaimed, but Perez shook his head; Joseph worked hard and would be sleeping now, so he shouldn't be woken. I would have loved to see him but had to respect the different priorities here. I was shown the new bathing facilities and the factories. The chicken coops where I had worked stood empty and neglected. 'Lull' (chicken coop) was still written on the door, the only reminder of the well-organised and modern chicken farm that once existed. Then I took a bus tour along the Sea of Galilee, as far as the bridge leading to Syria. I told the tourist guide that Kibbutz Beth Sera had once been shot at from here. It was a strange feeling. Of the American tourists on the tour, a couple from New York caught my attention. He wore long checked shorts and a white Panama hat and slept most of the time, his large belly acting as a cushion for his photographic equipment Whenever we stopped to admire something, his wife would shake his arm and shout: "Chaim, Chaim!" at which he would jump up, rush out of the bus and start clicking. Two ladies with pinned up, yellow-white hair and conspicuously white teeth came up to me: "We've noticed that you understand all three languages the guide uses. We get the feeling that we're missing out in English, as the German and Hebrew explanations take much longer." I reassured them that the content was the same in all three languages.

29. 9 Rona Road

Returning to England, I decided to give my life a new direction. Offers of marriage didn't attract me. I enjoyed my independence too much. Of course, I had to earn money, so buying a house and subletting part of it was once again on the agenda. It wouldn't be easy, as there was very little on the market. One morning, I set off along Parkway towards Camden Town and found myself standing in front of a somewhat dilapidated Victorian building with the sign: Arnold Willy – Estate Agent. Two or three properties were advertised in the window, but I ignored them. I walked into the office, where a plump, blonde, elderly lady dressed in black asked what she could do for me. I told her I was looking to buy a house and that I was a widow with no income. She gave me a friendly nod, picked up the telephone and said "We've got someone." And that was the start of the strangest of house purchases. I arranged to meet Mr. Willy, who looked like the saviour of all widows. He was small and dapper, with a white moustache, wore a black coat and bowler hat, and carried an umbrella and a briefcase – a phenomenon known in England as "a stockbroker". It transpired that Mr. Willy owned a house he wanted to get rid of. He was looking for someone that would be prepared to record a lower purchase price, in order to avoid capital gains tax. I pretended to agree to this, even though I had no intention of playing his game. When Mr. Willy showed me the house, I was unaware that Hampstead Heath was only ten minutes away. It was a typical London terraced house on several floors, very spacious and ideal for letting. I was smitten by it. As instinct always played a decisive part in my life, I was sure that this house would watch over me in the next phase of my life.

"Buy a house? It'll be an albatross!" came the warning cries from my cousin and well-meaning friends – I turned a deaf ear. Arnold Willy tried to get me a mortgage but nobody wanted to lend money to a widow with no income. Using various devices, he finally managed to arrange a local authority mortgage, which, fortunately, happened to be the cheapest available. I did, however, have to prove that my son was going to occupy one floor. There was a quantity of beautiful furniture in the house, some of antiquarian value, which I bought from him cheaply, and I reminded him to take out contents insurance as the house was unoccupied. The following day, he rang apologetically to tell me I had been right: a fridge and a rug had been stolen during the night. It was, of course, he who had removed the items, but I let him believe that I was unaware of his little ruse. Then came the move. It was my intention to occupy the third floor and the attic, so modifications were necessary. With the help of an Irish builder, a Mr. Trainer, I successfully applied for planning permission and moved temporarily into the ground floor, whilst three tenants – young university lecturers, one of whom was a friend of Stephen's – moved into the first floor. We called them "the three musketeers".

I may have realised my dream but there were still problems. Firstly, the whole house was clad in scaffolding. Mr. Trainer, a competent builder, then discovered that the roof beams were riddled with wet rot. The surveyor recommended by Mr. Willy had clearly been instructed to adopt a generous approach to certain defects! Mr. Trainer recommended that I take the matter to court. Yet again, my friends tried to dissuade me, suggesting that this would be throwing good money after bad. And, once again, I followed my instinct and initiated proceedings. I had a nice Jewish solicitor from Manchester, but I made sure I understood what was going on, which was just as well as I ended up having to do much of the work myself. At the hearing, we all sat round an enormous table. I had brought along one of my tenants, who had witnessed the surveyor's attempts to pressurise me into withdrawing my claim. My solicitor sent a representative whose sole contribution was to smile. This is what happened: a so-called mediator wearing a black gown, white bands and wig, rosy-cheeked, small in stature but very agile, sashayed through the door in my direction and relayed my opponent's offer to settle out of court. I was convinced of the rightness of my cause and so rejected every offer, insisting on a hearing. My witness said I was as steadfast as the Rock of Gibraltar. At last I was called into the courtroom. The judge gave me a kindly look and said: "Half a loaf is better than none" and ordered my opponent to pay damages – the amount I had hoped for. It ruined the surveyor, for whom I had some sympathy for because he, too, was a victim of Mr. Willy.

Gradually, I started to get to know my neighbours. To my right lived a couple of indeterminate age, who lived by the motto: Don't interfere in other people's business. The wife was a secretary at the BBC. Every Saturday morning, she would scrub the entrance to her house and we would talk at length about the weather, an inexhaustible topic for her, so there was never any danger that the conversation would dry up. Her husband was an electrician of an extremely nosy disposition. "How old are you?" "You go out a lot! Where d'you go? What do you do?" After the death of his wife, he seemed intent on getting his feet under my table; after all, he was extremely lonely. He died some years later and, one day, two young men knocked at my door. Could they ask me some questions about Mr Thomas, my former neighbour? Did I know he had been a multi-millionaire and had left everything to Dr. Barnardo's! I told them that we had got on well, although shortly after I had moved in, he had offered to fix my electric lawnmower when he saw I was having problems with it. He tightened the plug and returned the mower, saying "That'll be half-a-crown." At first I thought – wrongly – that he was joking. No wonder he was so rich!

On the other side lived a family with two children. He was Jamaican and had been in the RAF. One day, they took in an elderly relative who was ill with cancer. They put her up in a small room in the attic where – day and night – the poor woman screamed with pain. This went on for months and, as my bedroom was on the other side of the wall to hers, I asked them to take her to hospital; they insisted that she did not want to go. One day I fell ill. When my doctor heard about the situation next door, he arranged for the lady's immediate admission to hospital, where she died shortly afterwards. Soon afterwards the family moved away and the house was bought by the council. It had been empty for some time when squatters moved in. I approved, as there was still a housing shortage in London in 1970, despite the building of new housing. Large families were often accommodated in inadequate guesthouses. There was also countless supplies of empty old housing stock. The inhabitants of Rona Road were mainly older, conservative workers, who regarded me as a foreigner and, because my sympathies were with the squatters, gave me strange looks. However, once it became known that I had fought with the British during the war, I was declared to be 'OK' and was tolerated.

This was the era of the miniskirt, busking, hippies, drugs – in short, "Flower Power" – imported from San Francisco. Every celebrity had an Indian guru. My sons enlightened me on how squatters got by. One Sunday, one of the young men walked straight into my kitchen and helped himself to some of my roast. He didn't ask permission and I was outraged. David and Stephen explained that this was called having the 'mangies', a condition that kicks in after using drugs that makes one hungry and totally lacking in inhibition. The squatters soon moved out and the council allocated the house to a family with fourteen children. Some of the older girls had children of their own. Within weeks, the house became a scrap yard – the new neighbours were tinkers. When Stephen came to visit in his new car, the radio had been stolen by the next morning. Then they broke into the ground floor. When I challenged the boys next door about it, they sneered and called me a "dirty Jew woman!" How did they know I was Jewish? I only saw their mother once. She was standing outside her front door and called over to me: "Hello, I'm Mrs So-and-So!" She was petite, possibly about 38 and completely toothless. She told me that she had run away from her family and wasn't going back. Every word was preceded by the word 'bloody'. We all breathed a sigh of relief when the family was re-housed.

The workmen were still in the house. The foreman was a hard-working man; he converted the top floor – which is still my home – into a maisonette on three levels. Gradually, the problems were resolved and I concentrated full-time on the subletting project. I was extremely careful when selecting candidates and thought I was pretty good at judging people. But one should never judge a book by its cover. The young bank clerk that came for the interview dressed in a suit and tie with short, back and sides, suddenly appeared naked at my front door and I had great difficulty getting rid of him. But the boy with the long hair, whose trousers were held together with safety pins, who regarded himself as anti-establishment, and whose parents lived in the exclusive The Bishops Avenue, turned out to be an especially quiet member of our community.

After Ted died, I severed contact with my Freiburg friends; I found it hard to tell them that Ted was no longer alive. I made a few unsuccessful attempts, but the shock of his death had a paralysing effect on me. One day, Steve Ginn, one of my former tenants and a good friend, came to see me. He had been appointed a lecturer in mathematics at Birkbeck University. He had been invited to a conference near Freiburg and was intending to drive there. At some point, I had told him about the Borgmanns in Freiburg and he now suggested that I accompany him and his wife Jay and avail myself of the opportunity to see old friends. I saw it as a sign from on high, so wrote to the Borgmanns asking if they would like to see me and told them about Ted. Grete replied by return that I should come; they couldn't understand why they hadn't heard from me for so long. In August 1970, I travelled with Steven and Jay to the Black Forest. As our route took us via Bonn, I decided to visit Uncle Fritz and Aunt Marta. I didn't mention that my relatives lived in a mansion and that they had some preconceived ideas about the English, especially those with doctorates. We were invited for lunch and arrived punctually. Silver platters with selected delicacies were placed on the damask tablecloth, and Uncle Fritz produced a bottle of his best wine. After dinner, we were given a conducted tour of the house, after which my aunt said: "But you have all this in England, only even more beautiful." I made a few judicious changes in my translation; and, fortunately, my aunt and uncle never visited me in London so they had their own picture of my lifestyle.

It was wonderful to see the Borgmann family in Freiburg again, and I was happy to have renewed my contact with them. We turned a new page in our friendship. They invited me to their next New Year's Eve party and I stayed with them until Steven and Jay came to collect me.

ॐ

There were two tenants living on the ground floor at 9 Rona Road I regarded as part of my eccentric menagerie. One worked in television, the other was a nurse, a Buddhist with whom I had many deep conversations about Buddhism, although he often struck me as distracted. It was a sunny day when I returned from my Freiburg visit. Looking down from the roof terrace, I saw my Buddhist tenant lying on the grass, reading peacefully. I'll say hello to my tenants tomorrow, I thought. The next day, I was sweeping the stairs. The house was very quiet. I had an odd feeling when the telephone rang on the ground floor. Normally I didn't pay attention to what was going on in the house, but this seemed to be a warning. The ringing stopped. Then came the piercing sound of the doorbell. I opened the door and the Buddhist's girlfriend rushed past me and opened the door to his room. I followed and saw her leaning over the bed. He lay there motionless. She felt his pulse, turned to me and said: "He's dead! Could you please call his mother? Here's the number." I was shocked but managed to stay calm and inform his mother and the police. Then I called for Stephen to come downstairs, as Mr Miller had died. The door of the 'three musketeers' flat opened and a voice said: "If the ground floor flat becomes available – I assume his friend won't want to stay – could I possibly have it?" I was speechless. When the young man's mother and stepfather arrived, I invited them in. "My son was very intelligent", she said. "What a waste of all that studying." Again, I was lost for words. Two police officers came and inspected his room. They examined the body for signs of drug abuse. They told me that the corpse would be collected and that no one should enter the room in the meantime. It was then that I learned that my tenant was the son of a murderer and rapist – I had read about the trial in the newspapers – and had given evidence against his father. He had been the only one to maintain contact with his father. His mother had divorced and remarried. His girlfriend told me that he had been considering suicide for a long time. Only then did I understand some of his behaviour, which I hadn't been able to explain before. His friend did indeed move out and Keith, the musketeer on the first floor, took over the flat. On the instructions of the police, the room remained locked. One day, I caught Keith in there. He had obviously found a key and had let himself in. When challenged, he pretended to be searching for a pencil. Much later, it turned out that he had necrophiliac tendencies. It was years before we all recovered from the shock of the suicide.

Then came the joy of grandchildren. First came David's daughter Delia, followed two years later by her little brother Leo. The ten years that followed were, above all, dedicated to my family. David and his partner lived in a flat in my cousin Walter's house, not far from Rona Road. Between 1971 and 1981, my grandchildren came to me almost every weekend. We always made grand plans, in which Hampstead Heath played an important part. When they were a little older and more sure-footed, I showed them London. Leo was now four and I decided it was time to share my eagerness for culture with the children. One day, in the solemn silence of the National Gallery, Leo exploded: "I'm bored!" After that, I became less ambitious. I promised to show them Buckingham Palace. We walked from Trafalgar Square down The Mall, fed the ducks and arrived at the Palace. "Where's the Queen?" asked Delia, her disappointment evident. After all, she thought she was going to see the Queen, complete with crown.

One day, David telephoned and asked if I had any plans for the following Friday morning. I replied in the negative. "In which case, would you look after the children as Jenny and I want to get married." I was taken aback but agreed, provided his brother Stephen was a witness. And so the children came to me while my oldest son entered into matrimony. And, as I hadn't been invited, I saved myself the bother of a hat.

Stephen had always been very fond of Bob and often talked about him. One day, he surprised me by announcing that he had found Bob again. It seemed that Bob wanted us to meet. We took up where we had left off and his children were pleased, too. He worked in a bank; he was well but felt lonely. At first everything was as before. Bob had a car and we would go on holiday to the northern extremities of Scotland. He showed me Durham, with its cathedral, and the small village where he was from, and we visited his elderly mother and aunts. We had a wonderful time. Bob still wanted to marry me, but I was not prepared to give up my independence and so we parted again. Stephen maintained his friendship with Bob and with his daughter until Bob died of cancer, weakened by the infamous beriberi disease he had contracted whilst a Japanese prisoner-of-war.

Gradually, Christmas and New Year took on a regular pattern. I would always spend my birthday on Christmas Eve with friends and family. The party would start on the evening of 23 December, at midnight was the cutting of the birthday cake and everyone would sing 'Happy Birthday'. This was the moment that reminded me of my survival. On the 25th, I celebrated Christmas with the children and grandchildren. After that, I would travel to Freiburg to visit the Borgmanns, whose large family included at least 13 grandchildren. Over New Year, they always had guests from all corners of the globe. I enjoyed being there because there were always interesting people to meet and talk to.

One of the annual rituals in the Borgmann household was the carnival ball. As an old Rhinelander, I derived great pleasure out of dressing up, and this was usually the only festival I would go to during the year. The Rhenish spirit was something Grete and I had in common. At the last Ball, she dressed up as a man and I didn't recognise her. I was also invited to family celebrations during the summer and sometimes participated in events put on by the 'women's circle', of which Grete was the chair. I was especially interested in support for women in the developing world and learned a great deal from the project known as "A new start for the woman". I maintained my friendship with the Borgmann children as they grew up, went to university and got married. If there was one thing that helped me through difficult times, it was the understanding and affection I received from this family. There was always something to laugh about when we met. Once, I took Delia, then eleven, with me to Freiburg. As we sat down to lunch, I explained to her why one crossed oneself and thanked God. Delia crossed herself twice; when asked why, she replied: "Because the meal was so good!"

One of the highlights of New Year's Eve was my fortune-telling for the Borgmann family and friends. And despite some strange outcomes, considered by many of my friends and acquaintances to be unlikely, I was asked time and again to tell their fortunes. I was sometimes reluctant but always discreet. Sometimes I was able to help, especially young people with relationship problems. Some friends believed that Grete had a "direct line to God." I recall a particular experience with her in 1985 when, once again, I travelled to Freiburg for New Year's Eve. Grete told me that she and Karl were rather tired and didn't feel up to throwing a big party this year. I was invited to her daughter Eva's holiday home in the Vosges, and she would find me a cheap train to Colmar where I would be met. I went up to my room to pack my overnight bag and stowed away my travelling pack of Tarot cards, which Stephen had given me. I always put the pack in the same side pocket of my overnight bag. Whilst I was packing, I changed my mind and returned to the living room. "Grete – I would far rather spend New Year here with you and Karl" I told her. "Oh, that's nice," she said. "Go upstairs and unpack." And then she added; "Maybe you could do a Tarot reading for me." I went back to my room, unpacked, and reached into the side pocket for the cards – but they weren't there. In disbelief, I turned the suitcase upside down. Everything fell out except the cards. The next day, the housekeeper and I combed the whole room – in vain. Many months later, Delia, who always liked to take needy friends under her wing, telephoned me and asked if I would do a reading for someone who was in trouble. I invited them over for tea. Delia recounted how, one day, a pack of Tarot cards had suddenly appeared on her school bench. I asked her to bring the cards the next time she came – and, sure enough, they were the cards that had gone missing in Freiburg. There is no rational explanation, but it is possible that Grete – strong willed as she is – didn't really want to have her cards read that day.

Meantime, the attitude of the British towards the Holocaust had changed. Post-war films showed red-faced, thick-necked German soldiers, simple and stupid officers speaking comical English with a German accent, implied that these attributes had contributed to Germany losing the war. Then came the feature films and documentaries, mostly emanating from the USA, with gruesome images from the concentration camps. One could buy any number of books written by Holocaust survivors, but also by the second generation. All of this greatly interested me, and I went to lectures and took part in discussions. Although my family could understand that I was working for peace and reconciliation, they still laboured under a misapprehension. Only much later did I discover that David had long harboured the belief that I never spoke about the murder of my own parents because they had done something terrible. Otherwise, people just aren't killed! The British talked about the *Kindertransport* with pride . After the night of 9-10 November 1938 – *Kristallnacht* – the British government had responded to pleas from influential Jews and had agreed to accept German Jewish children up to the age of 17. The first *Kintertransport* left Berlin on 1 December 1938, bound for London. A total of 10,000 children were brought to safety. My thoughts went out to my parents, who had neither been granted permission to emigrate to Britain, nor benefited from the limited number of visas for Palestine, handed out by the British. At the time, the world had not been prepared to save the persecuted Jews, and especially not those without money. The affidavit of support signed by our American relatives reached Germany only after my parents' death. Television, too, aired documentaries and feature films, from *Holocaust* and *Shoah* to *Schindler's List*, the latter being particularly successful. It showed the cruelty realistically, as is only possible in film. The protagonist, Oskar Schindler, a German industrialist, had (partly for selfish reasons) saved the lives of a thousand Jews. Based on a true story, the film was shown in many schools.

In battling with my own demons, I was plagued with endless questions: how would I have behaved had I not been Jewish? Would I have supported the Nazis? Like many of my contemporaries, I belonged to the *Wandervogel* movement, and loved the close connection with nature, which was also promoted by the *Hitler Youth* and the *BDM*. This was something I had to grapple with – and I had my doubts.

30. Bearing Witness

In the 1980s, a letter arrived from the city of Bonn setting out plans for a *Begegnungswoche* (literally "Get Together Week") for its former Jewish citizens, those who had been forced to leave Bonn during the Nazi era. Having searched for me for some time, they had finally obtained my address from the Restitution Office. I wrote, as instructed, to a Mrs. Downing in Norfolk, expressing my interest and asking for more information. By return of post came the reply: If you are Margot Kober, then I am Marianne Katz! Marianne and I had been at school together. She told me that, somewhat apprehensively, she had accepted an invitation to a school reunion in 1981, but had been warmly welcomed.

The Bonn *Begegnungswoche* became an annual event. The costs of the first visit were borne by the city of Bonn. It was now 1983, and Stephen was prepared to accompany me. It was an unforgettable experience. Although I had often thought about my old school, I never had the courage to get in touch with my former classmates. And, having left Germany in 1936, I didn't know who was still alive. Stephen and I were put up in an exclusive hotel. Mayor Daniels hosted a reception at the town hall for all *Begegnungswoche* participants, after which we all met at the Königshof Hotel. There were familiar faces everywhere. Stephen whispered to me to look round: my former classmates had formed a guard of honour. I recognised them instantly, and we all embraced each other. From then on, some or all of my five Jewish classmates living abroad tried to meet every year. It was certainly an event in our lives that contributed to the healing process. Bonn was one of the first cities to organise a reunion of this nature; others followed suit. And the practice developed of inviting survivor witnesses into schools to tell their stories. The *Begegnungswochen* were happy occasions for the survivors, but they also had a positive political effect. For Stephen, the visit was an important experience – it gave him the opportunity for in-depth discussions with young Germans. In addition, he met some prominent West German politicians, amongst them the then Federal Chancellor Helmut Kohl, whose guests we were.

A reunion after so long also has its pitfalls. One automatically takes up where one left off. This meant that, for some of our group, I was still seen as the red-haired Zionist. For one of the reunions, I invited the group to London. Eight came and I arranged for them to stay in B&B accommodation not far from my home. Stephen was still working as the manager of a centre for the disabled and lived in a beautiful house in the attractive Oxfordshire countryside. He liked the whole idea so much that, through his work, he hired a minibus and collected the ladies from the airport. He also invited them to his home for lunch and took them on a sightseeing tour of Windsor Castle, a must for tourists! We painted the town red, went to see a Shakespeare play, and spent many happy hours in my home. Stephen thought it was interesting that we 'formers' met up in England, so he phoned the local paper. Although the editor was interested, at first, the interview was cancelled. The explanation we got was that they had too many Jewish readers that might not be too thrilled with the story.

Already, during my first visit to Bonn, one of the staff at the *Verein An der Synagoge* asked if I was willing to visit schools and talk about my life. I agreed and, in 1987, I visited a school for the first time and talked about my life in Beuel during the Nazi era, what happened to my parents and about my brother. At first, the children were shy and cautious, but they became increasingly interested and started asking questions.

The Spiro Institute in London is affiliated to Clemson University and offers courses in Jewish history, culture and language. It also organises visits by historical eye-witnesses to schools in Britain. I contacted the Institute and joined the school visits group. From the outset, the woman in charge of the group made her dislike for me clear. Against me was the fact that I talked to German children in Germany – she and some of members of the group found this unacceptable. Also against me was the fact that I hadn't been in a concentration camp. Furthermore, we differed on the rationale for the school visits. We had been told that our presentations were not intended to replace history lessons but rather, as eye witnesses to history, we should tell our personal story. It was my view that, whilst the eye witnesses' personal stories should take centre stage, young listeners lacked a deeper knowledge of the religious and historical connections, so it was essential to tell them about the history of the Jews in Europe, the pogroms, persecutions and discriminations. But then the Spiro Institute organised a three-day international conference, which I promoted in Bonn where I had met several teachers during my school visits. Six teachers from Bonn alone came to what was a very successful conference in London, and I also played my part as an eyewitness to history. Thereafter, the unfriendly attitude towards me gradually changed.

With the Bonn *Begegnungswochen* and my work in German and English schools, my life entered a new phase. As the work intensified, I realised that here was an opportunity for me to make a contribution to reconciliation with the past. This coincided with increasing interest in Germany for historical authenticity, not only in schools but also through organisations dedicated to anti-racism, peace and reconciliation. My first invitation came from a school whose pupils came from mainly problem families. The children sat there expectantly and thoroughly looked me up and down. No one wanted to ask the first question until, finally, some could no longer contain themselves: "How did you escape? Were you tortured? What else did they do to you?" were all accompanied by giggles, especially when a twelve-year old girl asked: "Is it true that, in the synagogue, the little Jewish boys have something cut off at the front?" I took a deep breath, and guided them away from the sensational back to a more serious track, so that they would learn that everything had a deeper meaning. I talked about my childhood in Beuel, about Jewish life, and about my own suffering. By the time I'd finished, they all seemed deeply moved.

The school visits in Germany increased over time, and I also started to speak regularly in English schools. Of course, British and German children differed in their attitudes toward me and what I represented. During the first few years, in particular, German children felt relieved to be able to talk openly about the past and to ask questions. They often complained that this was something they were unable to do at home. The British children were more influenced by the terrible pictures shown in the media, which played on sensationalism. Here, there was sometimes even greater ignorance. And it was far from easy to tell them my story. "Do you know the word anti-semitism?" "Do you know what Zionism is?" "Who was Jesus? Did you know he was a Jew?" They all looked at me wide-eyed. In one English classroom, during a religious studies lesson, it was only a 13-year-old Pakistani girl who was able to answer the question about Jesus: "I know who Jesus was. He was a Christian prophet." Although schoolchildren were supposed to have been properly briefed for our visits, and despite the fact that the Holocaust was part of the English school curriculum for this age group, most of the children knew only that Hitler had seized power in 1933, that he had started the Second World War, and had ordered the gassing of Jews. But, when I wanted to talk about specific events that resulted in the persecution of Jews, they wriggled uncomfortably in their chairs. The teachers, too, looked uncertain, because they were unprepared and obviously found it difficult to connect history and religion in a meaningful way.

My work with schools has resulted in many memorable experiences. On my arrival at a *Gesamtschule* (a comprehensive school) in Beuel, the teacher forewarned me with concern: "There are some badly behaved skinheads in the class." As I entered the room, a group of 15-year-old skinheads stood looking at me aggressively. At first they remained standing during my talk but eventually they sat down, listened attentively and even asked some good questions at the end. On another occasion, I was invited to visit an A-level class in Rudolf Hess's former school in Bad Godesberg. The headmaster warned me that there were some rightwing extremists in the class. "If they don't want to listen to you," he said, "just pick up your coat and leave!" I don't usually prepare for such lectures – after all, I know my own story – and adapt to the atmosphere I find. This was not the first time I had been warned in this way, so I didn't allow myself to be distracted and began with: "I have come to Germany voluntarily to tell you about my experiences as a Jew. If you don't want to listen, or if you get bored, just get out!" There was some nervous laughter, after which you could have heard a pin drop. At the end of the lesson, they asked me and the teacher of the subsequent class if we could continue. They wanted to hear more about Israel. Far from detecting any anti-semitic or extreme right ideas from the young men, I found them likeable, well-informed young Germans who treated me with respect and understanding.

If there was one event in my life my young listeners almost invariably sympathized with, it was that I had had to leave my parents at such a young age, never to see them again. The countless letters I received after each visit confirmed this. But there was also the surprising reaction of the 19-year-old who reproached me with the question: "How could you just desert your parents? You left them high and dry!" My attempt to explain how things were at the time and that my parents were probably relieved that at least their children were safe, was unsuccessful. Of course, the questioner couldn't know of my inner turmoil then and my sense of guilt. On another occasion, I was invited to speak to a group of young Catholic men. They listened attentively when I spoke of my church visits as a child, where we were always told that Jesus had been crucified by the Jews, a version that will have contributed significantly to violent anti-semitism. I explained that this version did not reflect the historical facts but was an anti-semitic interpretation. After all, Jesus himself had been a Jew and, what is more, it was the Romans and not the Jews who had crucified him. The young men listened with fascination. After a silence, one member of the audience burst out: "I've never heard it explained like that!" I experienced this reaction in German schools and also at an English convent school (who never invited me back).

When, in 1987, inexperienced in such things, I began the dialogues in German schools, I was extremely fortunate to be invited by one school that helped pave the way: the *Realschule* in Medinghofen near Bonn. I was made to feel welcome from the start and the teachers accepted me as one of their own. It was noticeable from the outset that the children had been well prepared. After my talk, it became a tradition that I joined the other teachers for a meal. I sensed their interest in the project, and we have stayed in touch to this day. A few years ago I was especially honoured when the school's director and the parents' association presented me with a certificate in recognition of my work. This school is representative of the many schools I have visited over the years that have been so committed to the principle of reconciliation. In my view, the mutual effort has resulted in awakening an understanding of the past and of the reconciliation process. Over the years, I have noticed that the younger generations are able to approach the issues without guilt and with the necessary objectivity, but also with seriousness and interest.

Of course, I encountered other reactions outside my work in schools. Travelling by train from Freiburg to Neustadt to visit friends, I was reading an English book. An elderly couple in hiking clothes sat down opposite me. I gathered from their whispered conversation that they were trying to guess where I was from. I didn't leave them in the dark for long and said: "Lovely weather today!" in German. The wife was pleased: "Yes, lovely." Then she came straight to the point: "You speak without an accent. Where are you from?" I didn't beat about the bush: "I'm Jewish – I emigrated to Palestine many years ago." She leaned forward and no doubt thought she was paying me a huge compliment when she exclaimed: "One would never have guessed!" Then there was the event that answered a question which had long preoccupied me. One day I received a telephone call from the Bonn Memorial Centre, which coordinated my school visits. A woman had apparently seen my picture in the newspaper and had left a message saying she had been at school with me. I didn't recognise the name but phoned anyway, because I thought it might be the girl who sat with us at lunch once a week and who had stood 'guard' in *BDM* uniform outside our door on that boycott Saturday, back in 1933. "I don't know your name and we didn't go to school together." We decided to meet up during my next visit to Bonn. When I entered the café, she recognised me instantly but I didn't recognise her. We sat opposite each other drinking coffee. "You look very like your mother," she said. "What a good woman she was! Your father and your brother were also really kind to me. It was so lovely in your house and so peaceful. But now…" She pulled a large photo album from her bag and showed me pictures of a house, a car, a husband and two grown-up daughters. "But now," she said raising her voice slightly, "as you can see, I am not so poor any more that I have to go to Jews to eat." I asked her "Don't you even want to know what happened to my poor parents? That they were gassed by the Nazis?" She was sorry to hear that. I asked why she had positioned herself outside our house, wearing the *BDM* uniform. "We all had to do it," she replied. "Not at that time," I said, to which she replied: "My husband mustn't find out that I was once so poor I had to eat at a Jew's house." I have never told anyone about it but I was shattered by the experience. Only later did I understand that, for her, my mother's goodness was a humiliation she was desperate to blot out.

A friend of the Borgmann family behaved in a similarly singular manner. I knew that the Borgmanns had helped Jews escape during the Nazi era, among them, the writer Lotte Paepcke. After Grete had told me, I started reading Lotte Paepcke's books and enjoyed them very much. In *Unter einem fremden Stern* she writes about being rescued but does not mention her rescuers' names, neither did she mention them when she talked about her life on TV. Lotte came to visit whilst I was staying with the Borgmanns. I liked her immediately. Of course, we knew about each other and it was as though nothing else needed to be said. She told us that she had registered for a place in a residential home so as not to be a burden on her children. Her manner towards Grete was not unfriendly but cool. If she was grateful to her rescuers she didn't show it. I didn't understand and was disappointed.

❧

Throughout the years during which I undertook the reconciliation work, I hoped for a rapprochement with my brother. When I went to my first *Begegnungswoche* with Stephen in Bonn, I was asked whether my brother might also be prepared to take part and I phoned Walter immediately. His spontaneous reaction was an outright refusal. He added that he couldn't leave his wife on her own as she wasn't well. I begged him to reconsider – it wouldn't cost him anything, apart from which, it would be an opportunity for him to meet my family. In 1989, he changed his mind and was prepared to come to Germany – but not England. He eventually agreed to this, too. but not before I had screamed hysterically down the telephone: "Don't you want to meet my family?" The children were very curious about meeting their uncle, but I also sensed a certain reticence: after all, he was a stranger. The day of his arrival dawned and I drove to collect Walter from the airport with Stephen. I was both excited and nervous; it was several years since we had last seen each other. What did he look like now? How would he react to my family and they to him? As the passengers streamed into the arrivals hall, Stephen suddenly shouted: "That's got to be your brother!" pointing to an Orthodox Jew who had just appeared. I was still laughing when, suddenly, there stood my brother, smiling. Much to Walter's delight, Stephen drove back through Central London. My brother had lived in London for a while, after fleeing Germany in 1937, and now he was revisiting some of his haunts. My family immediately took to him and he was thrilled with his new relatives. There was a lot of laughter and story-telling, and I couldn't have been happier. The Holocaust was never mentioned.

Then we travelled to Germany together. Many of the former Bonn Jews were still alive and came to the *Begegnungswoche*. Walter was put up in a hotel and I stayed with friends. By then, he was looking forward to meeting old acquaintances, and particularly enjoyed seeing our old teacher, Herr Hammerstein, with whom he had been interned in England. Hammerstein gave a talk about the teaching profession and teacher training, which was well received. Walter walked through the old, familiar streets of Beuel and knocked on the doors of former neighbours. They were very excited to see Walter Kober standing there and told him as much. But he seemed ill at ease. He wasn't 'coming home'; his memories were of a very different – and far more terrible – order than mine. My early emigration had spared me his terrible experiences. My brother always refused to discuss those years with me. What he did tell me was that, after *'Kristallnacht'* in November 1938, he had managed to get to Holland on a forged passport. It must have been terrifying, because he told me how his passport was checked repeatedly and, on each occasion, he was frightened to death. He worked for Uncle Leo, who had escaped from prison in Bonn and had fled to Holland, where he had opened another butcher's shop. Three months later, Walter was summoned by the police and informed that he would be deported to Germany because there were too many refugees in Holland. A police officer took Walter to the border by bicycle and warned him not to return to Holland. Once in Germany, he was taken to Herford prison where he received help from the outside. Ordinary people smuggled food into the prison in return for payment. Somehow, he got the address of a woman who helped him to escape to England, after which he was interned in Kent. It was from there that he had sent me the postcard to Palestine. He had wanted to join the British Army, but that wasn't possible. Together with other Germans, he was sent to Canada and interned again. My brother is also a victim of National Socialism and his experiences have shaped his life. Although it is sad that I know so little about him, at least I now understand why he has found it so difficult to talk about his traumatic past.

A few years ago, I was invited to Beuel to speak at a *Kristallnacht* commemoration event. I asked Walter to write something about his experiences that night in Krefeld. This is what he sent me in 1999:

I was woken in the early hours of the morning by the racket in the street. I just about had time to put some socks on, when some men

came running up the stairs. They forced the door open and threw
me down the stairs. My bedroom was on the third floor. I was in
my pyjamas and ran out on the street. A large crowd had already
gathered.
Someone screamed: "Shoot him!" I couldn't see my parents and ran
back into the house to their bedroom on the first floor. I grabbed one
of Father's jackets. He advised me to run to a friend's house.
There was a big lorry in front of our restaurant with about six
containers of petrol. Before I got to our friend's house I noticed that
the sky was lit up. The restaurant had gone up in flames. This was
because we had let a small room to a Jewish organisation. They had
a few Torah scrolls in the holy shrine,
prayed there and held services. That is why they burned our
restaurant to the ground.
We lost everything.

I was not surprised when, at the end of the Bonn *Begegnungswoche*,
Walter told me that he would never come to Germany again. He
has never been to Europe again, either. I visited him several times
in Montreal. Only once did we experience a closeness and speak
openly with each other. He asked me: "What would happen to your
forgiveness and reconciliation work if you came face to face with our
parents' murderers?" I couldn't answer his question.

After the *Begegnungswoche*, which I attended with Walter, I received a
letter from Agnes, who had lived opposite us in Beuel and with whom
I had spent almost every day of my childhood. We saw a little less of
each other after 1933, because I was busy with my Zionist activities,
but we still met quite often in the street and talked. We met once
more shortly before I emigrated. She told me that she was pregnant;
she had just turned 17. We were standing at our usual meeting point
by the fence when a young man walked past. "That is the father of my

child", she said, pointing to him and mentioning his name. The fact that she had signed her letter with the name of her boyfriend told me they were still together. She wrote that, having heard that my brother and I had been in Germany, she had summoned up the courage to get in touch with me. I was delighted and replied immediately. We met when I was next in Bonn and immediately felt a rapport. I think Agnes assumed that we would simply pick up where we had left off. When was that? And what was our situation at that time? "Why didn't you come and see us straight after the war? You knew we weren't Nazis," she asked. I had asked after her on my first visit to Beuel, in 1955; the neighbours had told me that she had moved away but that they didn't know where. For some incomprehensible reason, I hadn't dared to enquire further.

We talked at length about the past, and I stayed several nights in her attractive little house. Her husband was kind and sympathetic. Out of the blue, in the middle of a conversation, Agnes declared with great conviction: "Of course, you had everything: a house, a car, two children at secondary school, a maid – and we had nothing." Why was I so surprised? Why would she have thought differently? During my stay with her, I went to the school dialogues and other events. She told me that I was still in the prime of my life and that we no longer had anything in common. I was shocked. After that, we lost touch.

While I was busy with the educational work my family got on with their lives. There were the usual problems every now and then but, luckily, I was often able to help. Even though everyone led his or her own life, we were there for each other. I have an especially good relationship with my grandchildren. The highlights have included joint trips, visits to friends and relatives in America, and regular birthday parties in my flat. My home is their home and they feel completely at ease there. I lived in the belief that I had come to terms with my difficult past, the loss of my parents and relatives, deprivation, war and hunger, personal disappointments, and, not least, my husband's early death and the feeling of loneliness that had accompanied me since leaving Germany. I had made the right decisions: moving to London and finding a new circle of friends, and I had managed to keep my head above water financially. After retirement, I kept busy with the school visits and talks that gave my life a focus.

But then something happened that deeply traumatised me, and I discovered that my past had caught up with me with a vengeance. My youngest grandchild, Saul, a clever and attractive boy, suddenly started to complain of headaches and loss of concentration, to the extent that he had to interrupt his studies. Doctors were consulted and he was allocated a bed in a specialist clinic. At first, we thought it might be schizophrenia or epilepsy. Then it was thought to be a temporary condition. And so began a long battle with doctors, specialists and their misdiagnoses. Saul was literally fed on antipsychotic drugs without showing any sign of improvement. He was a frequent visitor to my home.

During one of his stays, he went out saying he would be back by 11 p.m. I went to bed. My bedroom was one floor above his. I didn't hear him return, neither did I hear him screaming for help. The neighbours did hear screaming and, thinking it was me, called the police because there was no response when they rang the doorbell. The police came immediately but were unable to gain entry, so called the fire brigade, who gained access to my flat from the back of the house. The firemen burst into my bedroom. I woke up to see two men in uniform – to me, they were Nazi uniforms – and I was convinced they had come to take me away. I became a young girl in her nightdress. I asked: "Is the house still on fire?" "Yes," replied one of the Nazis, and opened the door. I saw smoke filling the corridor. Submissively, I followed them downstairs. In the kitchen, I saw SS men (in reality, they were police officers in dark-blue uniform). At this point, Saul came out of his bedroom and didn't know what was going on. He had screamed in his sleep. I calmed him down and sat by his bedside until he fell asleep.

The next morning, I went to explain to the neighbours about what had happened and tried, in vain, to get to grips with the bewildering events of the previous night. Despite the fact that it had all taken place in my own flat, I had experienced it as if transported back to the Nazi era. There was clearly a psychological explanation for my reaction. Of course, I know that waking up to see two men standing in one's bedroom can cause shock, but I had clearly seen the smoke even though there was none. Every time I tried to envisage the firemen and the police, the images were always of Nazi uniforms.

The following year, Saul's parents bought a little house near Bristol for him and his younger brother. It was 2005 and, as always, I travelled to the *Begegnungswoche* in Bonn. I was thinking about Saul and hoping he could be helped. Returning to London on 7 July, I learned from the cab driver that bombs had exploded in the city centre. I telephoned my daughter-in-law in Bristol, who told me that Saul was staying with her because he wasn't feeling well but that he had decided to return to his own home. She was unsure whether to let him go in his condition. I thought she should – I had no premonition, no feeling of foreboding. At 7 o'clock the next morning, the telephone rang. It was David. There had been an accident. Saul had, as always, taken his medication. He had then lit a cigarette and fallen asleep. The sofa had caught fire and he had been terribly burned. The neighbours had initially ignored the fire alarm. The fire brigade arrived far too late. Saul was in hospital in a coma; his mother was with him.

Then began a terrible time for my little family: weeks of uncertainty as to whether Saul would survive. After weeks, the first sign of life: a movement of the eyelashes and the hope that he had been saved. Then came the question whether his legs would have to be amputated. In the event he lost both legs.

Describing the weeks and months that followed is far from easy. Saul's parents, his brother, the rest of the family and I were all trying to be very brave. I visited Saul in hospital as often as I could, and took him to nearby towns in his wheelchair, stopping every so often for a meal or a drink, and tried to distract him a little. After returning him to the hospital, I would be overcome with grief. There were times when I sank into a terrible depression, and I also suffered dizzy spells and was overcome by extreme fatigue. After a thorough examination, the doctors took the view that my condition was psychosomatic. Having never before experienced such anxiety, I was at a loss. I agreed to undergo counselling. In the six sessions I had with the young therapist, it became clear that my condition was connected with my past. To cope with daily life, I had suppressed the distressing experiences. When I visited schools and spoke about my life, I had held a tight rein on my emotions just to be able to tell my story. The therapist just listened to me, said little, but asked the right questions. The therapy liberated me from my fear. I feel strong again and look forward to continuing my mission, probably with added intensity, having gained a better understanding of myself through the therapy.

It is now clear to me that my past has always lain dormant in me and that it was re-ignited by my grandson's tragedy. Having regained my equilibrium, I look forward to continuing as before in the years which remain to me. One of my happiest moments was the celebration of my 88th birthday at home, surrounded by my family – all nine of us. Quite simply, it represented everything for which I had always lived, worked and fought.

Looking back at my life, I realise that despite my early opposition to my parent's middle-class way of thinking, it was the background of a loving family, and the values instilled in me by my parents in particular, which gave me the basis to make the right decisions in life. Sadly I never had the chance to thank them. I am happy to be able to do so now.

Glossary of Terms

Bar mitzvah The occasion of a Jewish boy's 13th birthday when he is considered to have attained manhood. Marked with the young man reading from the Torah scrolls in the synagogue and a celebration.

Bat mitzvah The equivalent of a Bar mitzvah for girls. It occurs usually when the young woman is 12 years old.

BDM Bund Deutscher Mädel (League of German Girls) was part of the Hitler Youth and was aimed at integrating all girls and young women between ages 10 and 21. As with the Hitler Youth, its pedagogical goal was to educate girls according to Nazi ideology, which, for girls, meant to prepare them for their future role as 'German mothers'. Founded in 1930, membership became compulsory in 1936.

British Mandate Created to govern Palestine after the First World War, when the Ottoman Empire was broken up. Palestine was originally part of Greater Syria.

Challah Plaited or round loaf baked for the Sabbath and festivals.

Chassidim Members of a branch of Orthodox Judaism that promotes spirituality and joy through music and dance and the popularisation of mysticism as a fundamental aspect of the Jewish faith. It was founded in 18th century Eastern Europe by the Baal Shem Tov (Rabbi Yisroel ben Eliezer) as a reaction against overly legalistic Judaism.

Chaverim Hebrew for companions or comrades.

Chumash The Jewish Bible, comprising the Five Books of Moses and the Prophets.

Der Spiegel German weekly founded in 1947 and published in Hamburg. It is one of Europe's largest publications of its kind, with a weekly circulation of more than one million copies.

Der Westdeutscher Beobachter A regional newspaper of the National Socialist movement circulated in the Cologne/Aachen area. After 1933, only approved pro-Nazi papers were permitted.

Dybbuk A famous Yiddish play written in 1914 by S. Ansky on the theme of spiritual possession. A dybbuk is a soul of a dead person that attaches itself to the body of a living individual.

Emek Yizrael The Jezreel Valley in northern Palestine.

Falafel Deep-fried, savoury balls made from chickpeas. Generally regarded as the national food of Israel, although it is originally an Arab dish.

Frankfurter Allgemeine Zeitung Respected national German broadsheet newspaper, founded in 1949. It is published daily in Frankfurt am Main.

Goebbels, Joseph Nazi head of propaganda and close associate of Adolf Hitler. As the Russians approached Berlin in 1945, Goebbels and his wife poisoned their six young children before themselves committing suicide.

Goy Hebrew for nation. Refers to non-Jews or gentiles.

Gymnasium The German equivalent of an English grammar school

Habima The Israeli national theatre, founded in Russia in the pre-Revolutionary period.

Habonim A Jewish Socialist-Zionist cultural youth movement, which exists to educate and bring Jewish culture to its members, both within Israeli society and in other parts of the world.

Haggadah The book containing the order of service for the *seder* on *Pesach*.

Hanukkah The festival of lights that occurs in December. An additional candle is lit each night on the special candelabra (or *chanukia*) until on the final night when all eight lights are burning. It celebrates the miraculous victory of the Macabees over the Greeks and the rededication of the Temple in Jerusalem, which reinstated Jewish religious and political sovereignty.

Hashomer Hatzair Left-wing secular Zionist labour movement that founded and ran many *kibbutzim*.

Hatikvah 'The Hope'. Officially declared the Zionist anthem in 1933. Composed by Naphtali Hertz Imber. Now the Israeli National Anthem.

Hechalutz A non-political youth movement whose aim was to encourage young Jews to go to Palestine to redeem the land.

Herzl, Theodor Hungarian-born, assimilated Viennese journalist and playwright (1860 –1904) who effectively founded the Zionist movement as a reaction to the experience of antisemitism as experienced in his coverage of the Dreyfus trial in France, in which a Jewish officer was wrongly accused of treason and imprisoned on Devil's Island.

Hess, Rudolf Hitler's deputy. Flew to Scotland on the eve of the invasion of the Soviet Union on a mission, apparently to sue for a separate peace. Sentenced to life imprisonment at the Nuremberg Trials and died in Spandau prison in 1987 aged 93 .

Hitler Youth Nazi youth movement for boys. Membership was obligatory for all 'Aryan' boys.

Hummus Paste made from ground chick peas and oil. Often served with *falafel*.

Irgun Zionist liberation movement that waged war against the occupying British forces in Mandate Palestine with the aim of creating an independent Jewish homeland. Led for much of its existence by former Israeli prime minster Menachem Begin.

Jecke (or Yekke) The term applied to German Jews in Palestine by their co-religionists. Probably derived from the German word for jacket and reflecting their formality.

Jewish National Fund (JNF) Set up in the late 19th Century as the fundraising arm of the Zionist movement. Originally concerned with the purchase and development of land for Jewish settlement. It still exists today.

Kameraden Founded in 1916. The largest non-Zionist Jewish Youth Movement in Germany.

Kibbutz Collective farms created to settle the land of Israel.

Kindertransport A rescue operation initiated in response to the events of 9-10 November 1938 (Kristallnacht). Sanctioned by the British government, it brought approximately 10,000 Jewish children from Central Europe to Britain.

Kristallnacht Also known as 'night of broken glass'. Nation-wide anti-Jewish pogrom organised by the Nazis in 1938 in revenge for the murder of a German diplomat in Paris. Synagogues throughout Germany were burned to the ground, Jewish businesses were ransacked and thousands of Jewish men taken to concentration camps.

Lehi Also known as the Stern Gang, a name given to it by the British after its original leader Abraham Stern. Like the Irgun it waged war against the the occupying British forces in Mandate Palestine, but was more radical in its activities, refusing to desist from military action against the British army during the War.

Pesach Also known as Passover, *Pesach* celebrates the Exodus from Egypt. Foods containing leaven are avoided during its eight-day duration.

Rassenschande Nazi term for marriage or sexual relations between 'Aryans' and 'non-Aryans', which was a criminal offence punishable by law.

Realschule A German secondary school more orientated towards trade and business than the more academic Gymnasium.

Reichsbund Juedischer Frontsoldaten Reich Federation of Jewish War Veterans (RjF). Association of German Jewish war veterans founded in February 1919 by Jewish soldiers who had served on the front lines of the German army during World War I. One of their main purposes was to disprove the popular belief that during World War I, Jews had either only held desk jobs or had avoided serving in the army altogether, attested to by the fact that 12,000 Jewish soldiers had died fighting for Germany.

Reichsmark The currency in Germany from 1924 until 1948.

Rosh Hashanah The Jewish New Year; a time of contemplation and asking God for forgiveness for one's sins.

Sabra One born in the land of Israel. The *sabra* is the fruit of the prickly pear cactus, which is hard on the outside but soft inside.

Scheitel A wig worn by strictly-Orthodox women to cover their hair for reasons of modesty.

Seder The order of service at the onset of *Pesach* (Passover) when Jewish people gather round the family table to recount the story of the Exodus from Egypt and enjoy a meal with foods that are special to the festival.

Sephardi Jews who originate from Spain and Portugal prior to the expulsion in 1492. Latterly used in Israel (incorrectly) to describe Jews of non-European origin.

Shabbat The Jewish Sabbath, runs from sunset on a Friday until nightfall on a Saturday.

Shofar The ram's horn that is blown in the synagogue during *Rosh Hashanah*, signalling the call for repentance.

Social Democrats The principal left-wing political party in Germany prior to Hitler's seizure of power. In common with all political parties (except the NSDAP), it was banned after 1933. The Nazis disbanded the party when they attained power. The party reformed after the War and continues to this day.

Spaetzle Type of soft, egg noodle found in the cuisine of Germany and Austria.

Torah The Five Books of Moses that form the basis for the Jewish religion. A portion of the *Torah* is read on the Sabbath, and festivals, from a hand-written parchment scroll.

Verdun One of the major battles on the Western Front, fought between the

German and French armies, in 1916 north of the city of Verdun-sur-Meuse in north-eastern France. The Battle of Verdun ended as a French tactical victory.

Verein an der Synagoge Holocaust remembrance centre in Bonn. Affiliated to the Task Force founded in post-War Germany for International Cooperation on Holocaust Education, Remembrance, and Research.

Von Hindenburg, Paul German general and hero of the First World War, who became president of the Republic in 1925 and invited Hitler to become Chancellor in 1933.

Wandervogel Literally 'rambling bird'. Name adopted by a popular outdoor movement of German youth groups from 1896 onward. Its ethos is to shake off the restrictions of society and get back to nature and freedom.

Weiberfastnacht A women's day, marking the start of carnival festivities in the Rhineland, when men can expect to have their ties cut off at work. A tradition that began 185 years ago with a group of washerwomen in Beuel.

Weimar Republic The name given to the German political regime between the end of the First World War and Hitler's seizure of power.

Willy Fritsch German theatre and film actor, who was among the most popular leading men in German silent films.

Wunderkind Literally 'wonder child'. Expression of adulation for one's child.

Yom Kippur Also known as the Day of Atonement, a 25-hour fast when Jewish people spend the entire day in the synagogue. It follows on eight days from *Rosh Hashanah*.

Youth Aliyah Organisation formed to assist young people to emigrate to Palestine.

Zapata Emiliano Salazar (1879 –1919). A leading figure in the Mexican Revolution, which broke out in 1910.